WORLD

Praise for the

'This book provides an excellent, informative introduction to the vexed question of English as a world language. It assesses the modern spread of the English language factually in an unbiased fashion and presents students with a wealth of exciting practical work that will enable them to develop a balanced perspective of the "global" language English.'

Richard Watts, University of Berne, Switzerland

Routledge English Language Introductions cover core areas of language study and are one-stop resources for students.

Assuming no prior knowledge, books in the series offer an accessible overview of the subject, with activities, study questions, sample analyses, commentaries and key readings – all in the same volume. The innovative and flexible 'two-dimensional' structure is built around four sections – introduction, development, exploration and extension – which offer self-contained stages for study. Each topic can also be read across these sections, enabling the reader to build gradually on the knowledge gained.

World Englishes:

❏ is a comprehensive introduction to the subject
❏ covers the major historical and sociopolitical developments in World Englishes from the reign of Queen Elizabeth I to the present day
❏ explores current debates in World Englishes from English in postcolonial America and Africa, and Asian Englishes in the Outer Circle, to creole development in the UK and US, English as a Lingua Franca (ELF) and the teaching and testing of World Englishes
❏ draws on a range of real texts, data and examples, including articles from *The New York Times*, *The Straits Times* and *The Economist*, emails, texts and transcripts of speech
❏ provides classic readings by some of the key names in the discipline including David Graddol, Ngũgĩ wa Thiong'o, Alastair Pennycook and Henry Widdowson
❏ is accompanied by a companion website featuring study questions for each unit, discussion and research questions for group and independent study, plus web links for online World Englishes resources.

Key features of this new edition include extended coverage of English as a Lingua Franca and China English. The units on Singlish and Estuary English have been updated and there are three new readings by David Crystal, Hu Xiao Qiong and Barbara Seidlhofer. The references have been updated and fresh examples and exercises have been included.

Jennifer Jenkins is Professor of English Language at the University of Southampton.

The accompanying website can be found at
http://www.routledge.com/textbooks/9780415466127

ROUTLEDGE ENGLISH LANGUAGE INTRODUCTIONS

SERIES EDITOR: PETER STOCKWELL

Peter Stockwell is Senior Lecturer in the School of English Studies at the University of Nottingham, UK, where his interests include sociolinguistics, stylistics and cognitive poetics. His recent publications include *Cognitive Poetics: An Introduction* (Routledge 2002), *The Poetics of Science Fiction*, *Investigating English Language* (with Howard Jackson), and *Contextualized Stylistics* (edited with Tony Bex and Michael Burke).

SERIES CONSULTANT: RONALD CARTER

Ronald Carter is Professor of Modern English Language in the School of English Studies at the University of Nottingham, UK. He is the co-series editor of the forthcoming *Routledge Applied Linguistics* series, series editor of *Interface*, and was co-founder of the Routledge *Intertext* series.

OTHER TITLES IN THE SERIES:

History of English
Dan McIntyre

Sociolinguistics 2nd edition
Peter Stockwell

Grammar and Vocabulary
Howard Jackson

Psycholinguistics
John Field

Practical Phonetics and Phonology 2nd edition
Beverley Collins and Inger Mees

Stylistics
Paul Simpson

Language in Theory
Mark Robson and Peter Stockwell

Child Language
Jean Stilwell Peccei

Pragmatics and Discourse 2nd edition
Joan Cutting

WORLD ENGLISHES

A resource book for students

A

B

C

D

JENNIFER JENKINS

Second Edition

Routledge
Taylor & Francis Group

LONDON AND NEW YORK

First published 2009
by Routledge
2 Park Square, Milton Park, Abingdon, Oxon OX14 4RN

Simultaneously published in the USA and Canada
by Routledge
270 Madison Ave, New York, NY10016

Routledge is an imprint of the Taylor & Francis Group, an informa business

Typeset in 10/12.5 pt Minion by
The Running Head Limited, Cambridge, www.therunninghead.com
Printed and bound in Great Britain by
TJ International Ltd, Padstow, Cornwall

British Library Cataloguing in Publication Data
A catalogue record for this book is available from the British Library

Library of Congress Cataloging-in-Publication Data
Jenkins, Jennifer
  World Englishes / Jennifer Jenkins. — 2nd ed.
    p.   cm.
  Includes bibliographical references and index.
  1. English language—Variation—English-speaking countries.   2. English language—
Variation—Commonwealth countries.   3. English language—Variation—Foreign
countries.   4. English language—English-speaking countries.   5. English language—
Commonwealth countries.   6. English language—Foreign countries. I. Title.
  PE2751.J46 2009
  427—dc22

                                                                              2008040871

ISBN10: 0–415–46611–3 (hbk)
ISBN10: 0–415–46612–1 (pbk)

ISBN13: 978–0–415–46611–0 (hbk)
ISBN13: 978–0–415–46612–7 (pbk)

HOW TO USE THIS BOOK

The Routledge English Language Introductions are 'flexi-texts' that you can use to suit your own style of study. The books are divided into four sections:

A Introduction – sets out the key concepts for the area of study. The units of this section take you step-by-step through the foundational terms and ideas, carefully providing you with an initial toolkit for your own study. By the end of the section, you will have a good overview of the whole field.

B Development – adds to your knowledge and builds on the key ideas already introduced. Units in this section might also draw together several areas of interest. By the end of this section, you will already have a good and fairly detailed grasp of the field, and will be ready to undertake your own exploration and thinking.

C Exploration – provides examples of language data and guides you through your own investigation of the field. The units in this section will be more open-ended and exploratory, and you will be encouraged to try out your ideas and think for yourself, using your newly acquired knowledge.

D Extension – offers you the chance to compare your expertise with key readings in the area. These are taken from the work of important writers, and are provided with guidance and questions for your further thought.

You can read this book like a traditional text-book, 'vertically' straight through from beginning to end. This will take you comprehensively through the broad field of study. However, the Routledge English Language Introductions have been carefully designed so that you can read them in another dimension, 'horizontally' across the numbered units. For example, units A1, A2, A3, and so on, correspond with units B1, B2, B3, and with units C1, C2, C3 and D1, D2, D3, and so on. Reading A5, B5, C5 and D5 will take you rapidly from the key concepts of a specific area, to a level of expertise in that precise area, all with a very close focus. You can match your way of reading with the best way that you work.

The Glossarial Index at the end, together with the suggestions for Further Reading which follow Section D, will help to keep you orientated. Each textbook in the series has a supporting website with extra commentary, suggestions, additional material and support for teachers and students.

World Englishes

World Englishes has eight units, each following the above four-part structure. Section A's units introduce the key topics in World Englishes from the sixteenth century to the present time and beyond. Section B develops these issues with additional detail and discussion. Section C offers opportunities for further study and your own research by following the latest works and controversies in the field. Finally, the readings in Section D take up the themes of each of the other three units in their respective section, and are accompanied by suggestions for further study and discussion.

The eight horizontal strands begin with the historical, social and political context (in units A1, B1, C1 and D1). Strand 2 explores pidgins and creoles; strand 3 follows the debate about English today; strand 4 investigates variation in Englishes across the world. The units in A5, B5, C5 and D5 examine the issue of standardisation in mother-tongue Englishes; strand 6 explores English as an international lingua franca; strand 7 focuses on Asian and European Englishes; and the final strand looks to the future of Englishes in the world.

Further material and activities can also be found on the website which accompanies the book: http//:www.com/textbooks/9780415466127

CONTENTS

C EXPLORATION
Current debates in World Englishes

D EXTENSION
Readings in World Englishes

**Further
Reading**

References

**Glossarial
Index**

FIGURES AND TABLES

Figures

Tables

PREFACE TO THE SECOND EDITION

While the overall structure of this new edition remains the same as that of the first edition, a number of other changes have been made. In a field as fast-moving as World Englishes, it was inevitable that there would be a need for extensive updating after only a few years. In addition, several units have benefited from substantial improvements in the light of new published evidence, particularly, but not exclusively, the units on Singlish and Estuary English (C4) and English as a Lingua Franca (C6). Some of the readings in section D have also been replaced or supplemented with more up-to-date material and, finally, many new activities and issues to consider have been added.

Lastly, a comment on the approach taken throughout this book: given the dramatic speed and nature of the developments in this field, particularly in the most recent decades, it has become essential for anyone involved in the study of English to become aware of the issues involved and it is precisely this kind of awareness-raising function that the book serves. Rather than presenting the author's perspective, it provides a range of positions on each topic, and asks you, the reader, to decide where you stand in the many debates and controversies that unfold in the pages that follow.

ACKNOWLEDGEMENTS

Acknowledgements (first edition)

A number of people far and near have contributed to this book in various ways. First all those who gave me food for thought through discussion (even if we did not always agree) and by providing useful material – especially Janina Brutt-Griffler, Clare Canton, Jenny Cheshire, Simon Elmes, Tony Hung, Ho Wah Kam, Thiru Kandiah, Constant Leung, Masaki Oda, Anne Pakir, Robert Phillipson, Edwin Thumboo, Chris Tribble, Henry Widdowson and Ann Williams. Special thanks to the second year undergraduates at King's College, London who studied World Englishes with me in 2001/2 and provided extensive feedback on the first draft: Natasha Ahuja, Chris Babidge, Laura Bolt, Emma Brown, Simon Felstein, Mark Gilbert, Rasheed Hassan, Beth Houghton, Mel Huntly, Hui Lai Ching (Chrissie), Becky Manley, Andy Mercer, Michelle O'Brien, Kristina Olsson, Bryony Rust and Huby Saroukhanoff. The book also benefited from the insights and constructive criticism of several readers, particularly Mark Sebba, Barbara Seidlhofer and Richard Watts. My thanks, too, to Susan Fearn and her many bilingual colleagues in the Language Section of the BBC World Service who gave generously of their time. I am greatly indebted to Louisa Semlyen, Christy Kirkpatrick and Liz O'Donnell at Routledge for their constant flexibility and patience, and to Ron Carter and Peter Stockwell, the series editors, who provided encouragement and useful comments throughout, and much practical help in the final stages. The writing of this book coincided with my move from the Language Centre to the Department of Education and Professional Studies. I would like to express my appreciation to colleagues in both departments for their support during this period, and especially to Sara Garcia-Peralta, Tony Thorne and Deryn Watson. Finally, as always, my immense gratitude to my family, John, Harriet and Nick. The book is dedicated to the memory of my husband, John, who died shortly before it went to press.

Acknowledgements (second edition)

In addition to all those who contributed in their various ways to the first edition of this book, others have made valuable contributions towards the updating and improving of the text for the second edition. I would like to express my thanks to the following people in particular: David Crystal, David Graddol and Braj Kachru, who generously spent time helping me sort out facts and figures; David Deterding, Clare Mar-Molinero, Barbara Seidlhofer and Henry Widdowson, who provided extensive help and comments on specific parts of the text, leading to much improved units on

Singapore English, English as a Lingua Franca, and Spanish as a global language; and John Wells, who directed me to the best available information on Estuary English. In addition, I am immensely grateful to Angelika Breiteneder and Marie-Luise Pitzl for the care and expertise with which they have put together the accompanying website. As before, I deeply appreciate the help that I have received from the editorial team at Routledge: above all, Nadia Seemungal for her constant help and advice, Louisa Sem-lyen for her encouragement from the start, and more recently, Eloise Cook who, as a student, studied World Englishes with me. I would also like to thank Carole Drum-mond for her patience and attention to detail in copy-editing the manuscript. Finally, my thanks to the University of Southampton for giving me the space, both metaphori-cal and physical, to further my interest in World Englishes and English as a Lingua Franca, to my colleagues in Modern Languages especially, and last but not least, to the MA, BA and Erasmus students on my current World Englishes courses for their feed-back on the manuscript. My thanks and appreciation to you all.

Permissions

Cambridge University Press. © Cambridge University Press 1998. Reproduced with permission.

McCarty, T. L. and Zepeda, O. (1999), 'Amerindians' in J. Fishman (ed.) (1999), *Handbook of Language and Ethnic Identity*, pp. 205–8. Reprinted with permission of Oxford University Press Inc.

Modiano, M. (1999), 'International English in the global village', *English Today*, vol. 15, no. 2, p. 25, figure ('The centripetal circles of International English'). © Cambridge University Press 1999. Reprinted with permission.

Modiano, M. (1999), *English Today*, vol. 15, no. 4, p. 10, figure ('English as an International Language illustrated as those features of English which are common to all native and non-native varieties'). © Cambridge University Press 1999. Reprinted with permission.

Ngũgĩ wa Thiong'o, 'The language of African literature' from *Decolonising the Mind: The Politics of Language in African Literature*, James Currey, 1986. Reprinted with permission of Boydell & Brewer Ltd.

'Oakland scratches plan to teach Black English', *The New York Times*, national section, vol. 1, no. 14, 1997, issue, pp. A, 10. Reprinted with permission.

Figure 'Three Circles of English' from *The Other Tongue: English across Cultures* edited by Braj B. Kachru; published by University of Illinois Press. Reprinted with permission.

Paynton, B. (1996) Article by Brenda Paynton, *Oakland Tribune*, 21 December, 1996. Reprinted with permission of the Oakland Tribune and the author.

Pennycook, A. (1998) *English and the Discourses of Colonialism*, Routledge, pp. 133–44. Reprinted with permission of Taylor & Francis UK.

Figure 'Representing the community of English speakers as including a wide range of proficiencies' by David Graddol, *The Future of English?*, 2006 p. 110. © The British Council 1997. Reprinted with permission of British Council and David Graddol.

Extract from 'The school board thought it might help if the slang these children used at home' *The Economist*, Editorial unsigned (in line with editorial policy) *The Economist*, 4 January, 1997. Reprinted with permission.

Seidlhofer, B. (2006) 'English as a lingua franca and communities of practice'. *Anglistentag 2006 Halle Proceedings*. Trier: Wissenschaftlicher Verlag, pp. 307–18. Reprinted with permission of WVT Wissenschaftlicher Verlag Trier and the author.

Extract from 'A sociolinguistically based, empirically researched pronunciation syllabus for English as an International Language' by Jennifer Jenkins, *Applied Linguistics*, vol. 23, no. 1, 2002, OUP. Reprinted with permission.

Short extract from *School Days* by Patrick Chamoiseau, translated by Linda Coverdale. © 1997 by the University of Nebraska Press, © Editions Gallimard, Paris, 1994. Reprinted with permission of University of Nebraska Press and Editions Gallimard, France.

Strevens, P. (1992) 'English as an international language' in Kachru (ed.) (1992) p. 33, figure ('British English and American English: the two branches of the family'). Reprinted with permission of the author and the University of Illinois Press.

Widdowson, H. (1994) 'Pragmatics and the pedagogic competence of language teachers' in T. Sebbage and S. Sebbage (eds) *Proceedings of the 4th International NELLE Conference* (Hamburg: NELLE), 1.10–1.13 © Henry G. Widdowson. Reprinted with kind permission of the author.

Widdowson, H. (1993) 'The ownership of English', *Annual Conference Report: Plenaries 1993*, IATEFL, pp. 5–8. © Henry G. Widdowson. Reprinted with kind permission of the author.

Section A

INTRODUCTION
KEY TOPICS IN WORLD ENGLISHES

A1　THE HISTORICAL, SOCIAL AND POLITICAL CONTEXT

Introduction to World Englishes

In the period between the end of the reign of Queen Elizabeth I in 1603 and the later years of the reign of Queen Elizabeth II at the start of the twenty-first century, the number of speakers of English increased from a mere five to seven million to possibly as many as two billion. Whereas the English language was spoken in the mid-sixteenth century only by a relatively small group of mother-tongue speakers born and bred within the shores of the British Isles, it is now spoken in almost every country of the world, with its majority speakers being those for whom it is not a first language.

Currently, there are approximately seventy-five territories where English is spoken either as a first language (**L1**), or as an official (i.e. **institutionalised**) second language (**L2**) in fields such as government, law and education. Crystal (2003) lists these territories, along with their approximate numbers of English speakers, in Table A1.1 (those countries where the variety of English spoken is a pidgin or creole are indicated by an asterisk.

Table A1.1 English-speaking territories (source: Crystal 2003a: 62–5).

Territory	Usage estimate		Population (2001)
	L1	L2	
American Samoa	2,000	65,000	67,000
Antigua & Barbuda*	66,000	2,000	68,000
Aruba	9,000	35,000	70,000
Australia	14,987,000	3,500,000	18,972,000
Bahamas*	260,000	28,000	298,000
Bangladesh		3,500,000	131,270,000
Barbados*	262,000	13,000	275,000
Belize*	190,000	56,000	256,000
Bermuda	63,000		63,000
Bhutan		75,000	2,000,000
Botswana		630,000	1,586,000
British Virgin Islands*	20,000		20,800
Brunei	10,000	134,000	344,000
Cameroon*		7,700,000	15,900,000
Canada	20,000,000	7,000,000	31,600,000
Cayman Islands	36,000		36,000
Cook Islands	1,000	3,000	21,000
Dominica	3,000	60,000	70,000
Fiji	6,000	170,000	850,000
Gambia*		40,000	1,411,000
Ghana*		1,400,000	19,894,000
Gibraltar	28,000	2,000	31,000
Grenada*	100,000		100,000
Guam	58,000	100,000	160,000
Guyana*	650,000	30,000	700,000

Hong Kong	150,000	2,200,000	7,210,000
India	350,000	200,000,000	1,029,991,000
Ireland	3,750,000	100,000	3,850,000
Jamaica*	2,600,000	50,000	2,665,000
Kenya		2,700,000	30,766,000
Kiribati		23,000	94,000
Lesotho		500,000	2,177,000
Liberia*	600,000	2,500,000	3,226,000
Malawi		540,000	10,548,000
Malaysia	380,000	7,000,000	22,230,000
Malta	13,000	95,000	395,000
Marshall Islands		60,000	70,000
Mauritius	2,000	200,000	1,190,000
Micronesia	4,000	60,000	135,000
Montserrat*	4,000		4,000
Namibia	14,000	300,000	1,800,000
Nauru	900	10,700	12,000
Nepal		7,000,000	25,300,000
New Zealand	3,700,000	150,000	3,864,000
Nigeria*		60,000,000	126,636,000
Northern Marianas*	5,000	65,000	75,000
Pakistan		17,000,000	145,000,000
Palau	500	18,000	19,000
Papua New Guinea*	150,000	3,000,000	5,000,000
Philippines	20,000	40,000,000	83,000,000
Puerto Rico	100,000	1,840,000	3,937,000
Rwanda		20,000	7,313,000
St Kitts & Nevis*	43,000		43,000
St Lucia*	31,000	40,000	158,000
St Vincent & Grenadines*	114,000		116,000
Samoa	1,000	93,000	180,000
Seychelles	3,000	30,000	80,000
Sierra Leone*	500,000	4,400,000	5,427,000
Singapore	350,000	2,000,000	4,300,000
Solomon Islands*	10,000	165,000	480,000
South Africa	3,700,000	11,000,000	43,586,000
Sri Lanka	10,000	1,900,000	19,400,000
Suriname*	260,000	150,000	434,000
Swaziland		50,000	1,104,000
Tanzania		4,000,000	36,232,000
Tonga		30,000	104,000
Trinidad & Tobago*	1,145,000		1,170,000
Tuvalu		800	11,000
Uganda		2,500,000	23,986,000
United Kingdom	58,190,000	1,500,000	59,648,000
UK Islands (Channel, Man)	227,000		228,000
United States	215,424,000	25,600,000	278,059,000
US Virgin Islands*	98,000	15,000	122,000
Vanuatu*	60,000	120,000	193,000
Zambia	110,000	1,800,000	9,770,000
Zimbabwe	250,000	5,300,000	11,365,000
Other dependencies	20,000	15,000	35,000

The total numbers of L1 and L2 English speakers amount to 329,140,800 and 430,614,500 respectively, and together these speakers constitute almost a third of the total population of the above territories (2,236,730,000 in total). However, as Crystal (2003a: 68) points out, the L2 total is conservative:

> The total of 430 million . . . does not give the whole picture. For many countries, no estimates are available. And in others (notably India, Pakistan, Nigeria, Ghana, Malaysia, Philippines and Tanzania, which had a combined total of over 1,462 million people in 2002) even a small percentage increase in the number of speakers thought to have a reasonable (rather than a fluent) command of English would considerably expand the L2 grand total.

He goes on to point out that whether or not pidgin and creole languages are included, the total number of L2 speakers in these regions is well above the total number of L1 speakers. And in fact, although all three totals (population, L1, L2) have increased since the first edition of Crystal's *English as a Global Language* (1997), the most substantial increase by far is in the number of L2 speakers, which have almost doubled from 235,351,300 in 1997 to over 430 million in 2003. And we should bear in mind that Crystal's figures are likely to have increased still further since the publication of his second edition in 2003.

The total number of L2 speakers is still more remarkable than Crystal's figures suggest. For, as he explains, they take no account of one further, and increasingly important group of L2 English speakers: those for whom English has little or no official function within their own countries. This group of English speakers, whose proficiency levels range from reasonable to bilingual competence, was originally described as speakers of **English as a Foreign Language** (**EFL**) to distinguish them from L2 speakers for whom English serves country-internal functions, that is, speakers of **English as a Second Language** (**ESL**). Since the mid-1990s, however, it has become increasingly common to find alongside EFL, the use of **English as a Lingua Franca** (**ELF**) or, less often, **English as an International Language** (**EIL**). The new term, ELF, reflects the growing trend for English users from, for example, Europe, China and Brazil, to use English more frequently as a contact language among themselves rather than with native English speakers (the EFL situation). It is impossible to capture the current number of EFL/ELF speakers precisely, because it is increasing all the time as more and more people in these countries learn English (particularly in China, partly as an outcome of its hosting of the 2008 Olympic Games). Current estimates tend to be around one billion, while Crystal (2008a) suggests that there may now be as many as two billion English speakers in the world as a whole.

A theme which recurs throughout the book and which it will therefore be useful to highlight from the start, is that of value judgements of these different Englishes. The negative **attitudes** which persist today towards certain varieties of English have their roots in the past and, especially, in the two dispersals of English (see next section). The British establishment still harbours the view of the superiority of British over American English. For example, in launching the British Council's English 2000 project in March 1995, Prince Charles was famously reported in the British press as follows:

The Prince of Wales highlighted the threat to 'proper' English from the spread of American vernacular yesterday as he launched a campaign to preserve the language as world leader. He described American English as 'very corrupting' and emphasised the need to maintain the quality of language, after giving his backing to the British Council's English 2000 project . . . Speaking after the launch, Prince Charles elaborated on his view of the American influence. 'People tend to invent all sorts of nouns and verbs, and make words that shouldn't be. I think we have to be a bit careful, otherwise the whole thing can get rather a mess.'

(*The Times*, 24 March 1995)

It should already be clear that there is scope for substantial disagreement as to whether the metamorphosis of *English* into *World Englishes* is a positive or negative phenomenon. And as can be seen in the reference to attitudes above, the use of English around the world has not proved uncontroversial or even, necessarily, beneficial. One of the purposes of this book, then, is to approach the controversies surrounding World Englishes from a wide range of perspectives in order to enable readers to draw their own conclusions.

The two dispersals of English

We can speak of the two dispersals, or **diasporas**, of English (see Figure A1.1*).* The **first diaspora**, initially involving the migration of around 25,000 people from the south and east of England primarily to America and Australia, resulted in new mother-tongue varieties of English. The **second diaspora**, involving the colonisation of Asia and Africa, led, on the other hand, to the development of a number of second language varieties, often referred to as 'New Englishes'. This is to some extent a simplification for it is not always an easy matter to categorise the world's Englishes so neatly (see A3). And, as was noted above, the whole issue has been further complicated since the twentieth century by the dramatic increase in the use of English first as a foreign language and subsequently as an international lingua franca (respectively EFL and ELF).

The first dispersal: English is transported to the 'New World'

The first diaspora involved relatively large-scale migrations of mother-tongue English speakers from England, Scotland and Ireland predominantly to North America, Australia and New Zealand. The English dialects which travelled with them gradually developed into the American and Antipodean Englishes we know today. The varieties of English spoken in modern North America and Australasia are not identical with the English of their early colonisers, but have altered in response to the changed and changing sociolinguistic contexts in which the migrants found themselves. For example, their vocabulary rapidly expanded through contact with the indigenous Indian, Aboriginal or Maori populations in the lands which they colonised, to incorporate words such as Amerindian *papoose, moccasin* and *igloo*.

Walter Raleigh's expedition of 1584 to **America** was the earliest from the British Isles to the New World, though it did not result in a permanent settlement. The

The first diaspora
Migrations to North America, Australia, New Zealand → L1 varieties of English

- ❑ USA/Canada: From early 17th century (English), 18th century (North Irish) to USA

  From 17th century, African slaves to South American states and Caribbean Islands.

  From 1776 (American Independence) some British settlers to Canada.
- ❑ Australia: From 1770
- ❑ New Zealand: From 1790s (official colony in 1840)

The second diaspora
Migrations to Africa and Asia → L2 varieties of English

- ❑ South Africa: From 1795. 3 groups of L2 English speakers (Afrikaans/ Blacks/from 1860s Indians).
- ❑ South Asia: India, Bangladesh, Pakistan, Sri Lanka, Nepal, Bhutan, from 1600 (British East India Company). 1765–1947 British sovereignty in India.
- ❑ SE Asia and South Pacific: Singapore, Malaysia, Hong Kong, Philippines from late 18th century (Raffles founded Singapore 1819).
- ❑ Colonial Africa: West: Sierra Leone, Ghana, Gambia, Nigeria, Cameroon, Liberia, from late 15th century (but no major English emigrant settlements → pidgins/creoles).

  East: Kenya, Tanzania, Uganda, Malawi, Zambia, Zimbabwe, from *c.* 1850

Figure A1.1 Summary of the two dispersals of English.

voyagers landed on the coast of North Carolina near Roanoke Island, but fell into conflict with the native Indian population and then mysteriously disappeared altogether, leaving behind only a palisade and the letters CRO carved on a tree. In 1607, the first permanent colonists arrived and settled in Jamestown, Virginia (named respectively after James I and Elizabeth I, the Virgin Queen), to be followed in 1620 by a group of Puritans and others on the *Mayflower*. The latter group landed further north, settling at what is now Plymouth, Massachusetts, in New England. Both settlements spread rapidly and attracted further migrants during the years that followed. Because of their different linguistic backgrounds, there were immediately certain differences in the accents of the two groups of settlers. Those in Virginia came mainly from the west of England and brought with them their characteristic rhotic /r/ and voiced /s/ sounds. On the other hand, those who settled in New England were mainly from the east of England, where these features were not a part of the local accent.

During the seventeenth century, English spread to southern parts of America and the Caribbean as a result of the slave trade. Slaves were transported from West Africa and exchanged, on the American coast and in the Caribbean, for sugar and rum. The Englishes which developed among the slaves and between them and their captors were initially contact pidgin languages but, with their use as mother tongues following the birth of the next generation, they developed into creoles (see strand 2). Then, in the eighteenth century, there was large-scale immigration from Northern Ireland, initially to the coastal area around Philadelphia, but quickly moving south and west. After the Declaration of American Independence in 1776, many Loyalists (the British settlers who had supported the British government) left for Canada.

Meanwhile, comparable events were soon to take place in Australia, New Zealand and South Africa (see Gordon and Sudbury 2002 on all three). James Cook 'discovered' **Australia** in 1770, landing in modern-day Queensland and the First Fleet landed in New South Wales in 1788. From then until the ending of transportation in 1852, around 160,000 convicts were transported to Australia from Britain and Ireland, and from the 1820s large numbers of free settlers also began to arrive. The largest proportion of settlers came from London and the south-east, although in the case of the convicts, they were not necessarily born there. Others originated in regions as widely dispersed as, for example, south-west England, Lancashire, Scotland and Ireland. The result was a situation of **dialect mixing** which was further influenced by the indigenous aboriginal languages.

New Zealand was first settled by European traders in the 1790s, though there was no official colony until after the British–Maori Treaty of Waitangi in 1840. Immigrants arrived in three stages: in the 1840s and 1850s from Britain, in the 1860s from Australia and Ireland, and from 1870 to 1885 from the UK, when their number included a considerable proportion of Scots. As in Australia, there was a mixture of dialects, this time subject to a strong Maori influence, especially in terms of vocabulary.

Although **South Africa** was colonised by the Dutch from the 1650s, the British did not arrive until 1795 when they annexed the Cape, and did not begin to settle in large numbers until 1820. The majority of Cape settlers originated in southern England, though there were also sizeable groups from Ireland and Scotland. Further settlement occurred in the 1850s in the Natal region, this time from the Midlands, Yorkshire and Lancashire. From 1822, when English was declared the official language, it was also learnt as a second language by blacks and Afrikaans speakers (many of whom were mixed race) and, from the 1860s, by Indian immigrants to the territory.

The second dispersal: English is transported to Asia and Africa

The second diaspora took place at various points during the eighteenth and nineteenth centuries in very different ways and with very different results from those of the first diaspora.

The history of English in Colonial Africa has two distinct patterns depending on whether we are talking about West or East Africa. English in **West Africa** is linked to the slave trade and the development of pidgin and creole languages. From the late fifteenth century onwards, British traders travelled at different times to and from the various coastal territories of West Africa, primarily Gambia, Sierra Leone, Ghana, Nigeria and Cameroon. However, there was no major British settlement in the area and, instead, English was employed as a lingua franca both among the indigenous population (there being hundreds of local languages), and between these people and the British traders. English has subsequently gained official status in the above five countries, and some of the pidgins and creoles which developed from English contact, such as Krio (Sierra Leone) and Cameroon Pidgin English, are now spoken by large numbers of people, especially as a second language.

East Africa's relationship with English followed a different path. The countries of Kenya, Uganda, Tanzania, Malawi, Zambia and Zimbabwe were extensively settled by British colonists from the 1850s on, following the expeditions of a number of explorers, most famously, those of David Livingstone. These six countries became British protectorates or colonies at various points between the late nineteenth and early twentieth centuries, with English playing an important role in the major institutions such as government, education and the law. From the early 1960s, the six countries one after another achieved independence. English remains the official language in Uganda, Zambia, Zimbabwe and (along with Chewa) Malawi and has large numbers of second language speakers in these places, although Swahili is more likely than English to be used as a lingua franca in Uganda, as it is in Kenya and Tanzania.

English was introduced to the sub-continent of **South Asia** (India, Bangladesh, Pakistan, Sri Lanka, Nepal and Bhutan) during the second half of the eighteenth century although, as McCrum et al. (1992: 356) point out, 'the English have had a toehold on the Indian subcontinent since the early 1600s, when the newly formed East India Company established settlements in Madras, Calcutta, and later Bombay'. The company's influence increased during the eighteenth century and culminated in a period of British sovereignty (known as 'the Raj') in India lasting from 1765 to 1947. A key point was the Macaulay Minute of 1835, which proposed the introduction in India of an English educational system. From that time, English became the language of the Indian education system. Even today, when Hindi is the official language of India, English is an 'associate official language' used alongside Hindi as a neutral lingua franca, and has undergone a process of Indianization in which it has developed a distinctive national character comparable to that of American and Australian English (see C7).

British influence in **South-East Asia**, **East Asia**, and the **South Pacific** began in the late eighteenth century as a result of the seafaring expeditions of James Cook and others. The main territories involved were Singapore, Malaysia, Hong Kong and the Philippines. Papua New Guinea was also, for a short time, a British protectorate (1884 to 1920), and provides one of the world's best examples of an English-based pidgin, **Tok Pisin**.

Stamford Raffles is the name most closely associated with British colonialism in South-East Asia. An administrator of the British East India Company, he played an important role in the founding of Singapore as part of the British colonial empire in 1819. Other major British centres were founded around the same time in Malaysia (e.g. Penang and Malacca), and Hong Kong was added in 1842. After the Spanish-American War at the end of the nineteenth century, the US was granted sovereignty over the **Philippines** which, although gaining independence in 1946, has retained a strong American-English influence.

In recent years, the use of English has increased in Singapore and a local variety has begun to emerge. On the other hand, the use of English has declined in **Malaysia** as a result of the adoption of the local language, **Bahasa Malaysia**, as the national language and medium of education when Malaysia gained independence in 1957. While still obligatory as a subject of study at school, English was regarded as useful only for international communication. However, there has recently been a change of policy, with English-medium education being reintroduced from 2003. And even before this development, the situation was complex with, for example, radio stations using English and Bahasa together for a local audience (Sebba, personal communication). Nowadays English is also learnt in other countries in neighbouring areas, most notably Taiwan, Japan and Korea, the latter two having recently begun to consider the possibility of making English an official second language.

Between 1750 and 1900 the English-speaking settlements of the first and second diasporas all underwent three similar and major changes. Up until 1750, as Strevens (1992: 29) has pointed out, the British settlers thought of themselves as 'English speakers from Britain who happened to be living overseas'. After this time, Strevens continues:

> First, the populations of the overseas NS [native speaker] English-speaking settlements greatly increased in size and became states with governments – albeit colonial governments – and with a growing sense of separate identity, which soon extended to the flavour of the English they used. Second, in the United States first of all, but later in Australia and elsewhere, the colonies began to take their independence from Britain, which greatly reinforced the degree of linguistic difference . . . And third, as the possessions stabilized and prospered, so quite large numbers of people, being non-native speakers of English, had to learn to use the language in order to survive, or to find employment with the governing class.

These Englishes have much in common, through their shared history and their affinity with either British or American English. But there is also much that is unique to each variety, particularly in terms of their accents, but also in their idiomatic uses of vocabulary, their grammars and their discourse strategies.

Since 1945, most of the remaining colonies have become independent states, with English often being retained in order to provide various internal functions and/or to serve as a neutral lingua franca.

THE ORIGINS OF PIDGIN AND CREOLE LANGUAGES   A2

Definitions and development

In an article describing the development of English during the colonial period, Leith (1996) identifies three types of English colony:

> In the first type, exemplified by America and Australia, substantial settlement by first-language speakers of English displaced the precolonial population. In the

second, typified by Nigeria, sparser colonial settlements maintained the precolonial population in subjection and allowed a proportion of them access to learning
English as a second or additional language. There is yet a third type, exemplified
by the **Caribbean** islands of Barbados and Jamaica. Here, a precolonial population was *replaced* by new labour from elsewhere, principally West Africa.

(Leith 1996: 181–2)

The first two types of English colony were the theme of A1. In A2 and the rest of
strand 2, we move on to look at the third type, whose linguistic consequences, as Leith
points out, are the most complex of all: pidgins and creoles.

Until very recently, pidgins and creoles were regarded, especially by non-linguists,
as inferior, 'bad' languages (and often not as 'languages' at all). In the later years of the
twentieth century, linguists working in the field of second language acquisition began
to realise what could be discovered about first and second language learning from the
way pidgins and creoles developed; meanwhile linguists working in the field of sociolinguistics began to appreciate the extent to which these languages reflect and promote the lifestyles of their speakers.

Nevertheless, as will be clear from the text on Cameroon Pidgin English in D2, this
view is not by any means universal, even today, and even among linguists themselves.
McArthur quotes from a review in *The Economist* of 11 May 1996 of the psycholinguist
Aitchison's 1996 book *The Seeds of Speech*, in which she argues that pidgins are illumi-
nations of linguistic evolution. This is how the (anonymous) reviewer responds:

> An examination of Tok Pisin [a variety of pidgin English spoken widely in Papua
> New Guinea], Ms Aitchison claims, illuminates the general story of linguistic evo-
> lution. But her claim is arguably mistaken. Pidgins and creoles do not clarify that
> story because they do not recapitulate that process. They are, instead, examples
> of a different process, one that can begin only from an already evolved language.
> For pidgins are corruptions – in the sense of simplifying adaptations – of existing
> languages. They offer evidence of degenerative change in existing languages under
> certain pressures, not of how language evolved . . . [P]idgins [are] simple, clumsy
> languages incapable of nuance, detail, abstraction and precision.
>
> (McArthur 1998: 161)

This is not a very long way from views such as that expressed by a Monsieur Bertrand-
Boconde in 1849, by coincidence quoted in an earlier book of Aitchison's:

> It is clear that people used to expressing themselves with a rather simple language
> cannot easily elevate their intelligence to the genius of a European language . . .
> the varied expressions acquired during so many centuries of civilization dropped
> their perfection, to adapt to ideas being born and to barbarous forms of language
> of half-savage peoples.
>
> (Aitchison 1991: 183)

While there is still a fair degree of disagreement among the wider population and
even among linguists as to the relative merits of pidgins and creoles, there is close

agreement as to basic definitions of these languages. The sociolinguist Wardhaugh, for example, defines them as follows:

> A *pidgin* is a language with no native speakers: it is no one's first language but is a *contact language*. That is, it is the product of a multilingual situation in which those who wish to communicate must find or improvise a simple language system that will enable them to do so . . . In contrast to a pidgin, a *creole*, is often defined as a pidgin that has become the first language of a new generation of speakers . . . A creole, therefore, is a 'normal' language in almost every sense.
>
> (Wardhaugh 2006: 61–3)

A pidgin arises in the first place to fulfil restricted communication needs between people who do not share a common language. This happened in the past mainly (though not exclusively) as a result of European expansion into Africa and Asia during the colonial period, with pidgins arising as a result of contact between speakers of a 'dominant' European language and speakers of mutually unintelligible indigenous African and Asian languages.

In the earlier stages of contact, communication tends to be restricted to basic transactions for which a small vocabulary is sufficient and in which there is little need for grammatical **redundancy**. For example, Todd (1990: 2) provides the example of the English phrase 'the <u>two</u> big newspaper<u>s</u>'. Here, the plural marking *–s* on 'newspapers' is redundant, since plurality is established by the word 'two'. In the French equivalent, 'le<u>s</u> deux grand<u>s</u> journ<u>aux</u>', there is still more redundancy (the marking of plurality not only on the word 'journaux' but also on 'les' and 'grands'). Cameroon pidgin, on the other hand, eliminates redundancy by rendering the phrase as 'di <u>tu</u> big pepa'.

In theory, a creole arises when the children of pidgin speakers use their parents' pidgin language as the mother tongue. In other words, a creole has native speakers. The simple structure of the pidgin is the starting point for the creole, but now that it is being acquired as a first language, its vocabulary expands and its grammar increases in complexity so that it is capable of expressing the entire human experience of its mother-tongue speakers. In practice, however, there are pidgin languages, such as Cameroon pidgin and some varieties of Tok Pisin, that have developed in this way without any intervention from child L1 learners.

In multilingual areas where a pidgin is used as a lingua franca for speakers of a number of mutually unintelligible languages, it is likely to develop over time and be used for an increasing number of functions. In this case, the early pidgin goes through a series of stages, becoming progressively more complex over one or two generations. This process is outlined in Type 3 in Figure A2.1. However, **creolisation** (the development of a pidgin into a creole) can occur at any point in a pidgin's lifespan, as shown in Types 1 and 2.

A final stage occurs if the creole continues to move in the direction of the standard dominant language, in other words, to become 'decreolised'. The process of **decreolisation** occurs when a creole comes into extensive contact with the dominant language as is the case, for example, with **African American Vernacular English** (**AAVE**, commonly known nowadays as **Ebonics** – see C2). On the other hand,

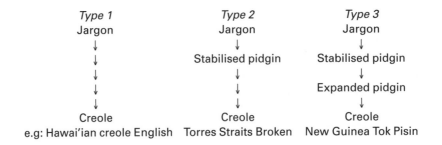

Figure A2.1 Pidgin lifespan (source: Mühlhäusler 1997: 9).

among younger speakers especially, the decreolised creole may show signs of moving back towards the creole, as is the case with the British-based patois known as 'London Jamaican'.

There are several hypotheses as to the origin of the term 'pidgin'. Romaine (1988: 12–13) lists five:

❏ a Chinese corruption of the English word 'business' as in 'gospidgin man' ('god-business-man') i.e. priest,
❏ a Chinese corruption of the Portuguese word 'ocupação' ('business'),
❏ from the Hebrew word 'pidjom' (meaning 'barter', 'exchange', 'trade'),
❏ from the word 'pidian' (meaning 'people') in Yago, a South American Indian language spoken in an area colonised by Britain, and
❏ from the two Chinese characters 'pei' and 'ts'in', meaning 'paying money'.

Aitchison (1991) suggests that these similar terms may have originated independently in different places and then reinforced each other, merging into the term 'pidgin' as we know it. Mühlhäusler (1997), on the other hand, rules out all but the first two as likely origins of the word.

The origins of the term 'creole' are less obscure, although they are nevertheless complex. Many authorities believe that the word comes from the Portuguese word 'criar' meaning 'to nurse, breed, nourish, bring up', itself deriving from the Latin 'creare', meaning 'to create'). According to Holm (2000: 9), '*Crioulo*, with a diminutive suffix, came to mean an African slave born in the New World in Brazilian usage. The word's meaning was then extended to include Europeans born in the New World' and 'finally came to refer to the customs and speech of Africans and Europeans born in the New World'. And as Mühlhäusler (1997: 6) points out, *crioulo* has acquired further meanings including 'locally-bred, non-indigenous animal'.

Theories of origin

Many theories have been advanced to explain how pidgin and creole languages arose in the first place, and there is still no final agreement. Here there is space for no more than a brief summary of some of the more prominent theories following Todd's (1990) account.

The earliest theory of pidgin origin to be advanced was that of the 'primitive native'. This belief is reflected in the quote from Bertrand-Boconde above. The attitude expressed is clearly naïve and no longer taken seriously by the majority of linguists, although it probably still represents the popular view.

Most other theories can be divided into three groups depending on whether they regard pidgins as having a single origin (**monogenesis**) or independent origin (**polygenesis**), or as deriving from universal strategies. Of the theories outlined below, the first two are polygenetic, the third monogetic, and the final two universal:

1 The independent parallel development theory

According to this theory, pidgins and creoles arose and developed independently, but developed in similar ways because they shared a common linguistic ancestor (European languages and hence an Indo-European origin) and, in the case of the Atlantic pidgins, they also shared West African languages. In addition, pidgins and creoles were formed in similar social and physical conditions.

2 The nautical jargon theory

This theory is based on the fact that European ships' crews were composed of men from a range of language backgrounds and therefore had to develop a common language in order to communicate with each other. According to the nautical jargon theory, the sailors' lingua franca was then passed on to the African and Asian peoples with whom they came into contact. The nautical jargon formed a nucleus for the various pidgins, which were subsquently expanded in line with their learners' mother tongues. Evidence for this theory is provided by the nautical element in all pidgins and creoles with European lexicons (e.g. the words 'hivim', 'kapsait' and 'haisim' meaning heave, capsize and hoist).

3 The theory of monogenesis and relexification

According to this theory, all European-based pidgins and creoles derive ultimately from one proto-pidgin source, a Portuguese pidgin that was used in the world's trade routes during the fifteenth and sixteenth centuries. This pidgin is thought to have derived, in turn, from an earlier lingua franca, Sabir, used by the Crusaders and traders in the Mediterranean in the Middle Ages. It was then, the theory goes, relexified by Portuguese in the fifteenth century. In other words, Portuguese lexis was introduced into Sabir grammar. This Portuguese version of Sabir would then have been used by the Portuguese in the fifteenth century when they sailed along the coast of West Africa, and would have been the first European language acquired by the indigenous population. Subsequently Portuguese influence decreased in the area and the pidgin began to be used increasingly in contact situations in which the dominant language could be English, Spanish, French or Dutch. Evidence for this theory is provided by the many linguistic similarities, both lexical and syntactic, between present-day Portuguese pidgins and creoles, and pidgins and creoles related to other European languages. For example, all pidgin and creole Englishes have a form of the Portuguese 'saber' meaning 'know' (e.g. 'savi', 'sabi') and of 'pequeno' meaning 'little' or 'offspring' (e.g. 'pikin', 'pikinini').

4 The baby-talk theory

This theory arose because of similarities that were identified between the early speech of children and the forms in certain pidgins, such as the large proportion of content words, the lack of structural words, the lack of morphological change, and the approximation of the standard pronunciation. It was also suggested that speakers of the dominant language, in using what is known as **foreigner talk** (simplified speech) with L2 speakers, themselves promoted the use of this type of speech among the latter.

5 A synthesis

Todd (1990) takes the 'baby-talk' theory much further in her proposal of a synthesis. She argues that instead of searching for a common origin in the past, we should approach the concept of common origin from a different perspective altogether: by seeking universal patterns of linguistic behaviour in contact situations. In her view, pidgins and creoles are alike because languages and **simplification processes** are alike. She cites as evidence the fact that speakers from different L1s simplify their language in very similar ways, be they children learning their L1, adults learning an L2, or even proficient speakers employing ellipsis (as in informal speech, e.g. 'Got a light?', creators of newspaper headlines, e.g. 'Air crash – fifty dead', and so on). In particular, Todd argues, these speakers all appear to have an innate ability to simplify by means of redundancy reduction when communication of the message is more critical than the quality of the language used. This suggests to Todd that there are inherent universal constraints on language.

The synthesis approach has the advantage of being able to account for the existence of pidgins in different types of contact situation, and both the independent origin of some pidgins and the related origin of others. This is because in each case people have responded to what Todd calls 'an innate behavioural blueprint'. Although it is not possible to prove this theory, given that it focuses on mental properties, Todd provides substantial evidence in its support:

❑ All children from all L1s go through the same stages in the mastery of speech (babble → intonational patterns of the speech community → individual words → short combinations of words)

❑ Children produce regular patterns across L1s which are not the same as adult norms, e.g. negator + sentence as in 'No I sit'.

❑ This type of simplified language is used in all speech communities by proficient to less proficient speakers, e.g. by parents to children, native speakers to non-fluent non-native speakers.

The fact that languages are simplified in similar ways suggests that all languages have a **simple register**, but that children swiftly move on from this register because of pressure to conform to the adult version of the language. Children of pidgin speakers, on the other hand, did not have this possibility, since there were no speakers of the non-simple register available to provide input. Hence, these children drew on their **innate bioprogram** (the genetic program for language that all children are believed to be born with and which they adapt to the language they hear around them) to transform the pidgins into creoles with minimum interference from adult language. In other words, this theory is simultaneously monogenetic and polygenetic: monogenetic in that creoles developed from pidgins by means of a single linguistic bioprogram common to all human beings, and polygenetic because of their independent origin in separate locations (see also Sebba 1997: 77–8, 95–7, on universalist approaches to pidgin and creole origins).

The strongest case for a synthesis approach is provided by **Bickerton**'s (1981, 1984) **Language Bioprogram Hypothesis** (**LBH**), based on his study of the development of Hawai'ian Creole. However, the LBH is criticised on a number of grounds. For example, it does not take into account the sociolinguistic realities of creole-acquiring children, who are likely to learn the language of one or both parents in addition to acquiring a creole. They thus grow up bilingual, with their two or more languages affecting each other as they acquire them simultaneously (see Sebba 1997: 176–82).

WHO SPEAKS ENGLISH TODAY?

ENL, ESL and EFL

The spread of English around the world is often discussed in terms of three distinct groups of users, those who speak English respectively as:

- ❑ a native language (ENL)
- ❑ a second language (ESL)
- ❑ a foreign language (EFL).

When we come to look more closely at this three-way categorisation and, especially, when we consider the most influential models and descriptions of English use, we will find that the categories have become fuzzy at the edges and that it is increasingly difficult to classify speakers of English as belonging purely to one of the three. Nevertheless, the three-way model provides a useful starting point from which to move on to the present, more complicated situation.

English as a Native Language (**ENL**) or **English as a mother tongue** as it is sometimes called) is the language of those born and raised in one of the countries where English is historically the first language to be spoken. Kachru (1992: 356) refers to these countries (mainly the UK, USA, Canada, Australia and New Zealand) as 'the traditional cultural and linguistic bases of English'. Their English speakers are thought to number around 350 million. English as a Second Language refers to the language spoken in a large number of territories such as India, Bangladesh, Nigeria and Singapore, which were once colonised by the English (see A1). These speakers are also thought to number around 350 million. English as a Foreign Language is the English of those for whom the language serves no purposes within their own countries. Historically, they learned the language in order to use it with its native speakers in the US and UK – though this is no longer the case. The current number of EFL speakers is more difficult to assess, and much depends on the level of competence which is used to define such a speaker. But if we use the criterion of 'reasonable competence', then the number is likely to be around 1 billion (although it should be said that this figure is not uncontroversial).

Even before we complicate the issue with changes that have occurred in the most recent decades, there are already a number of difficulties with this three-way categorisation. McArthur (1998: 43–6) lists six provisos which I summarise as follows:

1   ENL is not a single variety of English, but differs markedly from one territory to another (e.g. the US and UK), and even from one region with a given territory to another. In addition, the version of English accepted as 'standard' differs from one ENL territory to another.
2   Pidgins and creoles do not fit neatly into any one of the three categories. They are spoken in ENL settings, e.g. in parts of the Caribbean, in ESL settings, e.g. in many territories in West Africa, and in EFL settings, e.g. in Nicaragua, Panama and Surinam in the Americas. And some creoles in the Caribbean are so distinct from standard varieties of English that they are considered by a number of scholars to be different languages altogether.
3   There have always been large groups of ENL speakers living in certain ESL territories, e.g. India and Hong Kong as a result of colonialism.
4   There are also large numbers of ESL speakers living in ENL settings, particularly the US and, to a lesser extent, the UK as a result of immigration.
5   The three categories do not take account of the fact that much of the world is bi- or multilingual, and that English is often spoken within a framework of code-mixing and code-switching. (Note that a distinction used to be made between these two terms, whereas more recently they have tended to be used synonymously and interchangeably, see e.g. Y. Kachru and Nelson 2006: chapter 18).
6   The basic division is between **native speakers** and **non-native speakers** of English, that is, those born to the language and those who learnt it through education. The first group has always been considered superior to the second regardless of the quality of the language its members speak. This is becoming an ever more controversial issue and will be taken up in unit B6.

To the above points can be added two more. Firstly, in a number of the so-called ESL countries such as Singapore and Nigeria, some English speakers learn the language either as their first language or as one of two or more equivalent languages within their bi- or multilingual repertoires. And secondly, there are so-called EFL/ELF countries such as The Netherlands and Scandinavian countries where English is increasingly being used for *intra*national (i.e. country internal) purposes rather than purely as a foreign or international language. For example, English is fast becoming the medium of instruction in tertiary education, while in secondary and even primary education, school subjects are increasingly being taught through English as a means of learning both.

Models and descriptions of the spread of English

The oldest model of the spread of English is that of Strevens. His world map of English (see Figure A3.1), first published in 1980, shows a map of the world on which is superimposed an upside-down tree diagram demonstrating the way in which, since American English became a separate variety from British English, all subsequent Englishes have had affinities with either one or the other.

Later in the 1980s, Kachru, McArthur and Görlach all proposed circle models of English: Kachru's 'Three circle model of World Englishes' (1985/1988), McArthur's (1987) 'Circle of World English' and Görlach's (1988) 'Circle model of English'. McArthur's and Görlach's models are similar in a number of ways. Görlach's circle (not shown here) places 'International English' at the centre, followed by (moving outwards): regional standard Englishes (African, Antipodean, British Canadian, Caribbean, S. Asian, US), then semi-/sub-regional standard Englishes such as Indian, Irish, Kenyan, Papua New Guinean, then non-standard Englishes such as Aboriginal English, Jamaican English, Yorkshire dialect and, finally, beyond the outer rim, pidgins and creoles such as Cameroon Pidgin English and Tok Pisin.

McArthur's circle (see Figure A3.2) has at its centre World Standard English which, like Görlach's International English, does not exist in an identifiable form at present. Moving outwards comes next a band of regional varieties including both standard and standardising forms. Beyond these, divided by spokes separating the world into eight regions, is what McArthur (1998: 95) describes as 'a crowded (even riotous) fringe of subvarieties such as *Aboriginal English*, *Black English Vernacular* [now known as

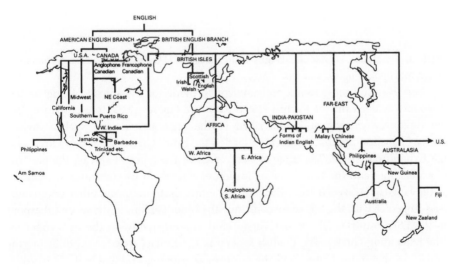

Figure A3.1 Strevens's world map of English (source: Strevens 1992: 33).

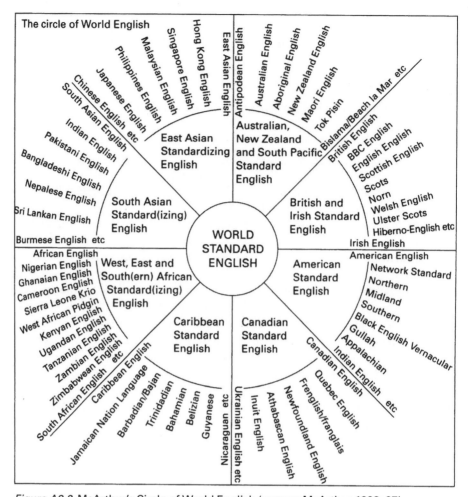

Figure A3.2 McArthur's Circle of World English (source: McArthur 1998: 97).

"African American Vernacular English" or "Ebonics"], *Gullah, Jamaican Nation Language, Singapore English and Ulster Scots*.

However, the most useful and influential, model of the spread of English has undoubtedly been that of Kachru (1992: 356) (see Figure A3.3). In accordance with the three-way categorisation described in the previous section, Kachru divides World Englishes into three concentric circles, the **Inner Circle**, the **Outer Circle** and the **Expanding Circle**. The three circles 'represent the types of spread, the patterns of acquisition, and the functional allocation of English in diverse cultural contexts', as the language travelled from Britain, in the first diaspora to the other ENL countries (together with the UK these constitute the Inner Circle), in the second diaspora to the ESL countries (the Outer Circle) and, more recently, to the EFL countries (the Expanding Circle). The English spoken in the Inner Circle is said to be 'norm-providing', that in the Outer Circle to be 'norm-developing' and that in the Expanding Circle to be 'norm-dependent'. In other words, while the ESL varieties of English have

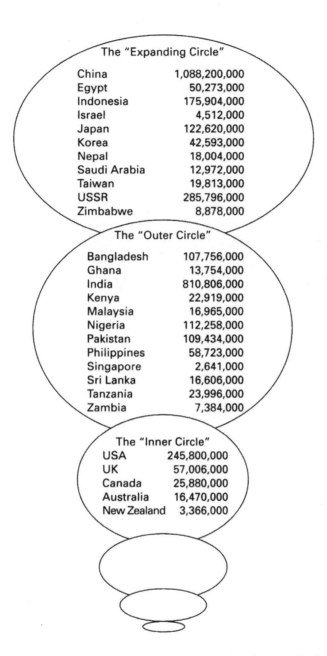

The "Expanding Circle"

China	1,088,200,000
Egypt	50,273,000
Indonesia	175,904,000
Israel	4,512,000
Japan	122,620,000
Korea	42,593,000
Nepal	18,004,000
Saudi Arabia	12,972,000
Taiwan	19,813,000
USSR	285,796,000
Zimbabwe	8,878,000

The "Outer Circle"

Bangladesh	107,756,000
Ghana	13,754,000
India	810,806,000
Kenya	22,919,000
Malaysia	16,965,000
Nigeria	112,258,000
Pakistan	109,434,000
Philippines	58,723,000
Singapore	2,641,000
Sri Lanka	16,606,000
Tanzania	23,996,000
Zambia	7,384,000

The "Inner Circle"

USA	245,800,000
UK	57,006,000
Canada	25,880,000
Australia	16,470,000
New Zealand	3,366,000

Figure A3.3 Kachru's three-circle model of World Englishes (source: Kachru 1992: 356).

Note: In this, the most frequently cited version of the model, the circles are oval rather than circular, and presented vertically rather than concentrically, with the lowest circles representing earlier versions of English. Note also that the model was first described in Kachru (1985) and published in diagrammatic form in Kachru (1988), and thus the numbers (which are for whole populations rather than English speakers alone) are now very out of date.

become institutionalised and are developing their own standards, the EFL varieties are regarded, in this model, as 'performance' varieties without any official status and therefore dependent on the standards set by native speakers in the Inner Circle.

Kachru argues that the implications of this sociolinguistic reality of English use around the world have gone unrecognised, and that attitudes, power and economics have instead been allowed to dictate English language policy. This situation, he considers, has been facilitated by a number of 'fallacies' about the users and uses of English in different cultures around the world. In B3 we will look further at this issue, which developed in the early 1990s into a major debate carried out in the pages of the journal *English Today*.

The three-circle model has been highly influential and contributed greatly to our understanding of the sociolinguistic realities of the spread of English. However, despite its influence, with many scholars, myself included, still using the three-circle model as their framework, over the past few years a number of World Englishes scholars have identified limitations with the model in its current form. Some of these limitations relate to recent changes in the use of English, while others concern any attempt at a three-way categorisation of English uses and users. The main points that have been raised by various scholars are the following:

❏ The model is based on geography and history rather than on the way speakers currently identify with and use English. Yet some English users in the Outer Circle speak it as their first language (occasionally as their *only* language). Meanwhile an increasing number of speakers in the Expanding Circle use English for a very wide range of purposes, including social, with native speakers and even more frequently with other non-native speakers from both their own and different L1s, and both in their home country and abroad. As Mesthrie points out, '[t]he German graduate students I taught in the cold Bavarian winter of 2005 seemed to be *thoroughly at home* in English' (2008: 32, emphasis added). In addition to this, English is increasingly being used as the medium of instruction in both schools and universities in many continental European countries, and more recently in Expanding Circle Asian countries such as China.

❏ There is often a grey area between the Inner and Outer Circles: in some Outer Circle countries, English may be the first language learnt for many people, and may be spoken in the home rather than used purely for official purposes such as education, law and government.

❏ There is also an increasingly grey area between the Outer and Expanding Circles. Approximately twenty countries are in transition from EFL to ESL status, including Argentina, Belgium, Costa Rica, Denmark, Sudan, Switzerland (see Graddol 1997: 11 for others).

❏ Many World English speakers grow up bilingual or multilingual, using different languages to fulfil different functions in their daily lives. This makes it difficult to describe any language in their repertoire as L1, L2, L3 and so on.

❏ There is a difficulty in using the model to define speakers in terms of their proficiency in English. A native speaker may have limited vocabulary and low grammatical competence while the reverse may be true of a non-native speaker. The fact that English is somebody's second or third language does not of itself imply that their competence is less than that of a native speaker.

❑   The model implies that the situation is uniform for all countries within a particular circle whereas this is not so. Even within the Inner Circle, countries differ in the amount of **linguistic diversity** they contain (e.g. there is far more diversity in the US than in the UK). In the Outer Circle, countries differ in a number of respects such as whether English is spoken mainly by an elite, as in India, or is more widespread, as in Singapore; or whether it is spoken by a single L1 group leading to one variety of English as in Bangladesh, or by several different L1 groups leading to several varieties of English as in India. Because of this, Bruthiaux argues that the model 'conceals more than it reveals and runs the risk of being interpreted as a license to dispense with analytical rigour' (2003: 161).

❑   The term 'Inner Circle' implies that speakers from the ENL countries are central to the effort, whereas their worldwide influence is in fact in decline. Note, though, that Kachru did not intend the term 'Inner' to be taken to imply any sense of superiority.

For more details concerning these issues see, for example, Bruthiaux (2003), Canagarajah (1999), Graddol (2006), Holborow (1999), Kandiah (1998), Kirkpatrick (2007a), Mesthrie (2008), Modiano (1999a), Pennycook (2006, 2007), Seidlhofer (2002), Toolan (1997), Tripathi (1998) and Yano (2001). Kachru, however, believes that the model has been misinterpreted. He defends it robustly point by point against the problems listed in the first edition of this book (Jenkins 2003: 17–18), arguing that the model has the capacity to encompass the kinds of sociolinguistic changes observed by his critics (Kachru 2005: 211–20). He concludes that the concerns raised in Jenkins (2003) 'are constructed primarily on misrepresentations of the model's characteristics, interpretations and implications' (Kachru 2005: 220). If you have access to Kachru (2005) and to some of the above sources, you may find it useful to read their authors' comments on the three-circle model, then Kachru's (2005) response, in order to help you decide on your own position.

Some scholars have since proposed different models and descriptions of the spread of English, sometimes in an attempt to improve on Kachru's model by taking account of more recent developments. Tripathi (1998: 55), for example, argues that the 'third world nations' should be considered as 'an independent category that supersedes the distinction of ESL and EFL'. Yano (2001: 122–4) proposes that Kachru's model should be modified in order to take account of the fact that many varieties of English in the Outer Circle have become established varieties spoken by people who regard themselves as native speakers with native speaker intuition. He therefore suggests glossing the Inner Circle as 'genetic ENL' and the Outer as 'functional ENL'. His model also takes account of the social dialectal concept of **acrolect** (standard) and **basilect** (colloquial) use of English, with the acrolect being used for international communication, and for formal and public intranational interaction, and the basilect for informal intranational communication. This is problematic in that it does not allow for the possibility of basilect use in international communication, whereas such use is becoming increasingly common. On the other hand, the attempt to remove any possible suggestion of a 'mandatory' genetic element from the definition of 'native speaker' is very welcome.

Another more recent attempt to take account of developments in the spread of World Englishes is that of Modiano (1999a, 1999b). He breaks completely with historical and geographical concerns and bases the first of his two models, 'The centripetal circles of international English', on what is mutually comprehensible to the majority of proficient speakers of English, be they native or non-native. The centre is made up of those who are proficient in international English. That is, these speakers function well in cross-cultural communication where English is the lingua franca. They are just as likely to be non-native as native speakers of English. The main criterion, other than proficiency itself, is that they have no strong regional accent or dialect. Modiano's next band consists of those who have proficiency in English as either a first or second language rather than as an international language. In other words, they function well in English with, respectively, other native speakers (with whom they share English as an L1) or other non-native speakers from the same L1 background as themselves. The third circle is made up of learners of English, i.e. those who are not yet proficient in English. Outside this circle is a final band to represent those people who do not know English at all (see Figure A3.4).

Although it makes good sense to base a modern description of users of English on proficiency and to prioritise (as McArthur and Görlach had done earlier) the use of English as an international or world language, there are certain problems with Modiano's model. In particular, where do we draw the line between a strong and non-strong regional accent? Presumably a strong regional accent places its owner in the second circle, thus categorising them as not proficient in international English. But as things stand, we have no sound basis on which to make the decision. And who decides? Again, given that international English is not defined, what does it mean to be proficient in 'international English' other than the rather vague notion of communicating well? Where do we draw the line between proficient and not proficient in international English in the absence of such a definition?

A few months later, Modiano redrafted his idea in response to comments which he had received in reaction to his first model. This time he moves away from intelligibility per se to present a model based on features of English common to all varieties of English. At the centre is EIL (English as an International Language), a core of features which is comprehensible to the majority of native and competent non-native speakers

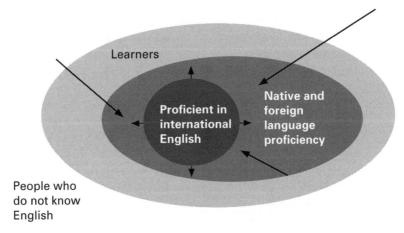

Figure A3.4 Modiano's centripetal circles of international English (source: Modiano 1999a: 25).

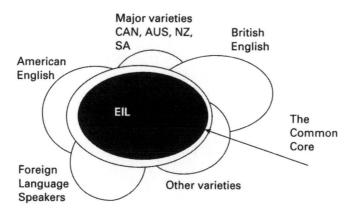

Figure A3.5 Modiano's English as an international language (EIL) illustrated as those features of English which are common to all native and non-native varieties (source: Modiano 1999b: 10).

of English (see Figure A3.5). His second circle consists of features which may become internationally common or may fall into obscurity. Finally, his outer area consists of five groups (American English, British English, other major varieties, local varieties, foreign varieties) each with features peculiar to their own speech community and which are unlikely to be understood by most members of the other four groups.

There are still problems. For example, the difficulty of determining what goes into his central category remains. In addition, some will find unpalatable the fact that Modiano equates native speakers with 'competent' non-natives, implying that all native speakers of English are competent users of English, which is patently untrue. There may also be objections to the designation of all the native varieties as 'major', but established Outer Circle varieties such as Indian English (spoken by a larger number than the NS (native speaker) populations of the US and UK combined) as 'local'.

Returning recently to Kachru's model, Graddol (2006: 110) points out that 'Kachru himself has recently proposed that the "inner circle" is now better conceived of as the group of highly proficient speakers of English – those who have "functional nativeness" regardless of how they learned or use the language'. Graddol demonstrates this in Figure A3.6, which he devised according to his interpretation of Kachru's words.

Graddol argues that '[i]n a globalised world . . . there is an increasing need to distinguish between proficiencies in English rather than a speaker's bilingual status' (2006: 110). This is similar to Rampton's (1990) notion of 'expertise', which, Rampton argues, is a more appropriate concept for English than that of nativeness (see unit B6 below). Degree of proficiency or expertise is an eminently (and possibly the most) useful way to approach the English of its entirety of speakers nowadays, regardless of where they come from and what other language(s) they speak.

The source for Graddol's presentation of functional nativeness in diagrammatic form was Kachru (2005) (Graddol, personal communication). However, it seems that Graddol's interpretation of the phenomenon of 'functional nativeness' may not be precisely the same as Kachru's. For when Kachru himself discusses functional nativeness

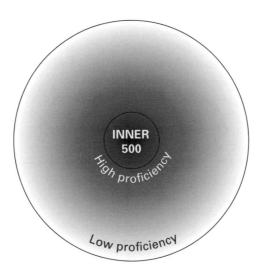

Figure A3.6 Representing the community of English speakers as including a wide range of proficiencies (source: Graddol 2006: 110).

(2005: 12, and see also Kachru 1997: 217), he explains it in terms of two variables: 'the RANGE and DEPTH of a language in a society' (capitals in the original), i.e. the 'domains' in which a language is used and 'the degree of social penetration of the language'. In other words, Kachru seems to be referring to the use of English in a society, and Graddol to the proficiency level of speakers of English within the entire 'community' of English speakers. The two overlap, but are not necessarily identical.

Most recently, Canagarajah (in a lecture, 'Developing a model for plurilingual competence', given at Southampton University, England, in July 2008) looked afresh at McArthur's circle model and argued that its world standard English centre is problematic. Canagarajah suggested replacing it with 'Pragmatics' – strategies of communication (see Canagarajah 2005: xxvi) – leaving the grammar to take care of itself. Still more controversially, as an alternative, he suggested leaving the centre completely empty. Either way, the implication is that it is impossible to capture the variability of English forms used in context around the world within a single term, a conclusion that is particularly consistent with the notion of English as a Lingua Franca (see strand 6).

A4 VARIATION ACROSS OUTER CIRCLE ENGLISHES

'New' Englishes and 'new' Englishes

The Outer and Inner Circle Englishes (British English apart) belong to one of two groups: the **new Englishes** which resulted from the first diaspora, or the **New Englishes** which resulted from the second, Note, though, that the two diasporas overlapped in time, with, for example, the Indian English of the second diaspora preceding the Australian English of the first (hence the scare quotes round 'New' and 'new' in the headings above and below). The former group consists primarily of North America (the US and Canada), Australia, New Zealand and South Africa. The Englishes in these territories developed independently of, and differently from, English in Britain partly because of the original mixtures of dialects and accents among the people who settled in these areas, and partly because of the influence of the languages of the indigenous populations. Nevertheless, because of their direct descendence from British English, and because they were spoken as mother tongues, there is a strong element of continuity in the use of these Englishes from pre-colonial days.

On the other hand, the latter group of Englishes, those commonly described as the 'New Englishes', were, and still are, for the most part, learnt as second languages or as one language within a wider multilingual repertoire of acquisition. This group includes, for example, Indian English, Philippine English, Nigerian English and Singapore English (the latter being one of the few New Englishes which are increasingly being spoken as a mother tongue). Strand 4 will not be concerned with the Englishes of the Expanding Circle, such as European Englishes and Japanese English, as these are the focus of strand 6.

The main reason for looking at a range of varieties of New English before tackling the complex issue of standard English, is to give a clear signal that the New Englishes should be considered in their own right, and not in terms of their differences from a particular native variety. This point is widely accepted in terms of American English, which is nowadays considered in the popular mind to be one of the world's two prestige varieties of English (the other being British English). On the other hand, as you will see in unit A5, Australian English has only recently begun to lose the negative connotations attached to its differences from British English. And the situation has not improved even to this extent for many of the Englishes of the Outer Circle, particularly (but not exclusively) those that have not yet been fully described and codified (see B5 for a discussion of the processes involved in standardisation).

Defining a 'New' English

The term 'New Englishes' covers a large number of varieties of English which are far from uniform in their characteristics and current use. They nevertheless share certain features. According to Platt et al. (1984: 2–3), a New English fulfils the following four criteria:

1   It has developed through the education system. This means that it has been taught as a subject and, in many cases, also used as a medium of instruction in regions where languages other than English were the main languages.
2   It has developed in an area where a native variety of English was *not* the language spoken by most of the population.
3   It is used for a range of functions *among* those who speak or write it in the region where it is used.

4   It has become 'localised' or 'nativised' by adopting some language features of its own, such as sounds, intonation patterns, sentence structures, words and expressions.

Another way of looking at a New English is to consider the status of its norms and the extent to which its innovative uses of the language are accepted despite their differences from native English norms. Bamgboṣe (1998: 3–4) outlines five internal factors that can be used to decide on the status of an innovation in English:

1   *the demographic factor*: how many speakers of the acrolect, or standard variety, use it?
2   *the geographical factor*: how widely dispersed is it?
3   *the authoritative factor*: where is its use sanctioned?
4   *codification*: does it appear in reference books such as dictionaries and grammars?
5   *the acceptability factor*: what is the attitude of users and non-users towards it?

Bamgboṣe points out that of these five, codification and acceptability are the most crucial as, without them, any innovation will be regarded as an error rather than as a legitimate form characteristic of a particular New English variety.

English was initially spoken in Africa and Asia only by the native English speaking colonisers from Britain and North America. They set up schools to teach first English, and then other subjects through English, in order to provide a local workforce able to communicate in the language. As time went on, and the number of students increased, the English-medium schools began to recruit local non-native teachers. Their English was, inevitably, different from that of their own native speaker teachers and the differences grew still more marked among the children who were taught by non-native speakers. Students were thus exposed to the language for several years during which time they used it for an ever increasing number of functions. In this way, the New Englishes evolved into varieties which served a wide or even full range of purposes and, at the same time, developed their own character.

Levels of variation

The main levels on which the new and New Englishes differ from the English of what Chinua Achebe has described as 'its ancestral home', i.e. Britain, and from each other, are the following: pronunciation, grammar, vocabulary/idiom, and discourse style. Although you should bear in mind that the different varieties of new and New Englishes are not internally uniform, nevertheless, as with British English, in the vast majority of cases there is sufficient common ground for us to be able to talk about a particular national English, be it Nigerian English, Indian English, American English or whatever. The following details draw mainly on Platt et al. (1984), supplemented where appropriate with more recent examples and commentary from Y. Kachru and Nelson (2006), and Kachru and Smith (2008) in particular.

Pronunciation

Consonant sounds

The dental fricative sounds /θ/ and /ð/ as in the words <u>th</u>in and <u>th</u>is when spoken with a British English **Received Pronunciation** (**RP**) accent (with the tongue tip vibrating against the upper teeth) are pronounced in various ways by speakers of New Englishes. For example, speakers of Indian, and West Indian Englishes use instead the sounds /t/ and /d/, so that these words are pronounced 'tin' and 'dis'.

On the other hand, speakers of Lankan (= Sri Lankan), Malaysian, Singapore and many African Englishes often use the sounds /tθ/ and /dð/, so that the same words sound closer to 't-thin' and 'd-this'. These substitutions would have started life as attempts to produce the 'correct' L1 English sound. However once L2-English-speaking teachers began to be employed, the sounds would have been produced as classroom models and imitated by pupils. Over time, they gradually became regarded as local variants, rather than incorrect attempts to conform, and in many cases are now in the process of being codified.

The same is true of a host of other consonant sounds of which the following are among those most frequently described:

- ❏ /w/ is pronounced as /v/ in Lankan and some Indian Englishes so that 'wet' sounds like 'vet'.
- ❏ The voiceless sounds /p/, /t/ and /k/ are pronounced at the beginnings of words without **aspiration** (a small puff of air) by speakers of Indian, Philippine, Malaysian and other New Englishes, so that they sound to Inner Circle speakers more like their voiced equivalents, /b/, /d/ and /g/ (e.g. the words 'pin', 'tin' and 'cap' sound closer to 'bin', 'din' and 'gap').
- ❏ Consonants at the ends of words tend to be unreleased or replaced with glottal stops in Englishes such as Ghanaian, West Indian and colloquial Singaporean, so that a word such as 'cat' may be pronounced either ca(t) with an unreleased final consonant, or ca' with a final glottal stop. The word-final **glottal stop** to replace a consonant sound, especially /t/, is also, of course, a feature of some non-standard varieties of British English such as Estuary English and Cockney.
- ❏ Several of the New Englishes, including Indian, West African and Papua New Guinean, use **voiceless** word-final consonants (that is, without vibration of the vocal cords) where RP would have a **voiced** one. Words such as 'feed', 'gave' and 'rob' may thus sound to an outsider as if they end in the consonants t, f and p, that is, as 'feet', 'gafe' and 'rop'.
- ❏ Clear and dark 'l' (as in '<u>l</u>ip' and 'pi<u>ll</u>') are not distinguished in most varieties.

Finally, there are two consonant features which occur less widely among the New Englishes, although, as you will see in A6, they feature in some of the Englishes of the Expanding Circle:

- ❏ there is a lack of distinction between /r/ and /l/ in Hong Kong, Singapore (of Chinese origin) and some East African Englishes (including Ngũgĩ's mother tongue, Gĩkũyũ), so that words such as 'red' and 'led' are interchangeable.

❑ /ʃ/ is pronounced as /s/ by speakers of some East African Englishes, and some (generally less well-educated) speakers of Hong Kong English, so that 'ship' sounds like 'sip'.

Vowel sounds

Vowel sounds vary across the New Englishes in terms of both their quality and their quantity; in other words, according to how high/low and forward/back the tongue is in the mouth, and the degree to which the lips are rounded or spread (these factors all relate to **vowel quality**), and to how long the sound is actually maintained (this factor relates to **vowel quantity**). Some of the main differences in vowel sounds across the New Englishes are as follows:

❑ Many of the New Englishes, e.g. Singapore, Indian and African Englishes, distinguish only minimally if at all between the short and long vowels /ɪ/ and /iː/ as in the RP pronunciation of the words 'sit' and 'seat', tending to pronounce both as /ɪ/. The same is often true of the sounds /ʊ/ and /uː/.

❑ Many New Englishes pronounce RP /aː/ without the length, e.g. Lankan, Singapore, Indian, Philippine and Jamaican Englishes, so that the word 'staff', for example, sounds closer to 'stuff' to an outsider.

❑ African Englishes tend to produce the **schwa** sound /ə/ as the full vowel [a] at the ends of words, so that 'matter' is pronounced [mata] where RP would be [matə].

❑ Diphthongs have a tendency to be pronounced both shorter and as monophthongs in several New Englishes including Indian, Lankan, Malaysian and African. For example, the diphthong /eɪ/ in the RP pronunciation of the word 'take' loses its second element, to become [eˑ] or the shorter [e] so that it sounds more like 'tek'. Similarly, in Lankan English the diphthong /əʊ/ in the word 'coat' tends to be pronounced either [oː] (by more educated speakers) or [ɔ] (by less educated speakers) so that, especially in the latter case, it sounds similar to RP 'cot'.

❑ Most New English varieties are **syllable-timed** (with *all* syllables occurring at regular intervals of time) rather than **stress-timed** (with *stressed* syllables falling at regular intervals), and as Mesthrie and Bhatt (2008: 129) point out, 'for these varieties vowel reduction is not as common as in RP and in some of them [ə] is rare'.

Grammar

Platt et al. (1984: chapter 4) sum up the main grammatical tendencies of the New Englishes in referring to people, things and ideas as follows:

❑ a tendency not to mark nouns for plural,

❑ a tendency to use a specific/non-specific system for nouns rather than a definite/indefinite system, or to use the two systems side by side,

❑ a tendency to change the form of quantifiers,

❑ a tendency not to make a distinction between the third person pronouns *he* and *she*, and

❑ a tendency to change the word order within the noun phrase.

The following is a selection from the many examples which Platt et al. (1984) cite for the five categories listed above. In each case, consider what the standard British/American English equivalent would be.

❏   Non-marking of plural forms:
         up to twelve *year* of schooling (India)
         and they know all four *dialect* (Jamaica)
         Pilipino is only one of the *subject* (Philippines)

❏   specific/non-specific system:
         Everyone has *car* (India)   } non-specific
         I'm not on *scholarship* (East Africa)
         I'm staying in *one* house with three other (Indian)   } specific
         There! Here got *one* stall selling soup noodles (Singapore)

❏   quantifiers:
         Don't eat so *much sweets* (Singapore)
         Some few fishermen may be seen (West Africa)
         I applied *couple of places* in Australia (India)

❏   pronouns:
         When I first met my husband, *she* was a student (East Africa)
         My mother, *he* live in kampong (Malaysia; a 'kampong' is a small settlement)

❏   word order:
         A *two-hour exciting* display (Ghana)
         Dis *two last* years (Papua New Guinea)
         Ninety over cheques (Singapore/Malaysia)

Moving on to verbs, these are the main tendencies that Platt et al. (1984: chapter 5) observe in many of the New Englishes:

❏   limited marking of the third person singular present tense form:
         She *drink* milk (Philippines)
         Every microcosm *consist* of many cells (India)

❏   limited marking of verbs for the past tense:
         Mandarin, I *learn* it privately (Hong Kong)
         My wife she *pass* her Cambridge (Singapore)

❏   tendency to use an aspect system (which shows whether an action is finished or still going on) rather than tense system (which shows the time an action takes place):
         I *still eat* (= I am/was eating in Malaysian English)
         I *have worked* there in 1960 (with use of has/have + past participle to indicate a time in the past in Indian English)

❏   a tendency to extend the use of be + verb + ing constructions to stative verbs, e.g:
       She *is knowing* her science very well (East African English)
       Mohan *is having* two houses (Indian English)

❏   the formation of different phrasal and prepositional verb constructions:
       Her name *cropped* in the conversation (East African English)
       I'm going to *voice out* my opinion (West African English)

Finally, a feature common to many New Englishes, such as Indian, Lankan and Malaysian Englishes, is the use of a general or undifferentiated question tag form, particularly 'is it?', 'isn't it?', or 'no?' where Inner Circle Englishes would repeat the tense and subject of the preceding statement in their tags. For example, an Inner Circle speaker would say 'Harriet will be home soon, <u>won't she</u>?', whereas a speaker of Lankan English might say (as my Sri Lankan neighbour actually did) 'Harriet will be home soon, <u>isn't it</u>?'. As Mesthrie and Bhatt (2008: 133) point out, 'these undifferentiated tags play an important pragmatic role . . . exhibiting how linguistic form is constrained by cultural constraints of politeness'. The general tag is seen as 'non-impositional and mitigating' whereas the canonical tag (the first type) is seen as 'assertive'.

Vocabulary/idiom

There are several respects in which we could study New English vocabulary, but we will restrict examples to locally coined words/expressions; borrowings from indigenous languages; and idioms. The examples below come from Platt et al. (1984) supplemented by Kachru and Smith (2008) and Trudgill and Hannah (2002).

Locally coined words/expressions

The creative capacity of speakers of New Englishes tends to be overlooked by speakers of Inner Circle varieties, with creativity still often being classified as error. This is an issue which you will be asked to respond to in B4. **Coinages** most commonly arise in one of two ways: by the addition of a prefix or suffix to an existing (British or indigenous) word, and by compounding, where a local concept is compounded from English items.

   Examples of the first kind of coinage are:

sting<u>ko</u>	colloquial Singapore English: 'smelly'
spac<u>y</u>	Indian English 'spacious'
heat<u>y</u>	Singapore/Malaysian English for foods which make the body hot, e.g. the stingko fruit, durian.
teacher<u>ess</u>	Indian English: 'female teacher'
jeep<u>ney</u>	Philippine English: 'a small bus' (army jeeps having been converted to buses)
<u>en</u>stool	Ghanaian English: 'to install a chief'
<u>de</u>stool	Ghanaian English: 'to depose a chief'

Examples of the second kind of coinage are:

peelhead	Jamaican English: 'a bald-headed person'
bushmeat	West African English: 'game'
dry coffee	East African English: 'coffee without milk and sugar'
chewing stick	African English: 'twig chewed at one end to clean one's teeth'
key-bunch	Indian English: 'bunch of keys'
dining leaf	Indian English: 'banana, lotus or other leaf used as a plate'
basket-woman	Lankan English: 'coarsely behaved woman'
high hat	Philippine English: 'a snob'

Borrowings from indigenous languages

East African English:	*chai*	'tea'
	duka	'shop'
	manamba	'labourer'
Indian English:	*bandh*	'a total strike in an area'
	crore	'ten million'
	swadeshi	indigenous, native, home-grown'
Philippine English:	*boondock*	'mountain'
	kundiman	'love song'

Idioms

Platt et al. (1984) distinguish between learners' unsuccessful attempts to use the idioms of native speakers of English, and stabilise New English idioms. They discount the first kind altogether, a policy on which you might or might not agree with them. However, they cite examples such as Singapore English 'gift of the gap' (for British English 'gift of the gab') and 'in lips and bounce' (for 'in leaps and bounds'), where the variation from the native speaker version is regular on account of pronunciation differences.

Some New English idioms are direct translations from indigenous idioms. For example, Singapore and Malaysian English 'to shake legs' comes from the Malay idiom 'goyang kaki', meaning 'to be idle'. Some New English idioms are based on native speaker English, e.g. the East African idiom 'to be on the tarmac', meaning 'to be in the process of seeking a new job'. Others involve combine elements from English with indigenous forms, e.g. the Nigerian 'to put sand in someone's gari' means 'to threaten someone's livelihood' ('gari' being a type of flour). Still other idioms are variations on native speaker ones, for example, the British English idiom 'to have your cake and eat it' becomes, in Singapore English, rather more effectively, 'to eat your cake and have it'. Presumably this began life as an unsuccessful attempt at the 'correct' British version and gradually became common Singapore usage. Another example from Singapore English is 'to be in hot soup', which has the same meaning as, and is a combination of, two British English idioms, 'to be in hot water' and 'to be in the soup' (i.e. to be in trouble). This highlights the difficulty in distinguishing between New English creativity and incorrectness, and it is important to bear in mind that most linguistic innovation begins life as something that would be considered an error in the standard form. This difficulty, as we shall see in unit 6, is even greater when in relation to Expanding Circle Englishes.

Discourse style

A feature of several New Englishes is that they have a more formal character than the Inner Circle Englishes. In particular, their vocabulary and grammatical structure are more complex. Indian English, in particular, favours 'lengthy constructions, bookish vocabulary and exaggerated forms which make even a formal style appear "more formal" to a speaker of another variety of English' (Platt et al. 1984: 149). Formality is, of course, a relative construct and, as the previous quotation implies, the language will only seem 'bookish' and 'exaggerated' to those who habitually use different forms.

Some Indian English stylistic features are logical extensions of British English strategies. For example, 'could' and 'would' are used in Indian English where British English would use 'can' and will', as in 'We hope that you <u>could</u> join us' or 'We hope that the Vice-Chancellor <u>would</u> investigate this matter' (Trudgill and Hannah 2002: 132). In both these cases, the past tense is used because it is felt to be more tentative and therefore more polite. The same strategy is regularly employed in British English. For example, in an instruction to a non-intimate, if the speaker wishes to appear more polite, he or she is likely to say 'Could you open the door?' rather than 'Can you open the door?'.

On the other hand, both Indian and African Englishes use a discourse style which cannot be found in Inner Circle Englishes, and here the indigenous culture is at least in part an influence. For example, certain aspects of Indian culture lead to expressions of thanks, deferential vocabulary and the use of blessings which would seem redundant or overdone to a speaker of an Inner Circle English: 'I am bubbling with zeal and enthusiasm to serve as a research assistant', or 'I offer myself as a candidate for the post of Research Assistant. Thanking you' (Platt et al. 1984: 150–1).

An area where the New Englishes differ very much from those of the Inner Circle is that of greeting and leave-taking. In the New Englishes, these are often direct translations from the indigenous language. Some examples of greetings are:

> Lankan English: So how? (translation from Sinhala)
> Nigerian English: You're enjoying? (translation from Yoruba)
> Singaporean/Malaysian English: Have you eaten already?
> West African English: How? How now?
> East African English: Are you all right?

and of leave-takings:

> Lankan English: I'll go and come
> Singaporean/Malaysian English: Walk slowly ho!

Finally, as is demonstrated by some of the preceding examples, the phenomenon of **code-mixing/code-switching** (using words, phrases, and longer stretches of speech in two or more languages) is characteristic of the speech of bi- and multilingual people. We will return to this phenomenon in unit B7.

STANDARD LANGUAGE IDEOLOGY IN THE INNER CIRCLE   A5

Standard language and language standards

Standard language and language standards are topics which excite an immense amount of controversy both inside and outside the linguistics profession. **Standard language** is the term used for that variety of a language which is considered to be the norm. It is the variety held up as the optimum for educational purposes and used as a yardstick against which other varieties of the language are measured. Being a **prestige variety**, a standard language is spoken by a minority of people within a society, typically those occupying positions of power. In other words, as Milroy (2001: 532) argues, 'varieties of language do not actually have prestige in themselves: these varieties acquire prestige when their *speakers* have high prestige'. Not surprisingly, then, as Mesthrie and Bhatt (2008: 14–15) point out, 'standard English has almost come to have a life and power of its own', with the ideology of standardisation 'presenting the standard as the primordial entity from which other dialects deviate' and, in turn, having 'important ramifications for the status of new varieties of English that developed . . . beyond the south of England and beyond the British Isles'.

    Language standards are the reverse side of the standard language coin. These are the prescriptive language rules which together constitute the standard and to which all members of a language community are exposed and urged to conform during education, regardless of the local variety. Because a living language is by definition dynamic, these rules are subject to change over time. During its earlier and transitional stages, language change is regarded as error by promoters of standard language ideology (lay as well as professional). It is the subject of much criticism from self-appointed guardians of 'correct' usage, who tend to hark back to a mythical linguistic 'Golden Age', often that of their own childhood.

    Because language standards seem not to function in the interests of certain groups, especially speakers of New Englishes, Parakrama argues that standards should be made more inclusive:

> Language standards are rarely contested, even by those who are engaged in radical and far-reaching social critique. Yet, standards discriminate against those who don't conform, and language standardisation has systematically worked against the underclass as well as women and minorities . . . The existence of standards, however objectionable, cannot be denied, so the only viable option, politically at any rate, is to work towards broadening the standard to include the greatest

variety possible, particularly the 'uneducated' arenas of usage which have so far been considered inappropriate, mistaken, even pathological.

(Parakrama 1995: back cover)

Hudson (1996: 32) describes standard languages as 'quite abnormal' in their development: 'Whereas one thinks of normal language development as taking place in a rather haphazard way, largely below the threshold of consciousness of the speakers, standard languages are the result of a direct and deliberate intervention by society'. Following Haugen (1966) he summarises this process of intervention as going through four stages, selection, codification, elaboration of function, and acceptance:

Selection

This is the most critical stage in the standardising process. It refers to the way in which one variety rather than any other is chosen as the one which will be developed as the standard language. Often, this is an existing variety which already has political and/or economic currency. Modern standard English, for instance, derives from Mercian, the East Midlands dialect favoured by the educated in London after the Royal Court was established there following the Norman Conquest, and the centre of power had moved away from Winchester and its West Saxon dialect (see Crystal 2003b: 29). On the other hand, the process could involve the selecting of features from several varieties or even, as in the case of Classical Hebrew in Israel, of a language variety that has no native speakers. Selection is, of course, a social and political process, since it is invariably led by those in power and subsequently reinforces and further promotes their interests over those of speakers of other (by definition 'non-standard') varieties.

Codification

Once selection has taken place, the variety chosen to represent the standard has to be 'fixed' in grammar books and dictionaries in order that those people who wish to use the language 'correctly' have access to its standard forms.

Elaboration of function

To fulfil its role, the standard variety has to be capable of performing a wide range of institutional and literary functions, particularly, though not exclusively, in government, law, education, science and literature. At this stage, then, new lexical items are added and new conventions developed to fill any gaps.

Acceptance

Clearly, unless the relevant population accept the selected variety as their standard and, most probably, their national language, then all will have been in vain. In practice, though, since those who make the selection tend to be, or to represent, those who have the right of veto, acceptance is unlikely to be an issue. Those who already lacked political and economic power will continue to do so, with their inferior status in society now being symbolised by their use of an 'inferior' language variety: a social, regional or ethnic dialect. For the time being, the standard variety, as Hudson (1996: 33) says, 'serves as a strong unifying force for the state, as a symbol of its independence of other states . . . and as a marker of its difference from other states'. On the other hand, it is quite possible that in times to come, there will be challenges to the 'accepted' variety from those both within and outside its users. This is currently the situation with English, as the next two sections will demonstrate.

What is standard English?

Standard English is by no means an easy language variety to identify. In the case of languages such as French and Italian, for which academies prescribe the forms that may and may not be codified in their grammars and dictionaries, the standard is evident. Even those people who do not themselves wish to promote it are able, year on year, to ascertain exactly what it is. All is less certain with standard English, not only in terms of its worldwide use (which is the subject of the following section) but also in its Inner Circle contexts.

The following are some of the main definitions of standard English which have been proposed in recent years. They are listed in chronological order of their first appearance in print, although as you will see, those that appear in later editions of the same publication have not altered. The first, third and sixth refer specifically to British English whereas the remaining three appear to include all Inner Circle Englishes.

1   The dialect of educated people throughout the British Isles. It is the dialect normally used in writing, for teaching in schools and universities, and heard on radio and television (Hughes and Trudgill 1979, repeated in the 2nd edition, 1996).
2   The variety of the English language which is normally employed in writing and normally spoken by educated speakers of the language. It is also, of course, the variety of the language that students of English as a foreign or second language (EFL/ESL) are taught when receiving formal instruction. The term 'standard English' refers to grammar and vocabulary (***dialect***) but not to pronunciation (***accent***) (Trudgill and Hannah 1982, and repeated in the 4th edition, 2002).
3   Standard English can be characterised by saying that it is that set of grammatical and lexical forms which is typically used in speech and writing by educated native speakers. 'It . . . includes the use of colloquial and slang vocabulary as well as swear words and taboo expressions' (Trudgill 1984).
4   The term 'standard English' is potentially misleading for at least two reasons. First, in order to be self-explanatory, it really ought to be called 'the grammar and the core vocabulary of educated usage in English'. That would make plain the fact that it is not the whole of English, and above all, it is not pronunciation that can in any way be labelled 'Standard', but only one part of English: its grammar and vocabulary (Strevens 1985).
5   Since the 1980s, the notion of 'standard' has come to the fore in public debate about the English language . . . We may define the standard English of an English-speaking country as a minority variety (identified chiefly by its vocabulary, grammar and orthography) which carries most prestige and is most widely understood (Crystal 1995, repeated in the 2nd edition, 2003b).
6   Traditionally the medium of the upper and (especially professional) middle class, and by and large of education . . . Although not limited to one accent (most

notably in recent decades), it has been associated since at least the nineteenth century with the accent that, since the 1920s, has been called *Received Pronunciation (RP)*, and with the phrases *the Queen's English*, *the King's English*, *Oxford English*, and *BBC English* (McArthur 2002).

These definitions bear certain similarities. For instance, there is a fair degree of consensus that accent is not involved in standard English, although as McArthur implies, the British general public associate the 'standard' with an RP accent. There is also general agreement that standard English is primarily a case of grammar and vocabulary, and that it is the variety promoted through the education system. Nevertheless, this does not help us to any great extent if we want to know what it all means in practice. Possibly the best attempt to provide such information is contained in an article by Trudgill, the originator of three of the above definitions. In 'Standard English: what it isn't' (1999), Trudgill demonstrates what may be the only feasible way of defining a 'non-academy' standard language such as English. That is, by what it is not:

❑ It is not a language: it is only one variety of a given English.
❑ It is not an accent: in Britain it is spoken by 12–15 per cent of the population, of whom 9–12 per cent speak it with a regional accent.
❑ It is not a **style**: it can be spoken in formal, neutral and informal styles, respectively:

> Father was exceedingly fatigued subsequent to his extensive peregrinations.
> Dad was very tired after his lengthy journey.
> The old man was bloody knackered after his long trip.

❑ It is not a **register**: given that a register is largely a matter of lexis in relation to subject matter (e.g. the register of medicine, of cricket, or of knitting), there is no necessary connection between register and standard English. Trudgill (1999: 122) provides this example: 'There was two eskers what we saw in them U-shaped valleys' to demonstrate 'a non-standard English sentence couched in the technical register of physical geography'.
❑ It is not a set of prescriptive rules: it can tolerate certain features which, because many of their rules are grounded in Latin, prescriptive grammarians do not allow. Trudgill (1999: 125) provides these examples: sentence-final prepositions as in 'I've bought a new car which I'm very pleased with', and constructions such as 'It's me', 'He is taller than me'.

Trudgill concludes that standard English is a dialect that differs from the other dialects of English in that it has greater prestige, does not have an associated accent, and does not form part of a geographical continuum. In other words, it is purely a **social dialect**. He goes on to point out that while standard English has many features in common with the other dialects of the country in question, there are certain differences and that these differences do not necessarily indicate the linguistic superiority of the standard forms.

Non-standard Englishes

It is not unusual for all the regional native speaker dialects of English to be lumped together with all the New Englishes (in both standard and non-standard versions) under the label **non-standard**, with the implication that all are inferior. Somewhat surprisingly, even educated Australian English belonged until recently to this category, only joining the ranks of standard English in the 1970s. Up to then, Australian English was evaluated in terms of its closeness to Standard British English (known locally as the 'colonial cringe'), with any distinctively Australian forms being regarded as 'bad' English. The first dictionary of Australian English to be edited within Australia's shores rather than in Britain was only published in 1976. Since then, educated Australians have developed a new confidence in their own identity which has translated linguistically into the celebration of their own ways of speaking and a new reluctance to hark back to their British roots and ape Standard British English.

If it was so difficult for a standard native speaker variety of English to gain acceptance, it is no surprise, then, that non-standard native varieties and both standard and non-standard non-native varieties have not so far met with similar success. In the case of the non-standard native varieties, lack of acceptance appears to have connections with attitudes towards race in the US and class in the UK. In her discussion of Standard American and British English, Milroy argues that people find it easier to identify the non-standard than the standard, and goes on to propose that

> in a sense, the standard [American English] of popular perception is what is left behind when all the non-standard varieties spoken by disparaged persons such as Valley Girls, Hillbillies, Southerners, New Yorkers, African Americans, Asians, Mexican Americans, Cubans and Puerto Ricans are set aside. In Britain, where consciousness of the special status of RP as a class accent is acute, spoken standard English might similarly be described as what is left after we remove from the linguistic bran-tub Estuary English, Brummie, Cockney, Geordie, Scouse, various quaint rural dialects, London Jamaican, transatlantic slang and perhaps even conservative RP as spoken by older members of the upper classes.
>
> (L. Milroy 1999: 174)

The New Englishes in both their standard and non-standard manifestations tend to be regarded in much the same way as the non-standard varieties of Inner Circle Englishes. In other words, Outer Circle Englishes which have undergone standardisation processes and codified their own standard, for example, Standard Singapore English and Standard Indian English, are nevertheless considered 'non-standard' by outsiders and it is not uncommon even for their own speakers to regard them as second-best in relation to the standard Englishes of the Inner Circle. This position is implicit, for example, in a letter to the editor of the British newspaper, *The Observer*, on 20 July 2008 from a correspondent in Bhopal, India, in response to an article the previous week that had bemoaned the so-called declining standards of British English speakers. The Indian correspondent told readers that he had been taught 'the Queen's English' in India as a child in the 1920s, had since 'been careful not to allow that standard to slip', and considered his use of English and that of other Indians to be 'exemplary'.

Then, in a reversal of traditional roles, he advised the British to raise the standard of their own English to that 'still held in other parts of the world'.

In several parts of the world including a number of African-English-speaking countries, standardisation processes are currently underway, and it will be some time before local standards can be codified in home-grown grammars and dictionaries. Even when this has been achieved, however, these standard Englishes are unlikely to attract the same prestige as their counterparts in Britain, North America and even, nowadays, Australia. This is because of attitudes held towards these varieties by many members of the Inner Circle, both the general population and even some linguists. Implicit in these attitudes is the belief that the New Englishes are the result of a process known as **fossilisation**. In other words, the learning of English is said to have ceased (or 'fossilised') some way short of target-like competence, with the target being assumed to be either Standard British or Standard American English. Of course, from a sociolinguistic perspective, however, the idea that the New Englishes should have as their target the standard Englishes of the Inner Circle is of dubious validity.

A6 THE SPREAD OF ENGLISH AS AN INTERNATIONAL LINGUA FRANCA

> Not only has 'English' become international in the last half century, but scholarship about English has also become international: the ownership of an interest in English has become international. We are no longer a language community which is associated with a national community or even with a family of nations such as the Commonwealth aspired to be. We are an international community.
>
> (Brumfit 1995: 16)

This quotation from Brumfit neatly encapsulates the changes that took place in the second half of the twentieth century, and that are beginning to impact on the way English is taught and spoken around the world in the early years of the twenty-first century. In A6, we will consider firstly, why it is that English has assumed the role of the world's major international language and secondly, the most serious issue which has to be addressed in the light of this role: the need to ensure mutual intelligibility across international varieties of English.

Why is English the international lingua franca?

Despite the fact that most of England's former colonies had become independent states by the mid-twentieth century, they retained the English language to serve various internal functions (see A1). So, by virtue of its colonial past, English was already well placed to become one of the world's main languages of international business and trade. But in the postcolonial period, English has spread well beyond its use as a second or additional language in the countries of the Outer Circle, to be adopted as an international lingua franca by many countries in the Expanding Circle for whom it performs no official internal functions (see A1 and A3 for numbers of speakers). Crystal (2003b) accounts for the present-day international status of English as the result of two factors, the first being its colonial past, which we have already noted. The second reason, and the one which has ensured the continuing influence of English throughout the twentieth century and beyond, is the economic power of the US:

> The present-day world status of English is primarily the result of two factors: the expansion of British colonial power, which peaked towards the end of the 19th century, and the emergence of the United States as the leading economic power of the 20th century. It is the latter factor which continues to explain the position of the English language today.
>
> (Crystal 2003b: 106)

Before we go on to consider the reasons why English remains the world's first international language into the twenty-first century however, it is important to acknowledge that this is not universally considered to be a beneficial state of affairs. Since the publication of his 1992 book, *Linguistic Imperialism*, Robert Phillipson has continued to argue against the desirability of the spread of English, especially where this spread has the potential to jeopardise the learning of other languages and the very existence of smaller languages (see unit 8 on the latter subject). Others have argued along similar lines; for example, following the events of 11 September 2001, Hilary Footitt, Chair of the University Council of Modern Languages, wrote as follows:

> One of the cultural shocks of September 11 is, overwhelmingly, that English is simply not enough. We cannot understand the world in English, much less search out intelligence, build ever larger coalitions of friends, and heal some of the long-standing wounds of the past. We need to be aware as never before of foreign languages and of the ways in which languages identify and represent their cultures.
>
> (*Guardian Education*, 23 October 2001, p. 15)

This is in direct contrast to the optimistic views regularly expressed by those who, like Telma Gimenez, regard the spread of an international language as wholly positive:

> [H]aving a common language helps us to see ourselves as human beings who live on the same planet, and to that extent can be said to form one community. The value of knowing English lies not only in the ability to access material things, but also in the possibility it offers for creating acceptance of, and respect for, the World's diversity. English allows us to advance toward global exchange and solidarity among the institutions of civil society, extending bonds between citizens far and wide across the globe. For this reason, considering English as an international language can also bring a sense of possibility in terms of strengthening what might be called 'planetary citizenship'.
>
> (*ELT Journal*, vol. 5, no. 3, July 2001, p. 297)

Beneficial or not, for the time being English as a Lingua Franca (ELF), or English as an International Language (EIL) as it is still sometimes known, is a fact of life. And the implications of this situation for L2 English are at last beginning to be addressed, with even the British press finally acknowledging that the English of its non-native speakers may be gaining acceptance in its own right, instead of being considered 'erroneous' wherever it differs from native varieties of English. *The Observer* newspaper, for example, in an article entitled 'Foreign tongues spread the English word', made the following point: 'The accented English of fluent foreigners such as Latino singer Ricky Martin or actress Juliette Binoche is usurping British and American English as the dominant form of the language' (29 October 2000, p. 1). The writer rather spoils his case by going on to report that the Education and Employment Secretary 'will tell a meeting of business leaders on Tuesday to capitalise on their advantage as native speakers', and even that 'the drive to make English the global lingua franca comes directly from Tony Blair [the British Prime Minister]' and is known as the 'Blair initiative'. To the extent that English is the 'global lingua franca' it is neither to the advantage of its native speakers nor controlled by them. These are both issues to which we will return later in strand 6, where we will also look in detail at what, precisely, the phenomenon of ELF is, and at the controversy its research is causing.

Activity ✪

For the moment, though, let us consider the possible reasons why those for whom English is not their mother tongue should wish to learn it, not only in countries such as India, where it is a nativised language that performs institutional functions, but increasingly in Expanding Circle countries such as Brazil, China and Italy. Crystal (2003b: 107) provides the following reasons. As you read through them, consider these two questions:

❏ Which, in your view, are most relevant to those who need or want to be able to communicate *internationally* in the English language?
❏ Are the scenarios that Crystal outlines still the same as they were in 2003 when his list was published, or are you aware of any changing circumstances in relation to your own and/or other countries?

Historical reasons

Because of the legacy of British or American imperialism, the country's main institutions may carry out their proceedings in English. These include the governing body (e.g. parliament), government agencies, the civil service (at least at senior levels), the law courts, national religious bodies, the schools, and higher educational institutions, along with their related publications (textbooks, proceedings, records, etc.).

Internal political reasons

Whether a country has imperial antecedents or not, English may have a role in providing a neutral means of communication between its different ethnic groups as it does, for example, in India. A distinctive local variety of English may also become a symbol of national unity or emerging nationhood. The use of English in newspapers, on radio or on television adds a further dimension.

External economic reasons

The USA's dominant economic position acts as a magnet for international business and trade, and organisations wishing to develop international markets are thus under considerable pressure to work with English. The tourist and advertising industries are particularly English-dependent, but any multinational business will wish to establish offices in the major English-speaking countries.

Practical reasons

English is the language of international air traffic control, and is currently developing its role in international maritime, policing, and emergency services. It is the chief language of international business and academic conferences, and the leading language of international tourism.

Intellectual reasons

Most of the scientific, technological, and academic information in the world is expressed in English, and over 80 per cent of all the information stored in electronic retrieval systems is in English (but see A8 for more recent statstics). Closely related to this is the concern to have access to the philosophical, cultural, religious and literary history of Western Europe, either directly or through the medium of an English translation. In most parts of the world, the only way most people have access to such authors as Goethe or Dante is through English. Latin performed a similar role in Western Europe for over a thousand years.

Entertainment reasons

English is the main language of popular music (particularly hip hop), and permeates popular culture and its associated advertising. It is also the main language of satellite broadcasting, home computers, and video games, as well as of such international illegal activities as pornography and drugs.

To the above points made by Crystal we could add **personal advantage/ prestige** since, in many cultures, the ability to speak English is perceived as conferring higher status on the speaker.

Crystal also adds a final section 'Some wrong reasons'. These concern beliefs that English is 'inherently a more logical or beautiful language than others, easier to pronounce, simpler in grammatical structure, or larger in vocabulary.' As Crystal points out, 'this kind of reasoning is the consequence of unthinking chauvinism or naïve linguistic thinking', and it is impossible to compare languages objectively in such ways. English, for example, may have few inflectional endings, but also has very complex syntax, and this has not prevented it from being learned and used around the world. So a third question for you to consider is:

❑   Why do you think beliefs about the intrinsic linguistic superiority of English persist?

The conflict between mutual intelligibility and group identity

If English is to fulfil its role as the world's international lingua franca, it goes without saying that it must be capable of achieving **mutual intelligibility** among speakers and writers from all first language backgrounds who wish to communicate in English. The main obstacle to such mutual intelligibility is identity. For, as Crystal (2003a: 127) points out, 'the need for intelligibility and the need for identity often pull people – and countries – in opposing directions'.

In essence, the problem is this. With the increase in the number of first language (L1) groups who speak English as an international language, the range of differences among their Englishes has also inevitably increased. These differences are particularly evident in the spoken language, and more so in terms of pronunciation than at the other linguistic levels, since it is on pronunciation that first language transfer has its greatest influence.

The demands of mutual intelligibility point to a need to decrease accent differences among speakers from different L1 backgrounds. This, however, does not necessarily involve encouraging L2 learners to imitate a native speaker accent. Indeed, such attempts have invariably failed. Accents may be closely bound up with feelings of personal and group **identity**, which means that people tend to resist such attempts, whether consciously or subconsciously. They may wish to preserve their mother-tongue accent in their L2 English or they may simply wish not to identify, through mimicking an L1 English accent, with native speakers of the language. And in the case of ELF (as contrasted with EFL), there is strong justification for not conforming to the accent (or even the lexicogrammar) of a native speaker group: the fact that the ELF community is by definition international rather than associated with any one national speech community. As Dörnyei et al. (2006: 110) point out in this respect, 'for a growing number of learners English now represents the language of the "world at large" rather than the language of a well-specified target language community.' They observe that '[t]his broadening view of ownership has had major consequences on L2 motivation research because the lack of a well-specified target language community undermines the attitudinal base of Gardner's (1985) traditional concept of **integrative motivation**' (2006: 9).

Integrative motivation involves the desire to come close to the target language community, and even complete identification with it. One of the current debates going on among ELF researchers is the extent to which English used in lingua franca contexts can be a language of identification and not simply one of communication. In other words, if ELF users no longer identify with an Inner Circle community of English speakers, is there a sense in which they identify instead with their own L1 group and/or a wider ELF community? Later in strand 6 we will consider this issue as well as exploring possible ways of preserving intelligibility in ELF communication that do not entail deferring to native English varieties, but enable ELF speakers to project their own identities in their English if they so wish.

Consider the roles of intelligibility and identity in your own language learning experience, as follows:

If you speak English as a second or subsequent language:

❏ Have you ever given thought to retaining your L1 identity in English?
❏ Is it important to you to retain your L1 identity in English?
❏ Are you more concerned to be intelligible to native speakers of English or to non-native speakers of English, or do you not distinguish between the two groups of listener?
❏ Do you believe it is appropriate to retain your L1 accent in your English or that you should attempt to sound 'native-like'?
❏ Do you believe it is possible to retain your L1 accent in English and still be intelligible to native-speakers?/to non-native speakers?

If you speak English as a first language and another language/other languages as second/subsequent languages:

❏ Have you ever given thought to retaining your L1 identity in the other language(s) you speak?
❏ Is it important to you to retain your L1 identity in the other language(s) you speak?
❏ Do you believe it is appropriate to retain your L1 English accent in your other language(s) or that you should attempt to sound like native speakers of the language(s)?
❏ Do you believe it is possible to retain your L1 accent in your other language(s) and still be intelligible to native speakers of that language? Have you had any personal experiences that support your view?

For both groups:

❏ What is your reaction to the following distinction which Prodromou makes between the learning/speaking of English and that of other modern foreign languages such as Spanish? Do you agree or not? Why/why not? If you do agree, what do you see as the most important implications for the speaking of English?

Most people quite simply do not learn English to speak to native-speakers. On the other hand, people learn Spanish, as I am doing at present, because they are interested in Hispanic culture for some reason (work or pleasure) and will therefore want a spoken and written model which will further this aim. There is a world of difference between English and, in fact, all other living languages at present.

(Prodromou 1997: 19)

~~GLISH IN ASIA AND EUROPE~~

~~Similarities and differences~~

used on two large non-Inner Circle regions in which English is
ope. In Expanding Circle Europe, while change is taking place
re several paces behind those of the Asian Outer Circle. In the
venty-first century, European English, or **Euro-English** as it is
increasing, s only just emerging as a distinctive variety or, more accurately,
group of varieties with its own identity which, like the Outer Circle Asian Englishes,
rejects the concept of having to defer to British English or American English norms
(see D7). What has already become clear is that English is evolving as a European
lingua franca not only in restricted fields such as business and commerce, but also in
a wide range of other contexts of communication including its increasing use as a language of socialisation. The progress of the codified Asian Englishes thus indicates the
likely future development of Euro-English.

A second similarity between Asian and Euro-Englishes is that both, by definition,
are evolving within contexts of bi- or multilingualism. This has implications not only
for the ways in which English is used by its majority (bilingual) speakers, but also for
the ways in which it is taught and tested (see C3).

A third similarity is one that Asian and European Englishes share with all non-
Inner Circle Englishes whether institutionalised or not. That is, they are 'linguistic
orphans in search of their parents' (Kachru 1992: 66). Kachru is referring here to the
still widespread – if slowly diminishing – belief that non-native and nativised English
varieties are deficient and unacceptable by virtue of the local characteristics they have
acquired in the process of being transplanted. Such attitudes in turn deter speakers of
non-native and even nativised English varieties from identifying with and promoting
their own local model. This issue will be taken up in the readings in D7.

English as an Asian language

Asian Englishes can be categorised both regionally and functionally. Regionally, they
are typically divided into three groupings, although the South-East and East Asian
varieties are sometimes grouped together (see Table A7.1).

Functionally, Asian Englishes are divided into two categories, depending on
whether they are institutionalised varieties of the Outer Circle or non-institutionalised
varieties of the Expanding Circle (see Table A7.2).

Table A7.1 Asian Englishes by region.

South Asian varieties	South-East Asian and Pacific varieties	East Asian varieties
Bangladesh	Brunei	China
Bhutan	Cambodia	Hong Kong
India	Fiji	Japan
Maldives	Indonesia	Korea
Nepal	Laos	Taiwan
Pakistan	Malaysia	
Sri Lanka	Myanmar	
	Philippines	
	Singapore	
	Thailand	
	Vietnam	

Table A7.2 Asian Englishes by use.

Institutionalised varieties (Outer Circle)	Non-institutionalised varietes (Expanding Circle)
Bangladesh	Cambodia
Bhutan	China
Brunei	Indonesia
Fiji	Japan
Hong Kong	Korea
India	Laos
Malaysia	Maldives
Nepal	Myanmar
Pakistan	Taiwan
Philippines	Thailand
Singapore	Vietnam
Sri Lanka	

Of the above territories, numbers of L2 English speakers with reasonable com-petence range from India (200 million), the Philippines (40 million) and Pakistan (17 million), to Hong Kong, Singapore and Sri Lanka each with around two million, Brunei with only 134,000 and Bhutan with only 75,000 (figures from Crystal 2003a; see A1 above). However, the figures disguise the fact that in some of these areas the L2 variety of English is spoken by a very large percentage of the total population. For example, almost half of Singaporeans speak L2 English, but this amounts to only two million of a population of 4,300,000. Again, just over two million Hong Kongese speak an L2 variety of English, but they constitute almost a third of the total Hong Kong population. On the other hand, less than a fifth of Indians speak L2 English with reasonable competence, but because the total population is over one billion, the number of L2 Indian English speakers is vast.

The South Asian Englishes (with the exception of the Maldives) belong to the Outer Circle. Indian, Lankan, Pakistani and Bangladeshi Englishes are often grouped together and known collectively as South Asian English(es) (see Crystal 2003a: 144). Within this group, Indian and Lankan Englishes are the most developed and well documented. At the other extreme, little information is available about the Englishes of Bhutan, the Maldives and Nepal. Even the weighty tome *The Handbook of World Englishes* (Kachru et al. 2006) is not able to enlighten us much. Bhutan is mentioned in a single sentence and the Maldives not at all. Only Nepal is given an entire (short) paragraph of its own, in which we learn that from 2005 to 2007 an Action Plan in primary education involved the teaching of three languages: Nepali, a local language, and English (Gargesh 2006: 100–1).

These Asian countries have much in common in terms of their history and culture, and in the way the English language is sustained within each one by similar groups of elites to perform similar roles (Kandiah 1991). On the other hand, there are differences. In postcolonial Bangladesh, for example, there has been relatively little interest in English beyond the utilitarian: that of widening access by bringing non-English speakers to a level of competence that will enable them to participate in those 'modern' spheres of activity traditionally dominated by the English language and its users. The same was true of Pakistan until recently, when the nation became interested in developing its own distinct variety of English. At present, though, the indications are that Pakistani English is developing still exonormatively (i.e. according to external norms), with British English as its reference point (Kandiah 1991). However, this may not remain the case for much longer in view of the (disconcerting) evidence that young educated Pakistani people are increasingly giving up the use of their local language, Urdu, in favour of English (Najma Husein, personal communication).

By contrast, English in India operates well beyond the confines of the practical uses for which it is learnt in Bangladesh and hitherto in Pakistan. This is to a great extent a function of the unifying role it plays as a neutral language of communication across a people of diverse mother tongues and, as a result, the way in which it has become bound up with Indian national consciousness and identity. Today Indian English performs a wide range of public and personal functions in a variety which has evolved its own phonological, syntactic, lexical and discoursal features rather than continuing to defer to those of its British past (see C7).

Like Indian English, Lankan English, too, has acquired a wide range of local functions both public and personal, though for political reasons it has so far not played the same neutral role in communication across speakers of different mother tongues in Sri Lanka as it has in India. In recent years the government has been promoting English as a link language between warring Sinhalese and Tamils, though this policy may not succeed because of differences in orientation towards the learning and use of English across the two ethnic groups (Canagarajah 1999: 82), as well as the fact that English is seen as 'a class marker (i.e. as the language of the educated and rich)' (Canagarajah 1999: 72).

Brunei, in common with most of the other Outer Circle territories, is linguistically diverse. Malay is the main language group, with Bahasa Melayu being the official language and Brunei Malay the most widely used. English is the most important non-native language as a result of colonial links with Britain, and plays an important role in education (where a bilingual system is in place), law and the media. Attitudes to English in the region are positive, with a study carried out in 1993 (Jones 1997) reporting that Bruneians want to study and be proficient in both Malay and English. Code-switching between Malay and English has become common among educated Bruneians. Saxena (2008) points out that Brunei increasingly perceives itself as part of the global economic and political system, and considers learning and using English essential for this purpose. It thus appears likely that in future there will be a further shift towards English, with Bruneian Malays, like Malays in Singapore, using English in their homes, and accompanied by the emergence of a more clearly identifiable variety of Brunei English.

Of Fiji's population of 850,000, just under 20 per cent, or 170,000, speak English as an L2. English is the national language of the territory, and is used in education, government and business. As in several other Outer Circle countries, it also serves as the language of communication among Fiji's different ethnic groups. From the limited data so far available, it nevertheless seems that Fiji English has already become a distinctive local variety characterised by a number of features which differ from L1 Englishes (see Siegel 1991).

Moving on to Malaysia, as Pennycook (1994: 217) tells us, 'The fortunes of English in Malaysia have waxed and waned and waxed again, and it never seems far from the centre of debate'. There are in fact eighty languages spoken in Malaysia, with Malay (Bahasa Malaysia) the national language and primary lingua franca across ethnic groups, English the second most important language, and Chinese, Tamil and other Indian languages used among ethnic communities – the latter two largely in family, social and religious domains. It is as a result of the success of nationalism and confidence in the stability of Bahasa Malaysia as the country's national language that English can once again be promoted in the Malaysian education system. However, because of the previous decline in English use, there is a wide range of proficiency among speakers. The most competent are the English-medium-educated Malaysian elite, and it is this group who will establish norms for Malaysian English and determine the target model for acquisition. Because these English speakers use English within a complex linguistic repertoire in which they engage in frequent codeswitching between English and Malay, there is considerable scope for borrowing from Malay into Malaysian English as the variety evolves. The current concern, as in a number of these regions, is to document the developed or developing 'standard variety that reflects their national identity as well as ensures international intelligibility', and that in Malaysia is described as 'Standard Malaysian English' (Gill 2002: 29).

The English of the Philippines is possibly the most comprehensively researched of all South-East Asian varieties of English including Singaporean (see Tay 1991, and Bautista et al. 2004, a special issue on Philippine English of the journal *World Englishes*). English is the second language of the Philippines, where a bilingual education policy – English and Filipino (based on Tagalog) – was adopted in 1972 and is now in place at all school levels, although Filipino remains the national lingua franca while English serves as the language of wider cross-cultural communication. A distinctive

Philippine variety of English has nevertheless been documented since the late 1960s, when idiosyncratic pronunciation and grammatical features began to be considered legitimate varietal characteristics rather than errors. There are considerable differences between the Philippine English of older and younger generations, along with variation in use among proficient English users ranging from informal (with patterned code-mixing known as 'Mix-mix') to establish familiarity and rapport, to standard Philippine English for careful speech and writing (see Tay 1991).

Thus, English is already well-ensconced in Asia, if more deeply in some of its regions than others. The greatest need now is for more research into the less well-documented Asian Englishes.

The changing role of English in Europe

The European Union (EU) is linguistically rich. When the first edition of this book went to press, eleven EU languages had official status. This number has since grown to twenty-three: Bulgarian, Czech, Danish, Dutch, English, Estonian, Finnish, French, German, Greek, Hungarian, Italian, Irish, Latvian, Lithuanian, Maltese, Polish, Portuguese, Romanian, Slovak, Slovene, Spanish and Swedish. Nevertheless, of these, just three languages dominate – English, French and German. Europe has become, in Graddol's (1997: 14) words,

> a single multilingual area, rather like India, where languages are hierarchically related in status. As in India, there may be many who are monolingual in a regional language, but those who speak one of the 'big' languages will have better access to material success.

By the end of the twentieth century, however, a single one of the three 'big' languages, English, had become the 'biggest', the de facto European lingua franca. And for the time being at least, it seems, those who speak English will have the best access to such material success, hence, in part, the current popularity of learning English among Europe's young that Cheshire (2002) documents.

Many scholars, most vociferously Phillipson (2003a), and including Cheshire herself, believe it is critical for all Europeans to learn each other's languages rather than for everyone to learn English. On the other hand, House (2001), whose position is for the most part diametrically opposed to Phillipson's, finds the EU's language policy hypocritical and ineffective. Rather than having several working languages and making heavy use of a translation machinery, she argues, the EU should opt officially for English as its lingua franca or, as she puts it, the 'language for communication'. On the other hand, House does not appear to consider the possibility that English can express the 'social identities' of its continental European English speakers. Instead, she believes that individual speakers' mother tongues will remain their 'language for identification' (House 2001: 2–3, and see D6). Cheshire (2002), by contrast, notes that European English appears to be developing the scope to 'express "emotional" aspects of young people's social identities' by means of phenomena such as code-switching and code-mixing (e.g. the use of half-German half-English hybrid compounds such as *Telefon junkie*, *Drogenfreak* and *Metallfan*, in German youth magazines). And subsequently, Seidlhofer et al. (2006) have documented a number of emerging features of Euro-English that could be seen as identity markers (see C6 below for further discussion of the ELF identity issue among Expanding Circle English speakers).

The positioning of English as Europe's primary lingua franca is so recent that it is too soon to be able to say with any certainty whether it will remain so, how it will develop, and whether it will expand to become fully capable of expressing social identity as well as performing a more transactional role in politics, business and the like. The linguistic outcome of European political and economic developments is predicted by some scholars to be a nativised hybrid variety of English, in effect, a European English containing a number of grammatical, lexical, phonological and discoursal features found in individual continental European languages along with some items common to many of these languages but not to standard British (or American) English.

Berns (1995: 6–7), for example, characterises the **nativisation** process that English in Europe is undergoing as follows: 'In the course of using English to carry out its three roles [native, foreign and international language], Europeans make adaptations and introduce innovations that effectively de-Americanize and de-Anglicize English'. She talks specifically of a 'European English-using speech community' who use English for intra-European communication, and for whom 'the label *European English* identifies those uses of English that are not British (and not American or Canadian or Australian or any other native variety) but are distinctly European and distinguish European English speakers from speakers of other [English] varieties'. In her view, it is possible that British English will eventually be considered merely as one of a number of European varieties of English alongside nativised varieties such as French English, Dutch English, Danish English and the like.

European English speakers are, nevertheless, as Berns (1995: 10) concludes, 'in the midst of an exciting, challenging, and creative social and linguistic phase of their history' in which 'they have the potential to have significant influence on the spread of English'. The situation is, as she puts it, one of 'sociolinguistic history-in-the-making' and one which will therefore need to be reviewed regularly as empirical evidence becomes increasingly available.

THE FUTURE OF WORLD ENGLISHES   A8

In A8, we consider the implications of English having become the language of 'others', along with the possibility that within the twenty-first century it may lose its position as principal world language to one or more of the languages of these 'others'. In B8, the first of these two themes is developed in a debate as to whether English, if it does remain the major world language, will ultimately fragment into a large number of mutually unintelligible varieties (in effect, languages), or will converge so that differences across groups of speakers are largely eliminated. In C8, the first theme is explored in terms of the extent to which English may either become a killer of other languages or evolve as a common language within a framework of world bilingualism. The strand ends in D8 with an extract from Graddol's meticulous study of English in its world context, *The Future of English?* which takes up many of these issues and leads us into the question-mark of the unknown. This is followed by Crystal's 2008 commentary on an article he had written in 1985, and points from Graddol's 2006 study, *English Next*. Taken together, these three publications demonstrate both how rapidly events are moving English-wise (even between the first and second editions of this book), and how little we can still predict.

English as the language of 'others'

I place 'others' in quotation marks to indicate that the term is, of course, culturally loaded and that my usage is ironic here. If English is already numerically the language of these 'others' and, as the century proceeds, is to become more overtly so, then the centre of gravity of the language is almost certain to shift in the direction of the 'others'. In the years to come we are very likely to witness increasing claims from English speakers outside the Inner Circle, especially in growing economies such as Brazil, Russia, India and China, for English language rights of the sort that were discussed particularly in A4, A6 and A7 (see Graddol 2006: 32–3 on 'the rise of the BRICs'). In the words of Widdowson, there is likely to be a paradigm shift from one of language *distribution* to one of language *spread*:

> I would argue that English as an international language is not *distributed*, as a set of established encoded forms, unchanged into different domains of use, but it is *spread* as a virtual language . . . When we talk about the spread of English, then, it is not that the conventionally coded forms and meanings are transmitted into different environments and different surroundings, and taken up and used by different groups of people. It is not a matter of the actual language being distributed but of the virtual language being spread and in the process being variously actualized. The distribution of the actual language implies adoption and conformity. The spread of virtual language implies adaptation and nonconformity. The two processes are quite different
>
> (Widdowson 1997: 139–40)

In this new paradigm in which English spreads and adapts according to the linguistic and cultural preferences of its users in the outer and expanding circles, many traditional assumptions about the language will no longer hold. The point is that if English is genuinely to become the language of 'others', then these 'others' have to be accorded – or perhaps more likely, accord themselves – at least the same English language rights as those claimed by mother-tongue speakers. And this includes the right to innovate without every difference from a standard native variety of English automatically being labelled 'wrong'. This is by definition what it means for a language to be international – that it spreads and becomes a global lingua franca for the benefit of all, rather than being distributed to facilitate communication with the natives. It remains to be seen whether such a paradigm shift does in fact take place.

The language(s) of 'others' as world language(s)

The other potential shift in the linguistic centre of gravity is that English could lose its international role altogether or, at best, come to share it with a number of equals. Although this would not happen purely or even mainly as a result of native speaker resistance to the spread of non-native speaker Englishes and the consequent abandoning of English by large numbers of non-native speakers, the latter could undoubtedly play a part. Because the alternatives to English as a world language are covered in detail in the first reading in D8, we will consider the issue only briefly here, by looking at two main factors: firstly the difficulties inherent in the English language, and secondly the arguments in favour of Spanish as the principal world language.

A piece in the *EL Gazette* in October 2001 (p. 3) under the heading 'It's now official: English is hard' announced: 'you can now motivate your students by telling them that English is the hardest European language to learn'. It went on to report a study carried out at the University of Dundee, Scotland, which compared the literacy levels of British primary school children with those from fourteen European countries (Finland, Greece, Italy, Spain, Portugal, France, Belgium, Germany, Austria, Norway, Iceland, Sweden, The Netherlands and Denmark). Children with one year's schooling had been presented with lists of common words in the mother tongue. It was found that all but the native English speakers were able to read 90 per cent of the words correctly, while the British children could only manage 30 per cent. The researchers concluded that the gap between the English-speaking children and those from the other fourteen countries was the result of difficulties intrinsic to the English language. And at a conference of the Spelling Society, held at Coventry University in the UK in June 2008, in which new research by the literacy researcher Marsha Bell was reported, the same point was made again, with English being described as the worst of all the alphabetical languages for children to learn.

Rather than 'motivate' learners, such difficulties could, if widely publicised, discourage them from attempting to learn the language at all. The difficulties divide into three main categories: orthographic, phonological and grammatical. **Spelling difficulties** are of various kinds although all relate to the fact that English orthography can often not be predicted from the way in which a word is pronounced. There are, for example, several ways of pronouncing the sequences 'ea' (e.g. as in 'bead', 'head', 'bear', 'fear', pearl), and 'ough' (e.g. as in 'cough', 'bough', 'tough', 'dough', 'through', 'thorough'). A large number of words contain silent letters, such as those which begin with a silent 'p' or 'k' ('psychology', 'pneumonia', 'pseud', 'knife', 'know', etc.), another group which end with silent 'b' ('comb', 'thumb', 'limb' 'climb', etc.), and a third with a silent medial letter (e.g. 'whistle', 'castle', 'fasten', 'muscle'). Other problems are doubled consonants (e.g. 'committee', 'accommodation', 'occasional', 'parallel'), and the spelling of unstressed vowels (e.g. the underlined vowels in 'woman', 'persuade', 'condition', 'success', 'infinity', all of which are pronounced as schwa in RP and many other, but not all, native accents).

As regards pronunciation, difficulties relate particularly to English vowels. Not only does native English have more vowel phonemes than many other languages (twenty in RP as compared with, for instance, five in Spanish and Italian), but it has a particularly large number of diphthongs (eight in RP) and makes extensive use of the central vowel, schwa, in unstressed syllables regardless of the spelling – as was demonstrated in the previous paragraph. In addition, many accent varieties of English including RP and **General American** (**GA**) make copious use of weak forms in connected speech. That is, schwa replaces the vowel quality in words such as prepositions ('to', 'of', 'from', etc.), pronouns ('her', 'them', etc.), auxiliaries ('was', 'are', 'has', etc.), articles ('a', 'the') and the like. There are also several other features of connected speech such as elision (loss of sounds), assimilation (modifications to sounds) and liaison (linking of sounds across words). All these aspects of English pronunciation conspire to make it more difficult both to produce and to understand than the pronunciation of many other languages.

Grammatically, difficulties relate very particularly to verb forms and functions. Firstly, English has a large number of tenses all of which have both simple and continuous aspect (present, past, perfect, past perfect, future, future perfect) and none of which have a straightforward link with time reference. Second, there are many **modal verbs** ('may', 'will', 'can', 'should', 'ought to', etc.) each with its own problems of form and function. Third, one of the most problematic areas for learners of English is that of **multi-word** (or **phrasal**) **verbs** such as 'get' ('get up', 'get down', 'get on', 'get off', 'get over', 'get through', etc.) and 'take' ('take up', 'take on', 'take in', 'take off', 'take out', etc.). Each has several meanings both literal and metaphorical, along with complicated rules as to whether the verb and particle can or must be separated for an object, depending on whether the verb is classed as adverbial or prepositional.

Because of these difficulties, it would not be surprising if there was eventually a move to abandon English in favour of an international language with fewer complicating linguistic factors along with a slightly less obvious colonialist discourse attached to it. Spanish appears to be a major contender, with its simpler pronunciation, spelling and verb systems, and its increasing influence in both the EU and America. As Moreno-Fernández and Otero (2008: 81) point out:

> The sum of native Spanish speakers and non-native Spanish speakers plus those learning the language gives a total figure of 438.9 million Spanish speakers according to the estimations based on the latest consolidated census information and on other sources such as the Cervantes Institute.

And according to an article in the *Times Higher Education Supplement* (14 December 2001 p. 23), 'Spanish is . . . the second international language of business as its importance in the United States grows'. In Europe, there is a massive increase in demand for Spanish, with the number of people travelling to Spain and sitting Spanish language examinations rising by 15 per cent a year, according to the Instituto Cervantes (Spain's equivalent of the British Council). In addition, the Dominican Republic, Cuba and Mexico are becoming increasingly popular tourist destinations, while the teaching of Spanish as a foreign language is spreading to many parts of the world. In this it is being 'overtly promoted by the Spanish government as part of its aim to strengthen and enhance a pan-Hispanic community across the world' as well as 'a desire to consolidate a power bloc with some claim to compete with the overwhelming march of global English' (Mar-Molinero 2006: 82). As Mar-Molinero continues, '[t]he Spanish language learning/teaching industry is thus a flourishing and expanding one' and 'whilst smaller in scale, in many senses it resembles the enormous EFL/ELT industry'.

Meanwhile, in the US it is predicted that there will be 51 million native speakers of Spanish by the year 2010, making this the second largest L1 group in the US after English, and comprising almost a fifth of the total population. Already non-Hispanic whites are in a minority in California and there are also particularly large numbers of Hispanics in Arizona and Texas. However, it is not only a case of numerical increase: the US Hispanic community appears also to be experiencing 'a resurgence of cultural pride and confidence' (*The Guardian*, 8 March 2001 p. 12), while politicians are beginning to pay far greater attention to the Hispanic community's needs than they have done hitherto. Meanwhile, Latinos such as the Puerto Rican Ricky Martin and Jennifer Lopez have, respectively, topped world pop music charts and won important film awards, and still more recently the Latin music of artists such as Daddy Yankee, Don Omar and Molotov has been achieving worldwide popularity (see Mar-Molinero 2008: 39–40).

Further evidence that English may eventually give way to another language (or languages – Mandarin Chinese is another strong contender) as the world's lingua franca is provided by the internet. As Crystal (2006: 229–31) points out,

[The Web] was originally a totally English medium – as was the Internet as a whole, given its US origins. But with the Internet's globalization, the presence of other languages has steadily risen. In the mid-1990s, a widely quoted figure was that just over 80 per cent of the Net was in English.

However, as he goes on to say,

The estimates for languages other than English have steadily risen since then, with some commentators predicting that before long the Web (and the Internet as a whole) will be predominantly non-English, as communications infrastructure develops in Europe, Asia, Africa, and South America.

Crystal also cites a 2004 Global Reach survey which found that 64.8 per cent of a total online population of 801.4 million was in countries where English is not the mother tongue, and he notes that Chinese is expected by most sources to become the majority language of internet users.

Graddol, likewise, considers the role of English on the internet to be 'only a very passing phase'. In his view, although the internet has been an important factor in the spread of English around the world, 'the biggest story is not the use of English on the internet but the use of languages other than English' because it is 'a technology that is very supportive of multilingualism' (in Elmes 2001: 114–15). In an address to the British Association of Applied Linguistics in 2000, Graddol discussed how the predominance of English on the internet was being lost. In particular, he pointed to the fact that on the one hand many multilingual sites were emerging within Europe, while on the other hand, sites which were not visible to American web users were developing outside Europe. In Japan, for example, only 15 per cent of users apparently wished to surf the internet in English.

A little over ten years ago (1997: 51), Graddol predicted that as computer use spreads around the world, its English medium content may fall to as little as 40 per cent. However, as he implies more recently (2006: 44), we need to distinguish between *users* and *material*. For while the proportion of English L1 internet users dropped from 51.3 per cent in 2000 to 32 per cent in 2005, and the proportion of English material has also been declining, he points out that 'there remains more English than is proportionate to the first languages of users'. This, Graddol observes, could be the result of a time-lag: 'internet sites in local languages appear only when there exist users who can understand them'. This is plausible given the fact that 'surveys of bilingual internet users in the USA suggest that their use of English sites declines as alternatives in their first language become available'. On the other hand, we cannot completely discount the possibility that a sizeable proportion of non-native English speakers may prefer to use English on the internet, even if this is more likely to be 'English in its new global form' rather than in its more traditional (native speaker) form (see Graddol 2006: 11 and C6 below).

It is probable, if not certain, that English-medium internet use has passed its peak. Meanwhile, the implications for both the spread and type of English used in other forms of communication are as yet far from clear.

Section B

DEVELOPMENT
IMPLICATIONS AND ISSUES

B1   THE LEGACY OF COLONIALISM

If you are to gain a full picture of the development of World Englishes, then the historical facts outlined in Section A cannot be divorced from the social and political contexts in which events took place. Nor can these 'facts' be taken at face value, but instead need to be problematised. For colonialism was neither a natural nor a neutral process, but one involving large-scale coercion and displacement, and one which inevitably impacted in major ways on the lives of those whose lands were colonised. Its effects have, in certain respects, lasted well into postcolonial times and may continue to affect people's lives far into the future. One result of colonialism is thought to be the endangering of many indigenous languages, a theme which will be taken up in B8. Here in unit B1, we will consider two other important and related effects of colonialism during the colonial and postcolonial periods: the denigrating of colonised peoples and their loss of identity (though the latter, of course, also has very close links with language loss).

The devaluing of local language and culture

One major legacy of the two diasporas of English is the assumption of the inferiority of the indigenous language, culture, and even character of the colonised, alongside the assumption of the superiority of the colonisers and their language. During the colonial period, this took an extreme form, and it is not uncommon in the literature to find references to the native populations of colonised lands as 'savages', to their languages as 'primitive' and to their cultures as 'barbaric'. The following three quotations illustrate this point:

> A knowledge of the English tongue and its authors, therefore, appears to hold a place of the first importance in a plan for the intellectual and moral elevation of the Hindoos. The English language will not only prove a more correct medium of giving public instruction to the students, but it will facilitate their progress in useful knowledge. All the Indian languages have been for so many ages the vehicle of every thing in their superstition which is morally debasing or corrupting to the mind, and so much is the grossly impure structure of heathenism wrought into the native languages, that the bare study of them often proves injurious to the mind of the European.
>
> (London Missionary Society 1826, quoted in Bailey 1991: 135–6)

> Fearful indeed is the impress of degradation which is stamped on the language of the savage, more fearful perhaps even than that which is stamped upon his form. When wholly letting go the truth, when long and greatly sinning against light and conscience, a people has thus gone the downward way, has been scattered off by some violent catastrophe from those regions of the world which are the seats of advance and progress, and driven to its remote isles and further corners, then as

one nobler thought, one spiritual idea after another has perished from it, the words also that expressed these have perished too. As one habit of civilization has been let go after another, the words which those habits demanded have dropped as well, first out of use, and then out of memory, and thus after a while have been wholly lost.

(Trench 1891, quoted in Bailey 1991: 278)

Probably everyone would agree that an Englishman would be right in considering his way of looking at the world and at life better than that of the Maori or Hotten-tot, and no one will object in the abstract to England doing her best to impose her better and higher views on those savages.

(Hobson 1902, quoted in Pennycook 1998: 52)

However, as the following example shows, the same sort of ethos still underlies much of what is written in supposedly 'neutral' language today:

To understand the momentous nature of the first English voyages to America, we have to appreciate the forlorn position of these weary travellers in a strange land-scape without a single reference point. We have to imagine a world in which all languages were foreign, all communications difficult, and even hazardous . . . Just as the Saxon English, confronted by the Norse languages, adapted their speech, so the settlers of Roanoke, Jamestown, and Plymouth, confronted by the need to communicate with Indians who could not speak a word of English, also adapted theirs.

(McCrum et al. 1992: 121)

Such disparagement of the non-Anglo (and, especially, non-white) 'other' slips in, it seems, even when writers appear to be attempting to produce an unbiased record of events. Note the words used here to describe the colonisers and their situation ('momen-tous nature', 'forlorn position', 'weary travellers', 'confronted by the need to communicate', 'adapted [their speech]'). Compare these with the references to the indigenous popula-tion and their situation ('strange landscape', 'all languages . . . foreign', 'communications difficult, and even hazardous', 'Indians who could not speak a word of English').

The same phenomenon can be seen at work in the regular references in McCrum et al. (1992), Crystal (2003a) and many other accounts, to the 'discovery' of lands, as though these territories were not already populated and often home to large numbers of human beings before the arrival of the colonisers. Again, the innocuous word 'set-tlers' is frequently used to describe people who were, in essence, invaders and annex-ers of lands belonging to others. And given contemporary attitudes towards the native languages of the indigenous populations in the colonised lands ('impure structure of heathenism', 'impress of degradation', etc.), it is not surprising that when colonised peoples made the effort to communicate in English, their English was denigrated as 'broken' and the like. The phenomenon persists to this day in attitudes towards the English of non-native speakers, and particularly towards their accents (see Jenkins 2007). For example, the Japanese Yoko Ono was criticised in two British newspapers, *The Guardian* of 7 January 1998 for 'her mauling of the English language', and the *Evening Standard* of 17 May 2001 for having 'the voice to be used against a peculiarly spirited inmate in a Khmer Rouge death camp'.

It is only in very recent times that L2 varieties of English have been accorded any sort of recognition whatsoever. Some former British colonies have embarked on the massive task of describing, standardising and codifying their local English (the so-called 'New' Englishes, see A4). Nevertheless, this is only the beginning, as they are still likely to meet resistance when they promote their Englishes as 'legitimate' standard varieties internationally. For the prevailing attitude of L1 speakers, as well as that of a sizeable majority of L2 speakers, is still that 'good English' is synonymous with that of educated native speakers born and bred in the United Kingdom or North America. This is an issue which we will examine more closely later on in the book, particularly in strands 3 and 6.

It is not surprising that after centuries in which non-Anglo languages and cultures and local L2 varieties of English have been undermined in this way, a lack of confidence pervades many L2 speakers' attitudes towards their use of English, even though they now constitute the majority of the world's English speakers. For example, Medgyes (1994: 40), a fluent bilingual speaker and teacher of English from Hungary, laments: 'we [non-native teachers of English] suffer from an *inferiority complex* caused by a glaring defect in our knowledge of English. We are in constant distress as we realize how little we know about the language we are supposed to teach' (see also 'linguistic security' in the Glossarial Index).

Activity

> ❑   To what extent do you believe that the attitudes towards certain non-English languages and cultures expressed by the nineteenth- and early twentieth-century writers above still exist at the start of the twenty-first century? What evidence is there for your answer?
>
> ❑   In your view, do non-native speakers of English suffer from an 'inferiority complex' over their use of English? Should they do so? Why/why not? How far do your answers depend on whether the speakers come from a country that was or was not once colonised by the British?
>
> ❑   What is your response to the following quotation?
>
> In the days of empire, the natives were the indigenous populations and the term itself implied uncivilized, primitive, barbaric, even cannibalistic . . . With the spread of English around the globe, 'native' – in relation to English – has acquired newer, positive connotations. 'Native speakers' of English are assumed to be advanced (technologically), civilized, and educated. But as 'NSs' lose their linguistic advantage, with English being spoken as an International Language no less – and often a good deal more – effectively by 'NNSs'. . . and as bilingualism and multilingualism become the accepted world norm, and monolingualism the exception . . . perhaps the word 'native' will return to its pejorative usage. Only this time, the opposite group will be on the receiving end.
>
> (Jenkins 2000: 229)

The loss of ethnic identity

A second major legacy of colonialism is the way in which it has led, either directly or indirectly, to the destruction of the ethnic identities of many whose lands were colonised. This is, in part, the consequence of the loss of indigenous languages, since identity and language are often closely interrelated. It also bears strong links with the undermining of the language and culture of colonised peoples that was discussed in the previous section. The situation, nevertheless, is not entirely hopeless. For as the following extract on the crisis among Native American communities demonstrates, it is possible to revive indigenous languages, or **heritage languages** as they are more commonly called today.

'If a Child Learns Only the Non-Indian Way of Life, You Have Lost Your Child.'

We turn now to the 'identity crisis' under way in indigenous communities today – a crisis suggested by the words of the Navajo elder that head this section. If it is indeed the stories, songs and daily interactions in the Native language that convey and transmit sense of place and sense of self, what happens when the language falls out of use?

This is the situation Native American communities now face. Of 175 indigenous languages still spoken in the United States, perhaps twenty are being transmitted to children. Languages in the U.S. Southwest are among the most vital – especially Navajo, Tohono, 'O'odham, Havasupai, Hopi and Hualapai – with a significant though declining number of child speakers. But by far the largest numbers of indigenous languages are spoken only by the middle-aged or grandparent generations.

Contemporary Native writers such as Ortiz, Momaday, Tapahonso, and others demonstrate that indigenous traditions *can* be represented in English. But Native speakers, particularly those immersed in the oral literature of their people, are quick to say, 'Yes, but the text is not the same. There is something missing.' In some cases, it is easy to point to words that lack even an approximate English equivalent. The 'O'odham *himdag*, for example, is often translated as 'culture'. But 'O'odham speakers say this is only a distant approximation; speakers understand this word to have various levels of complexity. As a consequence, they have taken up the practice of using the 'O'odham word when speaking about it in English.

This example highlights the fact that human cultures are not interchangeable; the loss of even one language and the cultural knowledge it encodes diminishes us all. Recognizing this, many tribes are actively engaged in language restoration efforts. In California, where fifty indigenous languages are spoken – none as a mother tongue by children – a bold language revitalization movement is under way. 'No one feels this impending loss more strongly than the Native Californians themselves,' linguist Leanne Hinton . . . maintains. 'Many are making enormous efforts to keep the language and cultural practices alive . . . even as they participate in the cultures and intercultures more recently derived from Europe and elsewhere' . . .

One such effort is the California Master-Apprentice Language Learning Program, in which Native speakers and younger apprentices live and work together over months or years, doing everyday things but communicating through the heritage language. Speakers from ten language groups have thus far been trained, and several apprentices have achieved conversational proficiency. In Hawai'i, language immersion programs have successfully revived Hawai'ian in dozens of homes. Language immersion programs also have been instituted on the Navajo Nation, among the Mohawks in New York, Ontario, and Quebec, and in numerous other indigenous communities throughout the United States.

The development of indigenous literacies has accompanied many of these efforts. As in many tribes, among the Hualapai of northwestern Arizona the development of a practical writing system grew out of local initiatives in bilingual education. There is now a significant body of Hualapai literature, including a grammar and dictionary, children's and adolescents' storybooks, poetry, teachers' guides, and anthologies of traditional stories and songs. All of this has raised support for larger, community-wide language maintenance efforts, including tribal sanctions for conducting tribal business in English, and the involvement of children, parents, and grandparents in language revitalization projects.

Literacy in indigenous languages, however, remains primarily restricted to schools, buttressing rather than replacing home- and community-based language transmission. Yet literacy is a powerful symbol of indigenous identity; it valorizes the community and publicly demonstrates the ways in which it is using its language in active and creative ways. By providing new forms for the preservation and transmission of traditional knowledge, indigenous literacy tangibly connects the language with the culture and history of its speakers. Finally, as the Hualapai example shows, indigenous literacy can stimulate other, more diffuse forces for language and culture maintenance. In all of these ways, literacy in indigenous languages is an asset and ally in the struggle to resist linguistic assimilation.

But the fact remains that there is an ever-decreasing pool of Native language speakers. This situation is a direct consequence of the history of colonialism and language repression that indigenous people have, for centuries, endured. Nonetheless, as Darrell Kipp of the Piegan Language Institute pointed out at a recent meeting of indigenous language activists, without their tribal languages, many indigenous communities 'will cease to be.' The loss of language, he states, 'is like throwing away your universe.'

(McCarty and Zepeda 1999: 207–8)

It is not only language, but also **place**, which provides people with a sense of identity. This is a song written in 1995 by Dan Hanna, a Havasupai medicine man, describing his native land:

The land we were given   *Down at the source*
the land we were given   *A spring will always be there*
It is right here   *It is ours*
It is right here   *It is ours*
Red Rock   *Since a long time ago*
Red Rock . . .   *Since a long time ago . . . .*

(McCarty and Zepeda 1999: 205)

McCarty and Zepeda point out that

What is interesting . . . is the fact that, in many cases, the places identified in the texts have been appropriated by others, disfigured, and even destroyed. Red Rock – the site to which Dan Hanna refers – is not included within the modern Havasupai reservation and is planned as the location of a uranium mine. Yet Hanna repeats, 'It is ours, it is ours, since a long time ago, it is ours'.

The authors conclude

It is the stories, the poetry, the prayers, and the songs that continue to fix these places in collective memory, recalling their images, commanding respect, and helping those for whom the narratives are intended to define who they are. Landscape or place sense is no more, or no less, important than language in this process. It is within the places in the stories that the 'sense of ourselves' resides.

(McCarty and Zepeda 1999: 205–6)

Activity

- ❏ To what extent do you believe it is possible for groups of people to retain their ethnic identity when (a) they are removed from their ethnic homeland and/or (b) they lose the use of their mother tongue?
- ❏ How strong a role do you think the written language plays in forming and retaining a sense of ethnic group identity? Does there in fact have to be a written language at all, or is oral communication sufficient? And what about the role of literature: how strong a part does it play in identity formation; and can it continue to promote ethnic identity if it is transmitted only orally or in translation?
- ❏ In the concluding comments to his edited volume, *Handbook of Language and Ethnic Identity*, Fishman (1999: 448–9) quotes a number of scholars who argue that those who feel more secure about their own identity are more tolerant of other ethnic groups and, at the same time, better placed to be an effective member of a cosmopolitan grouping. He finishes his discussion by quoting Haarmann (1997) on **European identity** as follows:

European identity includes cosmopolitan elements, but cosmopolitanism cannot serve as a simplistic substitute for traditional national identity . . . The recipe for a member of a national community to become a self-confident European lies not in the denial or neglect of his national collective identity . . . Somebody who considers him- or herself to be a cosmopolitan at the cost of national identity will hardly be in a position to appreciate the national components in other people's identity, and this can only weaken cooperation among Europeans.

(Haarmann 1997: 286)

Do you agree it is essential to retain one's own national identity in order to become a 'self-confident' member of a larger grouping such as Europe?

B2   CHARACTERISTICS OF PIDGINS AND CREOLES

This unit first takes you through the main formal features of pidgins and creole lexis, pronunciation and grammar, and then moves on to look at samples of texts serving a range of functions.

Lexis, pronunciation and grammar

Lexis

Generally, pidgin lexis is drawn from the dominant language, usually a European language such as English, French, Portuguese or Dutch (known as the **lexifier language**), while pidgin grammar is that of the indigenous African or Asian languages. Pidgin lexis is systematic and, like any language, has rules of use, although in the earlier stages of evolution, these rules are simpler. In particular:

❏ Concepts tend to be encoded in lengthier ways; for example, in Tok Pisin, an English-based pidgin in Papua New Guinea, the word 'bilong' (from 'belong') means 'of', so that 'papa bilong mi' means 'my father', and 'haus bilong yu' means 'your house'.

❏ There is extensive use of **reduplication**. This is partly to intensify meaning (e.g. 'tok' means 'talk' whereas 'toktok' means chatter, and 'look' means 'look' whereas 'looklook' means 'stare'), and partly to avoid confusions which could result from phonological similarity (e.g. in some Pacific pidgins, 'sip' means 'ship' whereas 'sipsip' means 'sheep', 'pis' means 'peace' whereas 'pispis' means 'urinate', and in some Atlantic pidgins, 'was' means 'watch' whereas 'waswas' means 'wash'; see Todd (1990: 53) for more examples).

Pronunciation

Pidgins have fewer sounds than those of the corresponding standard language, even at creole stages in their evolution. For example, Tok Pisin has only five vowel sounds [a] [e] [i] [o] [u] and most Caribbean creole speakers twelve, whereas American English (General American) has seventeen and British English (Received Pronunciation) has twenty. This means that in Tok Pisin there is, for example, only one sound /ɪ/ for the two British and American English sounds /ɪ/ as in the word 'dip' and /i:/ as in the word 'deep', and one sound /ɔ:/ for the BrEng sounds /ɜ:/ as in 'work' and /ɔ:/ as in 'walk'.

Moving to consonants, one feature of most pidgins and creoles is the **simplification** of consonant clusters so that, for instance, 'friend' becomes 'fren', 'cold' becomes 'col' and 'salt' becomes 'sol'. Another feature is **conflation**: most Caribbean creole speakers conflate the sounds /t/ with /θ/, /d/ with /ð/, and /tʃ/ with /ʃ/, while Tok Pisin speakers also conflate a number of other consonant sounds including /f/ and /p/, and /s/, /ʃ/ and /tʃ/. The result of this reduced phoneme inventory, even allowing for the effects of reduplication described in the section on lexis, is a much larger number of homophones (two words pronounced identically, e.g. 'pear' and 'pair') than exist in British or American English.

Grammar

Some of the main grammatical characteristics of pidgins and creoles are:

❑ They have few **inflections** in their nouns, pronouns, verbs and adjectives especially in pidgin phases. For example, nouns are not marked for number or gender and verbs have no tense markers. Pronouns are not distinguished for case, so that most pidgins use 'me' to indicate both 'I' and 'me'. However, Tok Pisin, like many other Melanesian languages, distinguishes between inclusive 'we', 'yumi' referring to the addressee and speaker, and non-inclusive 'we', 'mepela' (literally 'me and fellow') referring to the speaker and others, but not the addressee. The suffix '-fela' or '-pela' is also added to attributive adjectives describing people and things, e.g. 'naispela haus' ('nice house') and 'gutpela meri' ('good woman', 'meri' deriving from 'Mary').

❑ Negation is formed with a simple negative particle, often 'no' for English-based pidgins and 'pa' for French-based. For example, Krio from Sierra Leone uses 'no', as in 'I no tu had', while the French-based Seychelles Creole uses 'pa' as in 'I pa tro difisil'.

❑ In pidgin phases, **clause structure** is uncomplicated so that, for example, there are no embedded clauses such as relative clauses.

As pidgins develop into creoles, four main types of change take place:

❑ People begin to speak them much faster, so that they start employing processes of assimilation and reduction: Tok Pisin 'man bilong mi' (my husband) becomes 'mamblomi'.

❑ Their vocabularies expand:

New shorter words are formed alongside phrases: 'paitman' develops alongside 'man bilong pait' (fighter). Eventually the longer expression dies out.

The capacity for word-building develops, e.g. the suffix '-im' is added to adjectives to form verbs as in 'bik' (big, large), 'bikim' (to enlarge), 'brait' (wide), 'braitim' (to widen).

Technical words are borrowed from standard English

❑ They develop a tense system in their verbs, e.g. 'bin' is used to mark past tense and 'bi' (from 'baimbai') to mark future tense.

❑ They develop greater sentence complexity, for example their speakers are able to form relative clauses (Aitchison 1991: 190–1, and see Sebba 1997: 107–33).

Social functions

Extended pidgins and creoles perform a very wide range of **social functions** that go well beyond the original purpose of pidgins to serve as basic contact languages. They are used, for instance, in literature, both oral and written, in education, in the mass media, in advertising, and in the Bible. The important point to note about the scope of pidgins and creoles is that they are, or can easily become, capable of expressing all the needs of their speakers.

 Activity ★

Here are some samples of Tok Pisin translations of an excerpt from Shakespeare's *Julius Caesar*, The Lord's Prayer from the Gospel of Matthew in the Bible, and an advert for Colgate toothpaste. The translation of Mark Antony's famous speech from *Julius Caesar* was, in fact, undertaken by a European, Murphy, in 1943 for the specific purpose of demonstrating that pidgins are not inadequate languages. In each case, see how much of the pidgin text you are able to understand before turning to the English versions that follow the Tok Pisin group.

The Tok Pisin versions

1 The Lord's Prayer in the Tok Pisin Nupela Testamen translation, 1969

Fader bilong mifelo, yu stop long heven – Ol i santuim nem bilong yu – Kingdom bilong yu i kam – Ol i hirim tok bilong yu long graund olsem long heven. Tude givim mifelo kaikai bilong de – Forgivim rong bilong mifelo – olsem mifelo forgivim rong – ol i mekim long mifelo. Yu no bringun mifelo long traiim – tekewe samting no gud long mifelo. Amen.

(Mühlhäusler 1997: 329)

2 Excerpt from Julius Caesar

Pren, man bilong Rom, Wantok, harim nau. Mi kam tasol long plantim Kaesar. Mi noken beiten longen. Sopos sampela wok bilong wampela man i stret; sampela i no stret; na man i dai; ol i wailis long wok i no stret tasol. Gutpela wok bilongen i slip; i lus nating long giraun wantaim long Kalopa. Fesin biling yumi man. Maski Kaesar tu, gutpela wok i slip.

(Mühlhäusler 1997: 325)

3 Colgate toothpaste advertisement

Colgate i save strongim tit bilong yu
Lukaut: planti switpela kaikai na loli i savi bagarapim tit hariap

(Aitchison 1996: 142, reproduced from *Wantok*, Tok Pisin newspaper, 1980)

The British English versions

1 Our Father in heaven,
may your name be held holy,
your Kingdom come,
your will be done,
on earth as in heaven.
Give us today our daily bread.
And forgive us our debts,

B2

as we have forgiven those who are in debt to us.
And do not put us to the test,
but save us from the evil one.

(The Jerusalem Bible, Matthew 6, 9–13)

2 Friends, Romans, Countrymen, lend me your ears;
I come to bury Caesar, not to praise him.
The evil that men do lives after them;
The good is oft interred with their bones;
So let it be with Caesar.

(Julius Caesar, Act 1, Scene 2)

3 *Colgate strengthens your teeth*
Take care. Lots of sugary foods and sweets rot your teeth fast.
(Note: 'bagarapim' = the verb 'to destroy' from English 'bugger up', and 'hariap'
= the adverb 'fast', from English 'hurry up'.)

★ **Activity**

We finish this section with an example of contemporary Tok Pisin, a news item which appeared in the Papua New Guinean newspaper, *Wantok*, in April 1994:

Ol meri gat bikpela wari yet

Helt na envairomen em bikpela samting ol meri long kantri tude i gat bikpela wari long en.

Bikos dispela tupela samting i save kamap strong long sindaun na laip bilong famili na komyuniti insait long ol ples na kantri.

Long dispela wik, moa long 40 meri bilong Milen Be provins i bung long wanpela woksop long Alotau bilong toktok long hevi bilong helt na envairomen long ol liklik ailan na provins.

Bung i bin stat long Mande na bai pinis long Fraide, Epril 22. Ol opisa bilong Melanesin Envairomen Faundesen wantaim nesenel na provinsal helt opis i stap tu bilong givim toktok insait long dispela worksop.

Before you go on to compare the original with the verbatim and British English versions which follow, see how much of the text you can already understand, and make a note of any features of lexis, grammar and (by implication) pronunciation that fit into the categories described in the first part of this unit.

All women got big-fellow worry yet

Health and environment him all big-fellow something all woman along country today he got big-fellow worry along him.

Because this-fellow two-fellow something he know come-up strong along sit-down and life belong family and community inside along all place and country.

Along this-fellow week, more along 40 woman belong Milne Bay Province he meet along one-fellow workshop along Alotau belong talk-talk along heavy belong health and environment along all little island and province.

Meeting he been start along Monday and bye (-and-bye) finish along Friday April 22.

All officer belong Melanesian Environment Foundation one-time national and provincial health office he stop too belong give-him talk-talk inside along this-fellow workshop.

Women still have big worries

Health and environment are two of the major things which women in the country today have big concerns about.

Because these two things often have a strong effect on the situation and life of families and communities within villages and in the country.

This week, more than 40 women from Milne Bay Province are meeting in a workshop at Alotau in order to talk about the difficulties of health and environment in the small islands and provinces. The meeting began on Monday and will finish on Friday April 22.

The officers of the Melanesian Environment Foundation together with the national and provincial health office are there too in order to give talks in the workshop.

(Original text and translations from Sebba 1997: 20–1)

B3 THE *ENGLISH TODAY* DEBATE

With an ever-growing number of people speaking English in an increasing number of regions of the world, it is not surprising that the language is diversifying and 'English' has becoming 'Englishes'. Local conditions, including the influence of the other languages that English speakers of the Outer and Expanding Circle speak, are inevitably affecting the English that is evolving in different contexts around the world. Even within the Inner Circle countries, there are differences especially in accent, but also in vocabulary and, to a lesser extent, grammar, as well as input from increasing numbers of immigrants for whom English is not their mother tongue (e.g. there are over three hundred first languages spoken in London). Nevertheless, the standard varieties of English in the countries of the Inner Circle are regarded as 'legitimate' world norms, even if some ENL speakers regard their own country's standard forms as superior to those of the other ENL countries.

The situation is rather different for speakers of English in the Outer and Expanding Circles. World English scholars argue that the institutionalised varieties of English of countries in the Outer Circle should, in their standard (acrolect) forms, be seen as comparable with the standard Englishes of the Inner Circle countries, and so just as valid as local teaching models. On the other hand, many others consider differences from British or American standards to be not local innovations but errors and, as such, evidence of the substandard nature of these varieties. In other words, they regard English spoken in the Outer Circle as **interlanguage** (learner language which has not yet reached the target) or **fossilised** language (i.e. language used when learning has ceased short of nativelike competence – see B7). The situation is even more controversial in relation to English speakers in the Expanding Circle, and their position is not helped by the fact that those who argue for the recognition of Outer Circle varieties have been slow to extend the argument to the Expanding Circle. Because of the major changes currently taking place in the latter circle, it forms the topic of the entire strand 6, while much of what follows here in B3 is concerned mainly, though not exclusively, with Outer Circle Englishes.

Non-native Englishes as 'deficit'

The controversy over the legitimacy of non-native varieties of English is crystallised in a debate which took place in the pages of the journal *English Today* in the early 1990s. In 1990, the journal published an article by Quirk, 'Language varieties and standard language'. In essence, Quirk's position was that non-native Englishes are inadequately learned versions of 'correct' native English forms and therefore not valid as teaching models. Kachru's strongly worded response, 'Liberation linguistics and the Quirk concern', followed in 1991. Read through these points taken from Quirk's article and decide how far you agree or disagree with him:

❑ The native/non-native distinction is a valid one because research by Coppieters (1987) shows that native and non-native speakers have different intuitions about a language. For example, they differ in their judgements of the grammatical correctness of sentences. This research finding implies 'the need for non-native teachers to be in constant touch with the native language' (pp. 6–7). It also implies that natives and non-natives 'have radically different internalizations' of the language, so that it will be unwise to attempt to institutionalise non-native varieties.

❑ Learners of English outside Britain come to the language with little or no prior knowledge, and need to learn standard English in order to 'increase their freedom and their career prospects' (note that this is the argument used by Honey 1997 in his book *Language is Power*). The teacher's 'duty' therefore is not to question notions of correct and incorrect use, but to teach standard English (p. 7).

❑ There are no institutionalised varieties of English. In countries where these are claimed to exist, those in authority tend to protest that the so-called national variety of English is an attempt to justify inability to acquire what they persist in seeing as 'real' English . . . No-one should underestimate the problem of teaching English in such countries as India and Nigeria, where the English of the teachers themselves inevitably bears the stamp of locally acquired deviation from the standard

language ('You are knowing my father, isn't it'). The temptation is great to accept the situation and even to justify it in euphemistically sociolinguistic terms' (pp. 8–9).
❏ The teaching of English in the countries of the Expanding Circle should not involve any conflict over standards and where it does, is a reflection of 'half-baked quackery' and is mainly perpetuated by minimally trained teachers and 'academic linguists with little experience of foreign language teaching'. Just because, for example, the use of the phrase 'several informations' is intelligible, this is no reason to ignore the incorrect use of an uncountable noun (p. 9). (See Seidlhofer 2005, who responds to this particular point by arguing that it is in fact Quirk's view that is 'half-baked quackery', because it is grounded in an out-of-date monolithic view of English that fails to take account of the changing role of English not only in Outer Circle communities, but also as a lingua franca in the Expanding Circle.)

Quirk concludes

If I were a foreign student paying good money in Tokyo or Madrid to be taught English, I would feel cheated by such tolerant pluralism. My goal would be to acquire English precisely because of its power as an instrument of international communication. I would be annoyed at the equivocation over English since it seemed to be unparalleled in the teaching of French, German, Russian, or Chinese.

He recommends that while

it is not easy to eradicate once-fashionable educational theories . . . the effort is worthwhile for those of us who believe that the world needs an international language and that English is the best candidate at present on offer.

(p. 10)

 Activity

Non-native Englishes as 'difference'

Now read through some of the points Kachru (1991) makes in criticising what he describes as Quirk's **deficit linguistics** position:

❏ The solution of 'constant touch with the native language' does not apply to the institutionalised varieties for more than one reason: first, the practical reason that it is simply not possible for a teacher to be in constant touch with the *native* language given the number of teachers involved, the lack of resources and the overwhelming *non-native* input; second, the functional reason that the users of institutionalized varieties are expected to conform to local norms and speech strategies since English is used for interaction primarily in intranational contexts . . . The natives may have 'radically different internalizations [intuitions about grammaticality]' regarding their L1 but that point is not vital for a rejection of institutionalization. In fact, the arguments for recognizing institutionalization are that non-native users of English have internalizations which are linked to their own multi-linguistic, sociolinguistic and sociocultural contexts' (p. 5).

❑ Quirk seems to perceive the spread of English primarily from the perspective of monolingual societies, and from uncomplicated language policy contexts. The concerns he expresses are far from the realities of multilingual societies, and negate the linguistic, sociolinguistic, educational and pragmatic realities of such societies (p. 6).

Kachru goes on to argue (p. 10) that Quirk's approach is based on at least four false assumptions (see Kachru 1992: 357–9, where these are presented as 'Six Fallacies about the Users and Uses of English'):

1 that in the outer and Expanding circles . . . English is essentially learnt to interact with the native speakers of the language . . . The reality is that in its localized varieties, English has become the main vehicle for interaction among its non-native users, with distinct linguistic and cultural backgrounds – Indians interacting with Nigerians, Japanese, Sri Lankans, Germans with Singaporeans and so on. The culture-bound localized strategies of, for example, politeness, persuasion and phatic communion transcreated in English are more effective and culturally significant than are the 'native' strategies for interaction.

2. that English is essentially learnt as a tool to understand and teach the American or British cultural values, or what is generally termed the Judeo-Christian traditions . . . In culturally and linguistically pluralistic regions of the Outer Circle, English is an important tool to impart local traditions and cultural values.

3 that the international non-native varieties of English are essentially 'inter-languages' striving to achieve 'native-like' character . . . In reality, the situation is . . . that such institutionalized varieties are varieties of English in their own right rather than stages on the way to more native-like English.

4 that the native speakers of English as teachers, academic administrators and material developers are seriously involved in the global teaching of English, in policy formulation and in determining channels for the spread of language . . . In proposing language policies for English in the global context . . . there is a need for a 'paradigm shift' . . . reconsidering the traditional sacred cows of English . . . I am thinking of concepts such as the 'speech community' of English, 'ideal speaker-hearer' of English and the 'native speaker of English'. In the context of world Englishes, what we actually see is that diversification is a marker of various types of sociolinguistic 'messages' . . .

Kachru concludes that what Quirk describes in terms of 'deficit' is in the global context a matter of 'difference which is based on vital sociolinguistic realities of identity, creativity and linguistic and cultural contact'.

❑ Whose arguments do you find more convincing, Quirk's or Kachru's?
❑ How can we decide whether a non-standard English usage is an 'error' or an 'innovation'? Does it depend entirely on whether the speaker is native or non-native or are there other criteria such as frequency of use, number of users and so on?
❑ What is your response to these comments made by Bamgboṣe and de Klerk?

> The main question with innovations is the need to decide when an observed feature of language use is indeed an innovation and when it is simply an error. An innovation is seen as an acceptable variant, while an error is simply a mistake, or uneducated usage. If innovations are seen as errors, a non-native variety can never receive any recognition
>
> (Bamgboṣe 1998: 22)

> When does a substratal [indigenous] feature assert itself sufficiently to overcome the fear that if deviations are allowed, the rules will be abandoned and chaos will ensue? Is it when speakers use it often enough to silence or exhaust the prescriptors?
>
> (de Klerk 1999: 315)

❑ What do you see as the advantages and the disadvantages of a **pluricentric approach** to English, in which there are several global centres, native and non-native, each with its own standard variety of English? For example, how far is the way this enables a variety of English to express the culture of its speakers outweighed by problems such as the threat of fragmentation of English into mutually unintelligible languages? And if you think this is a realistic fear, what measures could be taken to prevent it from materialising?
❑ Kachru appears to be offended by Quirk's rejection of the distinction between speakers of English in the Outer Circle and those in the Expanding Circle, and the fact that he settles instead for a simple dichotomy between native and non-native speaker of English. In your view, are speakers of L2 Englishes in the Outer Circle 'privileged' over those in the Expanding Circle when it comes to English language rights?
❑ Mesthrie and Bhatt (2008: 208) consider that '[u]ltimately the Kachru–Quirk controversy can only be resolved outside the ivory tower, by the attitudes and actions of parents, pupils, teachers, administrators and the like. Linguistic hegemony power can be contested, but it is seldom dismantled by reason alone'. How far do you agree with them?

THE LEGITIMATE AND ILLEGITIMATE OFFSPRING OF ENGLISH   B4

The naming of the New Englishes

Unit B4 takes its title from that of an article by the World Englishes scholar Mufwene. In the article, he argues that the way in which New Englishes are named 'has to do more with who have appropriated and speak them than with how they developed and how different they are structurally from each other, hence with how mutually intelligible they are' (Mufwene 1997: 182, and see also Mufwene 2001: chapter 4).

In particular, Mufwene attacks the view of many western linguists that the 'legitimate offspring' of the English language are those varieties spoken by descendents of European speakers of English while its 'illegitimate offspring' are the varieties spoken by those who are not. In other words, the Englishes of the Inner Circle have the right to be named 'English', while those outside this charmed circle forfeit that right. The most extreme group of 'illegitimate offspring', according to this view, argues Mufwene, is that of the English-based pidgins and creoles. These are often classified as separate languages or even, in the case of pidgins, considered not to be entitled to the name 'language' at all. Also disenfranchised are the indigenised New Englishes of the Outer Circle. Despite the fact that they are used for a wide range of daily purposes in many countries of the Outer Circle and have developed their own varietal characteristics (i.e. have become **nativised**), the New Englishes are to this day called 'non-native' Englishes by western linguists.

Mufwene goes on to argue that this classification of Englishes into 'legitimate' and 'illegitimate' is based on a mistaken belief about language contact. According to this belief, a **mother language** gives birth to **daughter languages** without the intervention of any other languages prior to the production of the 'offspring', that is, without any language contact. Mufwene points out that **language contact** was in fact a feature of the development of the 'legitimate' Englishes, but that this is generally overlooked. For example, Irish and Scots-Irish Englishes were influenced by contact with Gaelic. However, because the latter Englishes are spoken almost entirely by communities of native speakers, they are not termed creoles, even in their most non-standard forms, despite the contact involved in their development.

Mufwene provides examples of a range of Englishes past and present, to demonstrate his point that the sharing of an identifiable ancestor does not at all guarantee the intelligibility of a variety: 'if mutual intelligibility were such a critical criterion over sharing an identifiable ancestor, there would be more reasons for treating Modern English varieties and creoles as dialects of the same language than for lumping the former together with Old English while excluding creoles' (1997: 190). In the next section, some of the examples used by Mufwene to support his argument are reproduced, along with further examples from other sources.

A range of Englishes

> As you read through the following extracts, assess how easy it is to make sense of each one and, if you can, identify the time and place in which each one is/was written or spoken. Finally, before you consult the key and discussion which follows the extracts, decide which you consider to be 'legitimate' and which 'illegitimate' Englishes. You will need to think here about the criteria on which to base your decisions, e.g. degree of (evident) contact with other languages, intelligibility and suchlike.

Extract 1

Nu scylun hergan hefænricæs Uard,
Metudæs mæcti end His modgidanc,
uerc Uuldurfadur, sue He uundra gihuæs,
eci Dryctin, or astelidæ.
He ærist scop ælda barnum
heben til hrofe, haleg Scepen.
Tha middungeard moncynnæs Uard,
eci Dryctin, æfter tiadæ
firum foldu, Frea allmectig.

Extract 2

O dronke man, disfigured is thy face,
Sour is thy breeth, foul artow to embrace,
And thurgh they dronke nose semeth the soun
As though thou seydest ay 'Sampsoun, Sampsoun';
And yet, god wot, Sampsoun drank never no wyn,
Thou fallest, as it were a stiked swyn.

Extract 3

JR: You trow way . . . trow way wha? En one day, I gone down deh, en talk bout shrimp bin a bite! I bin on dat flat, en I had me line, I done ketch couple a whiting . . . I say, I ga put up da drop net . . . when I look up, duh look from yah to your car deh, I see sompin on da damn side da shoulder comin, like a damn log. I watch um, en when I see him gone down . . .

EL: Hm hm!

JR: En dat tide bin a comin in . . . en dat sucker swim close, closer en closer, den I look en I see dat alligator open e damn mout!

Extracts 4

Well, I seen the time you'd buy a farm for . . . five or six hundred . . . Seen farms selling and I young lad.

But when the house is quiet and us alone you never heard such talk that's going on there

He fell and him crossing the bridge.

Extract 5
Went down there and he's a-holding three dogs in one hand and the coon in the other hand. And they's all a-trying to bite the coon and the coon a-trying to bite Jack and the dogs, and Jack pulled out a sack and it wasn't a dang thing but an old pillow case that Maggie had used, his wife, it was about wore out.

Extract 6
Owar ya? Ts goota meecha mai 'tee.
Naluk. Djarem membah dabrah nai dul? Tintin zluk infu rit'h. Kanyah elpim? Dabrah nai dul? Oi, oi! Slaika toljah. Datrai b'gib dabrah nai dul ta'Walker. Ewuz anaisgi. Buttiz'h felaz tukahr presh usdjuel. Enefda Arumbayas ket chimdai lavis gutsfa gahtah'z. Nomess in'h!

Extract 7
When it was early in the morning of the next day, I had not palm-wine to drink at all, and throughout that day I felt not so happy as before; I was seriously sat down in my parlour, but when it was the third day that I had no palm-wine at all, all my friends did not come to my house again, they left me there alone, because there was no palm-wine for them to drink.

Extract 8
In the upgrowth o a leid ti haill matuirity o lettirs, the staiblishin o an exponent prose is aften deimit a determant stage. A leid may hae a weil-founnit tradeition o hameilt sang, leirit indyte, an ein nerratif prose; but wantan a registir conding for academic screivins, hit maun bide be a 'hauf-leid'.

Extract 9
A no wahn a ting tu du wid yu bika yu kom . . . lang taym an yu no kom luk for Titi. Hu iz dis, Pap?

Key

Extract 1
This is Cædmon's Hymn, an early Old English religious poem composed by the poet Cædmon, and dating from 657 to 680. The above version of the text is in a Northumbrian dialect. It has been translated as follows:

Now must we praise the Guardian of heaven,
The power and conception of the Lord,
And all His works, as He, eternal Lord,
Father of glory, started every wonder.
First He created heaven as a roof,
The holy Maker, for the sons of men.

Then the eternal Keeper of mankind
Furnished the earth below, the land for men,
Almighty God and everlasting Lord.

(R. Hamer (ed.): 1970, A Choice of Anglo-Saxon Verse,
London: Faber & Faber: 122–3)

Extract 2

This extract is by the Middle English author Geoffrey Chaucer. It comes from the 'Pardoner's Tale', one of Chaucer's *Canterbury Tales* (*c.* 1386–1400), and tells the story of a fraudulent preacher who preaches against avarice, a sin which he himself commits. The section of the tale provided in extract 2 comes from part of the Pardoner's sermon in which he rails against drunkenness (lines 223–8). The language is clearly considerably closer to modern English than is the Old English example which precedes it, but not necessarily any closer than some of the contemporary New English extracts, such as the one which follows it.

Extract 3

This conversation comes from Mufwene's field records (1997: 191) gathered in the 1980s. The language exemplified is the creole, Gullah, spoken along the US coast from Florida to South Carolina and the Sea Islands.

Extracts 4

This set of extracts is also taken from Mufwene's article (though the original sources are Odlin 1992 and Filppula 1991). They all exemplify spoken Hiberno-English, that is, Irish English. Only the third one may need translating: 'He fell while crossing the bridge'.

Extract 5

This is an example of Appalachian speech from West Virginia in the US. It is from a study carried out by the sociolinguist Walt Wolfram (cited in Crystal 2003b: 315). Appalachian speech is considered to represent a very conservative dialect of American English and therefore to be closer than others to the speech of the original Elizabethan settlers. Despite certain features that are not used in modern English dialects, e.g. the a-prefix with *–ing* forms, you should find the extract intelligible.

Extract 6

This is another of the examples cited by Mufwene (1997: 193). Once you work out the 'system', you should be able to understand it without translation. If you have not yet managed to do so, read through the translation, return to the original, and all should become clear:

How are you? It's good to meet you, matey.
Now look. Do you remember the brown idol? Tintin's looking for it. Can you help him?
The brown idol? – It's like I told you. The tribe gave the brown idol to Walker. He was a nice guy. But his fellows took our precious jewel. And if the Arumbayas catch him, they'll have his garters. No messing!

The extract is from 'The Arumbaya language according to Leslie Lonsdale-Cooper and Michael Turner, the translators of Hergé's *The Adventures of Tintin: The Broken Ear* (1975)'. It is, then, fictional and, as Mufwene points out, 'perhaps the only development which one may consider unnatural in settings where English has been appropriated by a foreign group'. He comments that his eight-year-old daughter could not interpret it because she could not recognise any English words which, in turn, is because the creators of the language have 'segmented the phonetic strings in ways that violate English word boundaries'. Mufwene adds that there are no pidgin or creole languages which restructure English in this way.

Extract 7

This sample (cited in Platt et al. 1984: 179) remains in the realms of literature. This time, it comes from the Nigerian author, Amos Tutuola's work, *The Palm-Wine Drunkard*. Tutuola's English is influenced by his mother tongue, Yoruba (an indigenous Nigerian language), and this comes across in his writing. While exhibiting features not found in the English of native speakers (e.g. 'all my friends did not come. . .'), Tutuola's English should be perfectly intelligible to those who speak other varieties.

Extract 8

These are the opening lines of a journal article on Scots, published in the journal *English World-Wide* in 1981 (cited in Crystal 2003b: 333), and originally presented at the symposium '*Our ain lied?*' ('Our own language?'). This is one of the few extracts for which you will probably need a translation. This is how Crystal translates it:

> In the development of a language to full maturity of literature, the
> establishment of an expository prose is often judged a crucial stage. A language
> may have a well-founded tradition of domestic song, learned poetry, and even
> narrative prose; but lacking a register suitable for academic writers, it must
> remain a 'half-language'.

Extract 9

This extract exemplifies the variety of English spoken by the Miskito Indians on the Miskito coast of Nicaragua. According to McCrum et al. (1992: 219–20), from whom the extract is taken, the Miskito Indians 'use a variety of English that has evolved from a unique collision of languages: the speech of seventeenth- and eighteenth-century British settlers, their African slaves, the Indians themselves, and later the Spanish-speakers who seized the area at the end of the nineteenth century'. Miskito was isolated from mainstream English for almost two hundred years and, as a result, evolved differently from the latter, although it also has features in common with both more standard varieties and with West African pidgins. The extract is translated by McCrum et al. as: 'I want nothing to do with you because you have not come for a long time to see Titi. Who is this?'

- ❏ Try to pick out any features of lexis, grammar, pronunciation or discourse style which characterise the variety in each extract.
- ❏ Kachru (1997: 228) distinguishes between *innovation, deviation* and *mistake*. An **innovation** is concerned with creativity which, as Kachru points out, the gatekeepers of English in the UK have been reluctant to accept even from speakers of English in the other Inner Circle countries, let alone in the countries of the Outer Circle. A **deviation** involves a comparison with another variety, normally one from the Inner Circle, while a **mistake** (or 'error') relates to acquisitional deficiency. To what extent would you describe the characteristic features you were able to identify as representing innovations, deviations, or mistakes in the varieties of English concerned?
- ❏ Which extracts did you originally decide represented 'legitimate' and which 'illegitimate' varieties of English? What were your criteria? Did your decision depend to some extent on whether you thought the sample was spoken or written (or a literary representation of speech or writing)? To what extent did your decision depend on the degree of standardness? Having read the key, have you changed your mind in any respect? If so, why?

STANDARDS ACROSS SPACE

Standard English across regions

This section is divided into two parts, and in both we will be focusing primarily on English spoken in Britain, North America and Australia, and looking in particular at vocabulary and grammar. In the first part we will be concerned with the similarities and differences across the Englishes designated 'standard' in each of these three regions, while in the second, attention will shift to the similarities and differences across varieties of English within two of the regions, Britain and North America.

Although the differences across the standard native speaker varieties of English are far outweighed by the similarities, each of these three standard Englishes has certain features which characterise it as specifically British, American or Australian. The most noticeable level of divergence is that of vocabulary, with lexical differences between British and American Englishes far exceeding those between Britain and Australia. In the case of British and **North American English** (US and Canadian English) thousands of words either do not exist at all in one or other variety, or have completely or partially different meanings. The main reasons for this are to some extent obvious. Firstly, the early settlers needed to name those items for which they did not already have names. They did this by extending the meaning of existing English words, creating new words, or borrowing items from the indigenous population, the **Native Americans**. Examples of words with extended meaning are *corn* (referring to grain in Britain, maize in North America) and robin (a small red-breasted warbler in Britain, a large red-breasted thrush in North America). An example of a new creation is *butte* (an isolated hill with a flat top). Examples of borrowing are *moccasin*, *squash* and *toboggan* (see McCrum et al. 1992). Secondly, developments taking place since North American English separated from British English have led to further divergences between the two varieties. This is particularly true of vocabulary resulting from technological innovation, such as car-related words. For example, North American English has *windshield*, *hood* and *trunk* for the items which in British English are designated *windscreen*, *bonnet* and *boot*.

★ **Activity**

Trudgill and Hannah (2002: 85–8) divide **English English** (their preferred term for **Standard British English**) and US English differences into four main categories:

1   Same word, different meaning.
2   Same word, additional meaning in one variety.
3   Same word, difference in style, connotation, frequency of use.
4   Same concept or item, different word.

The following is a selection of items from Trudgill and Hannah's lists. Can you place them in the correct categories and explain the difference in British/American use? (Note that one word fits two categories.) Think about the sorts of communication problems that might arise as a result of these differences. Which category, in your view, has the greatest potential to cause miscommunication between speakers of English from the UK and the US? The key is given in Figure B5.1 (p. 78).

faucet	smart	autumn	regular	bathroom
pants	sophomore	to fancy	a queue	pavement
homely	school	quite (as in *quite* good)		

Category 1 probably has the greatest potential to cause miscommunication. This is because the difference in meaning may never be appreciated and clarified, and so the miscommunication is more likely to remain unresolved.

The differences between **Australian English** and British English lexis are relatively few in number except at the level of idiomatic language and slang. One source of Australian lexical innovation was initially borrowings into English from the Australian aboriginal languages. These include words like *kangaroo* and *boomerang* which are widely known outside Australia, as well as some which are less well known, such as *gibber* (a rock), *corroboree* (a large gathering) and *jumbuck* (a sheep). Many are words for the indigenous flora and fauna, e.g plants such as *calombo*, trees such as *mallee* and

Key

Category 1: same word, different meaning

Word	EngEng meaning	USEng meaning
homely	down to earth, domestic	ugly (of people)
pants	underpants	trousers
pavement	footpath, sidewalk	road surface

Category 2a: additional meaning in USEng

Word	Meaning in common	Additional meaning in USEng
bathroom	room with bath or shower and sink	room with toilet only
regular	consistent, habitual	average (as in size), normal
school	institution of education at elementary level	all institutions of education including universities

Category 2b: additional meaning in EngEng

Word	Meaning in common	Additional meaning in EngEng
smart	intelligent	well-groomed

Category 3: same word, difference in style, connotation, frequency of use

Word	EngEng usage	USEng usage
autumn	common; all styles	uncommon; poetic or formal ('fall' used instead)
to fancy (to like, want)	common, informal	uncommon
quite	negative or neutral	positive

Category 4: same concept or item, different word

USEng only	Corresponds to EngEng
faucet	tap
sophomore	second-year student

EngEng only	Corresponds to USEng
queue	line
pavement	sidewalk

Figure B5.1 British English/American English lexical differences.

birds such as *kookaburra*. Oddly, although the number of borrowings from aboriginal languages into Australian English was small, these words are now regarded as 'quintessentially Australian' (Elmes 2001: 66).

Other Australian English lexical innovations are intra-English in origin, the result of adaptations in form or range of meaning of words already in existence in English English. For example:

Australian English	English English
barrack for	support
footpath	pavement
parka	anorak
sedan	estate car
station	stock farm
stroller	push-chair
bludger	loafer, sponger
singlet	vest
station wagon	saloon car
paddock	field

By far the majority of lexical differences across varieties of English are in their colloquial usage, especially in often-ephemeral slang words and phrases. The following are examples of Australian English slang items which are not used in English English (from Elmes 2001 and Trudgill and Hannah 2002):

a dag (an affectionate term meaning an eccentric person)
a drongo (a fool)
a galah (a fool)
a chine (a mate)
an offsider (a partner or companion)
a sort (an attractive person)
a sheila (a girl)
tucker (food)
splosh; *boodle* (money)
spiflicated; *rotten*; *full as a boot* (drunk)
crook (ill, angry)
to spit the dummy (to lose your temper)
to bot (to cadge, borrow)
to gammon (to fool someone into thinking something)
to front up (to arrive, present oneself somewhere)
to fine up (to improve – used of weather)
to retrench (to sack, make redundant)
to shout (to buy something for someone, e.g. a round of drinks)
shooting a fairy (farting)
she'll be apples (everything is going to be okay)

> Are you familiar with equivalent slang words and expressions in other (Inner or Outer Circle) varieties of English? For example, British English has words such as 'rat-arsed' and 'legless' for the adjective 'drunk', and 'to con' for 'to fool someone into thinking something'. If you are using this book in a class where students come from a range of English speaking backgrounds, select a number of categories (e.g. drink, money, weather, etc.) and compare slang words and expressions across Englishes for lexical items within these categories. How do you account for any cross-cultural similarities and/or differences that emerge?

Another feature of Australian lexis is the love of abbreviations. There is a tendency among all speakers of English to shorten words, a process known as 'clipping', to the extent that the original word may no longer be known to most speakers, e.g. 'pants' is an abbreviation of 'pantaloons', and 'bus' of 'omnibus' (see Gramley 2001: 94). However, it seems that Australians engage in clipping more frequently than do speakers of other Englishes. In Australian English, again more so than in other Englishes, the clipped word may then be given a diminutive suffix, especially *–ie* or *–y* but also *–o*. For example, the word 'barbecue' becomes 'barbie', the word 'Australian' becomes 'Aussy', and the word 'afternoon' becomes 'arvo'.

Turning to grammar, the grammatical differences between English English and Australian English are relatively few in number at the level of educated speech and writing and, as Trudgill and Hannah (2002: 18) point out, it is often impossible to tell, unless there is distinctive use of vocabulary, whether a text was written by an Australian or British writer.

The grammatical differences between English English and US English, however, are far more wide-ranging. It is only possible to single out some of the main categories of difference here (see Trudgill and Hannah 2002: 55–79 for details).

Verbs

❏ Morphology: differences in past and participle endings, e.g. English English: 'dived', 'sneaked', 'got'; US English: 'dove', 'snuk', 'gotten'.

❏ Auxiliaries: use of epistemic 'must': English English uses 'can't' in the negative, e.g. 'He <u>can't</u> be in – his car has gone', whereas US English uses (uncontracted) 'must not' (not to be confused with 'mustn't' meaning 'not be allowed').

Nouns

❏ Greater use of certain noun endings in US English, e.g. *–ee* (retiree, draftee), *–ster* (teamster, gamester).

❏ Difference in derivational ending, e.g. English English: 'candidature', 'centenary'; US English: 'candidacy', 'centennial'.

❏ Greater tendency to use verbs as nouns in US English, e.g. 'to run down', 'to be shut in', to try out', become 'the rundown', 'a shut-in' ('an invalid'), 'a try-out' ('an audition').

Adjectives and adverbs

❑ The comparative adjective 'different' is followed by 'than' in US English and by 'from' (or more recently, 'to') in English English, e.g. 'This one is different <u>than/from</u> (to) the last one'.

❑ The adverbs 'yet' and 'already' cannot occur with the simple past tense in EngEng, whereas they can do so in US English. In such cases, English English uses the present perfect tense: US English: 'I didn't buy one yet', 'Did you read it already?'; English English: 'I haven't bought one yet', 'Have you read it already?'.

Prepositions

❑ A few prepositions differ in form in the two varieties, e.g. English English: 'behind'; US English: 'in back of' ('I put it <u>behind/in back of</u> the shed').

❑ Differences in preposition in specific contexts, particularly in expressions of time, e.g. English English: 'I haven't seen him <u>for</u> ages/weeks'; US English: 'I haven't seen him <u>in</u> ages/weeks'.

❑ Clock time: English English: 'twenty <u>to</u> three', 'five <u>past</u> eight'; US English: 'twenty <u>of/till</u> three', 'five <u>after</u> eight'.

❑ Different uses of 'in' and 'on': English English: 'to live <u>in</u> a street', 'to be <u>in a</u> sale'; US English: 'to be <u>on</u> a street', 'to be <u>on</u> sale' (whereas in English English 'on sale' means 'for sale').

If you are familiar with both British English and either New Zealand English or South African English, which grammatical features would you single out as differing most from English English? In your view, do any of these differences have the same degree of potential for miscommunication as lexical differences do? Have you had any personal experience of miscommunication arising from grammatical differences in your own and an interlocutor's English?

Standard English and dialect

The differences between standard and non-standard Inner Circle Englishes receive much comment, with the non-standard Englishes (or 'dialects' as they are often called) being stigmatised in so far as they diverge from the variety regarded as the standard. Despite this, and the extent of the stigmatising which continues to this day, Trudgill and Chambers regard the grammatical and lexical differences in the regional and social varieties of English spoken by its native speakers as trivial:

> The vast majority of native speakers around the world differ linguistically from one another relatively little, with more differentiation in their phonetics and phonology than at other linguistic levels. Most English people, for example, betray their geographical origins much more through their accents than through their vocabulary or grammar. This vast majority speaks mainstream varieties of

English, standard or non-standard, which resemble one another quite closely, and which are all reasonably readily mutually intelligible. Differences between these mainstream varieties may be regionally and socially very diagnostic, but they are generally linguistically rather trivial, and where not trivial, quite regular and predictable. Grammatically, in particular, these varieties are very close to standard English.

(Trudgill and Chambers 1991: 2)

The linguist Stubbs provides evidence of the truth of Trudgill and Chambers' claim by showing how working-class speech in many regions of Britain differs morphosyntactically from Standard British English in only a few ways. These are among the examples he cites:

1. Multiple negation:
   I didn't do nothing.
2. Ain't as a negative form of be or auxiliary verb have:
   I ain't doing it.
   I ain't got one.
3. Never used to refer to a single occasion in the past:
   I never done it (SE: I didn't do it).
4. Extension of third person –*s* to first and second person verb forms:
   I *wants, you wants, he wants.*
5. Regularisation of be:
   We was, you was, they was.
6. Regularisation of some irregular verbs:
   I draw, I drawed, I have drawed.
   I go, I went, I have went.
   I come, I come, I have come.
7. Optional –*ly* on adverbs:
   He writes real quick.
8. Unmarked plurality on nouns of measurement after numerals:
   twenty year, ten pound.
9. Different forms of the relative pronoun:
   The man as/what lives here.
10. Regularisation of reflexive pronouns:
    myself, yourself, hisself, herself; ourselves, yourselves, theirselves.
11. Distinction between main and auxiliary verb do:
    You done it, did you? (SE: You did it, did you?).

(Mitchell 1993, selected from Stubbs 1986)

Activity

> If a speaker uses certain of the above features even once – a double negative, for example – he or she will be 'diagnosed' as a speaker of a non-standard English. On the other hand, other features, such as the –*ly* ending on adverbs (no. 7), seem to be slowly dying out of common usage, in this case perhaps

by analogy with forms such as 'fast' and 'hard' which do not take the *–ly*, or because of complications with adverb forms of adjectives such as 'friendly' which already end in *–ly*. Presumably when sufficient numbers of educated speakers of English have dropped the *–ly* adverb ending, it will no longer be considered a dialect marker. A similar case is no. 8, unmarked plurality, with a number of educated speakers of British English using 'pound' singular in phrases such as 'ten pound'. Do you envisage this happening in the reasonably short term to any other items on Stubbs's list? If so, do you think that the change will be restricted to the spoken language or that it will eventually work its way into the written standard?

Despite claims that standardness is not an issue in the US to the same extent as it is in Britain (see, for example, Baron 2000: 134–5), the evidence provided by Bonfiglio (2002), Lippi-Green (1997), Wolfram and Schilling-Estes (2006) and others suggests otherwise. The difference is that attitudes towards standardness are connected in the US with race rather than class, with the dialects spoken by speakers of Hispanic English and Black English (AAVE) being the most highly stigmatised. The following extract in which members of the studio audience and telephone callers participate in a screening of the Oprah Winfrey show demonstrates this point:

1

2nd caller. Hi, Oprah?

Winfrey. Yes

2nd caller. I guess what I'd like to say is that what makes me feel that blacks tend to be ignorant is that they fail to see that the word is spelled A-S-K, not A-X. And when they say aksed, it gives the sentence an entirely different meaning. And this is what I feel holds blacks back.

Winfrey. Why does it give it a different meaning if you know that's what they're saying?

2nd caller. But you don't always know that's what they are saying.

2

9th audience member. The problem seems to be that everybody tries to push something down your throat by arrogance. That's not the way to get something done. You could speak your own language, you could have your own way, but don't force someone else to have to suffer and listen to it.

Winfrey. You say what?

10th audience member. Well I'm an accountant and –

Winfrey. Well, wait, wait, let me get back to you. What is causing you to suffer?

9th audience member. Well I think there is a certain way of speaking that has been considered the acceptable way of speaking. And because of that this is the type of language you speak when you're out in the world. If you want to speak Spanish at home that's fine. If you want to speak black with your friends that's fine. But don't insult someone else's ears by making them listen to it.

(both extracts in Milroy and Milroy 1999: 152–3)

> If you were Oprah Winfrey, how would you have responded to the 2nd caller and 9th audience member?

According to Wolfram and Schilling-Estes (2006: 131), '[d]ialect difference in America is by no means a thing of the past, and there is every indication that the boundaries whose foundations were laid when the first English colonists arrived in Jamestown in 1607 will continue to exist in some form long into the current millennium'. They also point out that the vowel systems which distinguish the north cities and the south from one another are in the process of diverging further rather than converging, while both are becoming more distinct from the vowel systems of the Midland area.

As with the British English dialects, it is only possible to summarise some of the main socially diagnostic grammatical structures. The following items are all taken from Wolfram and Schilling-Estes (2006: 370–84):

The verb phrase

1 Irregular verbs
The majority of vernaculars in the north and south exhibit the following features:

- ❏ past as participle form, e.g. 'I had <u>went</u> down there',
- ❏ participle as past form, e.g. 'He <u>seen</u> something out there', and
- ❏ bare root as past form, e.g. 'She <u>come</u> to my house yesterday'.

Some rural vernaculars in the south may also exhibit this pattern:

- ❏ different irregular form, e.g. 'Something just <u>riz</u> (rose) up right in front of me'.

2 Completive 'done'
In southern European and African American (AAVE) vernaculars, the form 'done' may mark a completed action or event in a different way from a simple past tense form by emphasising the 'completedness' of the action, e.g. 'I <u>done</u> forgot what you wanted'.

3 Habitual 'be'
In AAVE as well as in some rural European American varieties, the form 'be' occurs in sentences such as 'She usually <u>be</u> home in the evening'.

4 A-prefixing
In vernacular Southern mountain speech, as well as in many other rural dialects, an a-prefix may occur on *–ing* forms functioning as verbs or adverbs, e.g. 'She was <u>a</u>-coming home', 'He starts <u>a</u>-laughing'. This form cannot occur with *–ing* forms which function as nouns or adjectives, and is also restricted phonologically in that it can only occur on forms whose first syllable is accented. It is also preferred on items which begin with a consonant sound.

5 Double modals

In some Southern vernacular varieties, combinations of two modal verbs, e.g. 'I <u>might could</u> go there', 'You <u>might oughta</u> take it', are widespread. They are apparently not particularly stigmatised, perhaps because, as Wolfram and Schilling-Estes (2006 374) point out, 'they lessen the force of an attitude or obligation conveyed by single modals'.

Adverbs

-ly absence

In Southern-based dialects, especially upper Southern vernacular varieties such as Appalachian and Ozark English, the *–ly* adverb ending is being lost, e.g. 'They answered <u>wrong</u>', 'She enjoyed life <u>awful</u> well', 'I come from Virginia <u>original</u>'.

Negation

Multiple negation and *ain't* are the two major negation features of vernacular varieties of US English.

1 Multiple negation

Almost all vernacular varieties of American English make use of multiple negation of type 1; most Southern and restricted Northern vernaculars make use of type 2; most Southern vernaculars make use of type 3; and restricted Southern and AAVE varieties make use of type 4:

> *Type 1*: marking of the negative on the auxiliary verb and the indefinite following the verb, e.g. 'The man <u>wasn't</u> saying <u>nothing</u>'.
> *Type 2*: negative marking of an indefinite before the verb phrase and of the auxiliary verb, e.g. '<u>Nobody</u> <u>didn't</u> like the mess'.
> *Type 3*: inversion of the negativised auxiliary verb and the pre-verbal indefinite, e.g. '<u>Didn't</u> <u>nobody</u> like the mess?'
> *Type 4*: multiple negative marking across different clauses, e.g. 'There <u>wasn't</u> much that I <u>couldn't</u> do' (meaning 'There wasn't much that I could do').

2 ain't

This item may be used instead of certain standard forms including forms of *be* + *not*, e.g. 'She <u>ain't</u> here now'; forms of *have* + *not*, e.g. 'I <u>ain't</u> seen her in a long time'; and *did* + *not*, e.g. 'I <u>ain't</u> go to school yesterday'.

Pronouns

The first four types of pronominal difference are found in most vernacular dialects of American English, and the fifth is specifically a Southern feature:

- ❏ regularisation of reflexive forms by analogy with other possessive pronouns, e.g. 'He hit <u>hisself</u> on the head', 'They shaved <u>theirselves</u>',
- ❏ extension of object forms to co-ordinate subjects, e.g. '<u>Me and him</u> will do it',
- ❏ adoption of a second person plural form: (a) <u>Y'all</u> won the game (Southern);

(b) <u>Youse</u> won the game (Northern); (c) <u>You'uns</u> won the game (used in an area extending from southern Appalachia to Pittsburgh),

❑ extension of object forms to demonstratives, e.g. '<u>Them</u> books are on the shelf' (note: this is also a common feature of non-standard British English), and

❑ a special personal dative use of the object pronoun form, e.g. 'I got <u>me</u> a new car', 'We had <u>us</u> a little old dog'.

<hr />

Activity

Williams (2007: 402) argues that

> [i]n spite of the efforts of linguists to educate the public about the regular, rule-governed nature of NS [non-standard] dialects, the view that such dialects are inferior and full of errors, 'bad' or 'incorrect' English still prevails, even among some speakers themselves. The role that standard English has traditionally played in education, literature and in the media on the other hand, means that it is often considered to be a linguistically superior variety and that speakers of SE [standard English] speak 'good' or 'correct' English.

Williams is referring specifically to the British context. If you are familiar with this context, do you agree with her assessment, and/or does it reflect the situation in any other Inner Circle contexts with which you are familiar?

If you agree with Williams, do you think that the attitudes towards non-standard varieties to which she refers are in some way bound up with attitudes towards their speakers? Before you decide, look again at the extracts from the Oprah Winfrey show above, and then at the following three quotations. To what extent, in your experience, are they typical of the general public's attitudes towards speakers of non-standard Englishes?

> Boys from bad homes come to school with their speech in a state of disease, and we must be unwearied in the task of purification.
>
> (Sampson 1924, quoted in Crowley 2003: 204)

> Why should we consider some, usually poorly educated, subculture's notion of the relationship between sound and meaning? And how could a grammar – any grammar – possibly describe that relationship?
>
> As for 'I be,' 'you be,' 'he be,' etc., which should give us all the heebie-jeebies, these may indeed be comprehensible, but they go against all accepted classical and modern grammars, and are the product not of a language with roots in history but of ignorance of how language works.
>
> (US journalist John Simon speaking of AAVE, quoted in Pinker 1994: 385)

> If you allow standards to slip to the stage where good English is no better than bad English, where people turn up filthy at school . . . all these

things tend to cause people to have no standards at all, and once you lose standards then there's no imperative to stay out of crime.
(Norman Tebbit, a (British) Conservative MP speaking on BBC Radio 4 in 1985, quoted in Cameron 1995: 94)

NATIVE AND NON-NATIVE SPEAKERS OF ENGLISH

B6

As Mesthrie and Bhatt (2008: 36) observe, '[t]he distinction between a native and non-native speaker of English – long taken for granted in Linguistics – is being increasingly called into question in World English research'. Mesthrie and Bhatt are referring here to the use of 'native' and 'non-native' in relation to the 'New' Englishes of the Outer Circle (see A4). However, a growing number of scholars (e.g. Jenkins 2000, McKay 2002, Seidlhofer 2001) have, for several years, been articulating a similar position in respect of the Expanding Circle. Their point is that when English is used as an international lingua franca among Expanding Circle speakers, then these speakers 'own' their lingua franca English, or ELF, and it therefore makes no sense to describe them as 'non-native' English speakers. In other words, according to this perspective, while the native speaker/non-native speaker distinction holds good for English as a *foreign* language and for other modern foreign languages (i.e. any second language learnt primarily for communication with its L1 speakers), it does not hold good for ELF, which is used mainly among L2 speakers of English, often with no L1 English speaker present at all.

Is nativeness a viable concept for English as a Lingua Franca?

⭐ **Activity**

So what are the arguments against the use of the terms 'native' and 'non-native' speaker of English? The following have been suggested. Do you agree with them? If not, what are your reasons? Most of these arguments were originally made in relation to speakers of Outer Circle Englishes. Which of them do you regard as most relevant to ELF?

❑ The term 'native speaker' perpetuates the view that monolingualism is the world's norm when, in fact, the majority of people are multilingual, and switch appropriately from one language to another according to the situation.
❑ It ignores the fact that because English is often one of several languages available in the repertoires of the multilingual populations of countries such as India, it is often difficult to decide which language is a speaker's first, second, third, and so on.
❑ It implies that the most important criterion for language proficiency is

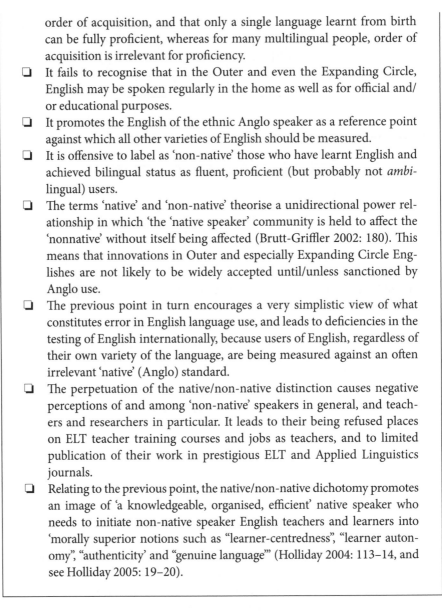

order of acquisition, and that only a single language learnt from birth can be fully proficient, whereas for many multilingual people, order of acquisition is irrelevant for proficiency.

❏ It fails to recognise that in the Outer and even the Expanding Circle, English may be spoken regularly in the home as well as for official and/or educational purposes.

❏ It promotes the English of the ethnic Anglo speaker as a reference point against which all other varieties of English should be measured.

❏ It is offensive to label as 'non-native' those who have learnt English and achieved bilingual status as fluent, proficient (but probably not *ambilingual*) users.

❏ The terms 'native' and 'non-native' theorise a unidirectional power relationship in which 'the 'native speaker' community is held to affect the 'nonnative' without itself being affected (Brutt-Griffler 2002: 180). This means that innovations in Outer and especially Expanding Circle Englishes are not likely to be widely accepted until/unless sanctioned by Anglo use.

❏ The previous point in turn encourages a very simplistic view of what constitutes error in English language use, and leads to deficiencies in the testing of English internationally, because users of English, regardless of their own variety of the language, are being measured against an often irrelevant 'native' (Anglo) standard.

❏ The perpetuation of the native/non-native distinction causes negative perceptions of and among 'non-native' speakers in general, and teachers and researchers in particular. It leads to their being refused places on ELT teacher training courses and jobs as teachers, and to limited publication of their work in prestigious ELT and Applied Linguistics journals.

❏ Relating to the previous point, the native/non-native dichotomy promotes an image of 'a knowledgeable, organised, efficient' native speaker who needs to initiate non-native speaker English teachers and learners into 'morally superior notions such as "learner-centredness", "learner autonomy", "authenticity' and "genuine language"' (Holliday 2004: 113–14, and see Holliday 2005: 19–20).

On the other hand, some do not agree that the native/non-native speaker distinction is untenable in relation to the use of English in the Expanding Circle:

> In the Expanding Circle . . . the ideal goal is to imitate the native speaker of the standard language as closely as possible. Speaking English is simply not related to cultural identity. It is rather an exponent of one's academic and language-learning abilities. It would, therefore, be far from a compliment to tell a Spanish person that his or her variety is Spanish English. It would imply that his or her acquisition of the language left something to be desired.
>
> (Andreasson 1994: 402)

The previous quotation raises a number of questions, which are listed below. What is your reaction to them? Are there any other questions that you would wish to raise in response?

1   Who is 'the native speaker of the standard language'? Defining both 'native speaker' and 'standard language' (see A5), as you will have realised, is far from unproblematic. And even if we focused on one specific group, e.g. educated middle-class speakers of British English, we would still need to distinguish between, for example, speakers with different accents (RP is used by only a tiny and ageing minority), speakers from different age groups (there are major differences in the speech of younger and older educated middle-class British-English speakers), and formal and informal use. All this makes it difficult to identify precisely who and what Expanding Circle speakers should 'imitate'.

2   Does one's use of English really exemplify no more than one's 'academic and language-learning abilities'?

3   Is it a fact that 'speaking English is simply not related to cultural identity'?

4   Does it seem reasonable that mother-tongue speakers of English should (generally) be comfortable with the idea that their accents reveal their geographical origins, while non-mother-tongue speakers should equate regional accents with poor acquisition of English and regard them as an embarrassment?

5   Compare the view expressed in the above quotation with that of an Austrian teacher of English in an Austrian university. Which view do you have greater sympathy with?

I've been here [name of institution] very, very long and this has been a tradition that you're supposed to approximate the native speaker, and unless you approximate the native British speaker you are sort of regarded as inferior . . . I don't see why a good EFL teacher, Austrian English teacher, shouldn't have a trace of an accent of his local variety of English. We're talking about international English . . . and we're still keeping to this idea that the Austrian teacher . . . you must sound more British than the British.

(quoted in Jenkins 2000: 30)

6   The quotation by Andreasson could be said to represent the views of those who see English in the Expanding Circle as a **foreign language**, and the second quotation to represent the views of those who see it as a **lingua franca**. How important or unimportant do you think this distinction is?

What are the alternatives?

If we abandon the use of the terms 'native' and non-native' in relation to EIL, what are the alternatives?

Rampton (1990: 98–9; Leung et al. 1997) proposes the use of the term 'expert' to describe all accomplished users of English, arguing that expertise has the following advantages over nativeness:

1   Although they often do, experts do not have to feel close to what they know a lot about. Expertise is different from identification.
2   Expertise is learned, not fixed or innate.
3   Expertise is relative. One person's expert is another person's fool.
4   Expertise is partial. People can be expert in several fields, but they are never omniscient.
5   To achieve expertise, one goes through processes of certification, in which one is judged by other people. Their standards of assessment can be reviewed and disputed. There is also a healthy tradition of challenging 'experts'.

On the other hand, the use of the term 'expert' for fluent speakers of English implies the use of 'non-expert' to describe less fluent speakers. This, it could be argued, imposes something of the value judgement of the term 'non-native'. For this and other reasons, I prefer to reconceptualise the issue by turning the traditional terminology upside down and propose the following system:

1   for speakers of English who speak no other language, **monolingual English speaker** (**MES**)
2   for proficient speakers of English and at least one other language, regardless of the order in which they learned the languages, **bilingual English speaker** (**BES**)
3   for those who are not bilingual in English but are nevertheless able to speak it at a level of reasonable competence, **non-bilingual English speaker** (**NBES**).

These are what I see as the two main advantages of my reconceptualisation (for fuller details, see Jenkins 1996; 2000: 8–10):

1   MES as an epithet is considerably less favourable than BES given that it signals the greater linguistic competence of the BES and the lesser of the MES. Thus, this system of labelling reflects the fact that monolingualism is not the preferable condition – and neither is it the world norm.
2   BES removes the artificial distinction – in an international context – between speakers of L1 and L2 varieties of English. This should, in turn, eventually lead to the end of discrimination against teachers of English on the grounds that they are not 'native speakers' of English (see unit C3 for more on this issue and, in particular, the advantages of being a bilingual teacher of English).

On the other hand, this system is not without its disadvantages. In particular, there is the problem of what counts as bilingual competence, and where to draw the line between non-bilingual and bilingual competence (and, of course, who should be responsible for drawing it). At the time of writing, these problems are far from being resolved. However, one suggestion (Ayako Suzuki, personal communication) is to replace NBES with 'Potential BES' which, while still not solving these problems, at least removes the negative associations of the prefix 'non'.

★ **Activity**

❏ What do you consider to be the pros and cons of each of these attempts to replace the terms 'native' and 'non-native' speaker? Do you agree with the advantages and disadvantages already mentioned? Can you think of others? Which of the two approaches do you prefer overall, and why? Do you prefer the second approach with or without Suzuki's modification? Alternatively, can you devise another solution?

❏ If you were made responsible for deciding how to distinguish between Jenkins's BES/NBES competence or Rampton's expert and, by implication, non-expert speaker of English, what would your criteria be?

❏ McKay (2002: 27) is in favour of using the term 'bilingual user of English' to describe a wide range of proficiency because of the difficulty in drawing a line between more and less proficient speakers. Do you think this is a viable alternative?

EN ROUTE TO NEW STANDARD ENGLISHES

B7

In unit B7 we will be looking at Asian Englishes in relation to the codification process (see A5) and the problems they are encountering on the way to achieving fully-standardised and codified status.

As D'Souza (1999: 271) has pointed out, codification is 'the crux of the matter'. Without codification, the Outer and Expanding Circle Englishes will continue to lack prestige not only in the eyes of speakers of 'accepted' (i.e. Inner Circle) standard varieties, but also among their own speakers. In order for local classroom models in Asia (and Europe) to be considered acceptable internationally as alternatives to British and American models, it must be possible to find their grammatical, lexical, phonological and discoursal characteristics in widely respected works of reference such as grammars and dictionaries. Even then, it will be difficult, yet vital, to ensure that learners of World Englishes are not 'victims of a system that has one *de jure* model but a somewhat different de facto one' (D'Souza 1999: 272), that is, that they are not taught local norms which remain unacceptable to Inner Circle gatekeepers. In this respect, selection is critical, and one of the main tasks for the codifiers of World Englishes in the twenty-first century will be to distinguish between items for local informal use and those which have the 'right' to international status.

Codifying Asian Englishes

One of the greatest obstacles to the codifying of Asian Englishes in recent years has been the claim of a large number of **second language acquisition (SLA)** scholars in the Inner Circle that these **nativised** or **indigenised varieties of English (IVEs)** along with the African IVEs of the Outer Circle are 'interlanguages', that is, 'learner' languages characterised by 'errors', rather than legitimate L2 varieties of English containing forms which happen to differ from forms used in L1 English varieties (see also unit B3). Because this issue is still not resolved, because it has been so hotly debated, and because it has been represented on the IVE 'side' largely by speakers of Asian IVEs, we will look at what has been said before moving on to consider codification itself.

Sridhar and Sridhar (1992: 97) discuss the 'IVE = Interlanguage' claim in terms of the 'dangers of an uncritical application of the current SLA paradigm'. They argue that SLA researchers have neglected the IVEs as a result of certain assumptions which underpin their perspective on SLA, chiefly:

1   that the goal of SLA is (or ought to be) native-like competence,
2   that the (native speaker) input available to learners is sufficient to allow acquisition of full active competence,
3   that the SLA process can be studied without reference to the functions which the L2 will serve for the learner in his/her community,
4   that the 'role' of the learner's L1 should be evaluated only in terms of its contribution in 'interfering' with and (less often) facilitating the acquisition of L2 structures, with no interest in its contribution to the communicative function involved, and
5   that the ideal motivation for success in SLA is 'integrative', i.e. 'one that involves admiration for the native speakers of the language and a desire to become a member of their culture'.

(adapted from Sridhar and Sridhar 1992: 93–4)

However, as Sridhar and Sridhar point out, IVE settings have a very different character from those typical of most SLA research. Firstly, the communicative target is no longer native speakers but other non-native speakers. This in turn renders the native speaker norm against which non-native speaker performance is measured in a traditional SLA paradigm irrelevant. Instead, the optimum model of instruction and reference point for performance evaluation derives from IVE norms. Secondly, the input available to learners is an IVE, not a native variety of English. In fact most learners of IVEs have no contact with native-speaker-English and often the latter is barely understandable to them. Thirdly, learners of IVEs go on to use their English in multilingual settings in a distribution comparable to that of the high variety in a diglossic situation (**diglossia** being the use of a high variety for some functions and a low variety for others). Thus their English does not serve all the functions that it does in the case of monolingual native English speakers, and nor should it be expected to. Fourthly, the motivation of most IVE learners is instrumental rather than integrative. That is, it is learnt as a result of the desire to achieve some functional goal (e.g. to pass an exam, to participate in a particular field of employment, whether local or international) rather than to identify with the target-language culture. According to a traditional SLA perspective, this should mean a low level of success in acquiring the L2, and yet the opposite is often the case.

Interlanguage (a term coined by Selinker 1972) is defined during the language learning phase by its instability, in that a learner's interlanguage (IL) passes through a range of intermediate systems between the native and target languages before reaching a point where it stabilises. Because it rarely stabilises with a competence identical to that of a native speaker of the language, IL is said to 'fossilise' at the point of stability (Selinker 1972), with fossilisation clearly implying deficit rather than difference. IL is thus one of two things: unstable learner language or fossilised learner language. Since most IVEs are stable (to the extent that any bona fide language is stable), the only way SLA can apply the concept 'interlanguage' to IVEs is to claim that competence 'in whole groups of individuals' can become fossilised, 'resulting in the emergence of a new dialect ([such as] Indian English), where fossilized IL competences may be the normal situation' (Selinker 1972). In other words, entire communities' varieties of English are being characterised as 'fossilized IL competences'.

World Englishes scholars (see, for example, Y. Kachru 1994, Sridhar and Sridhar 1986, S. Sridhar 1994) have for many years pointed out that this view of the IVEs is unsatisfactory on account of both the unprincipled way in which it assigns the term 'fossilised', and the failure to take account of the bi- or multilingual context in which IVEs are acquired and used, including the fact that the goal of SLA is by definition bilingualism (see C7 for discussion of the latter issue). As regards the first point, Y. Kachru argues:

> The question of why a stable system should be characterized as an IL is not answered. It is also not clear what the difference is between 'stable' and 'fossilized': that which is fossilized is surely unchanging and therefore stable! Additionally, if 'an entirely fossilized IL competence' refers to a community . . . it is difficult to see why it is an IL and why it is 'fossilized'. Presumably American English developed as an IL among a large portion of the immigrant population from the non-English-speaking parts of Europe. Does this mean that American English represents an 'entirely fossilized IL'?
>
> (Y. Kachru 1993: 266)

On the second point, Canagarajah has this to say:

> Often the speaker's L1 is considered to be the culprit in creating fossilized items. Furthermore, code-mixed versions of bilingual communication can be stigmatized as fossilized forms that prevent progression towards native-speaker competence. This means that the unilateral movement towards native norms, and the uniform criteria adopted to judge the success of acquisition, ignore the positive contributions of L1 in the construction of unique communicative modes and English grammars for periphery speakers.
>
> (Canagarajah 1999: 128)

As Y. Kachru (2005: 159) points out, one source of the problem is the confusion of attitudes with sociolinguistic reality: '[t]here are Americans, just as there are Indians or Singaporeans, who think their own variety is not as "pure" or "elegant" as British English . . . That, however, does not lead to questioning the existence of a standard variety of American English, nor should it result in denying the status they deserve to the standard varieties of the Outer Circle'. Brutt-Griffler (2002) adds to the debate by arguing that another source of the problem is SLA scholars' exclusive focus on individual acquisition of English and hence their ignoring of its acquisition by bilingual speech communities.

The IL debate is not yet fully resolved. Nevertheless, the IVEs, particularly those of several Asian Outer Circle countries, are increasingly being recognised as fully-fledged language varieties, if not yet by the majority of SLA researchers. But even where the derogatory interlanguage label has been removed, there is still the problem of deciding on what is to be included in the standard version of a variety, a decision involving factors and challenges which codifiers of the traditional (Inner Circle) varieties have not hitherto had to face. In particular, codifiers of Asian Englishes are having to establish a novel set of criteria as the basis on which they make their selection, since the native speaker English standard varieties of the US and UK are of minimal relevance in the standard *Asian* English selection process. Instead, local educated varieties are (or should be) the focus of attention. However, in these countries there are often a number of educated varieties each influenced by the mother tongue of its speakers, which means that difficult and sometimes controversial decisions are having to be taken. And these decisions cannot even be tackled yet in a few Asian countries such as Hong Kong (see C7), because of the remaining strength of attachment to native speaker English norms. The issue of the choice of standard in Asia, as Pakir (1997: 175) argues, 'can only be resolved when the myth of the Native Speaker Interlocutor has been laid to rest'.

A second major challenge facing Asian English codifiers is the resolution of the conflict between centripetal forces pulling them inwards towards local needs and centrifugal forces pushing them outwards towards international intelligibility and acceptability. A codified Asian English will need to combine local features that signal its difference from other Englishes and perform the functions required by its *intranational* community, with available modifications to render it intelligible and acceptable to English speakers (primarily non-native, but not forgetting the native speaker minority) *internationally*. In other words, while for many Expanding Circle speakers, international communication is their primary or even sole use of English, it should not be forgotten that Outer (and Inner) Circle speakers also use English as a Lingua Franca.

This is a mammoth task, one far more complex than that of Inner Circle codifiers, who up to now have worked on the assumption that whatever they deem standard at the national level will also be intelligible and acceptable internationally. Asian English intranational needs involve, for example, the acceptance of local (Asian) innovations in English including the standardising in the English lexicon of non-English words for which there is no precise English equivalent. For instance, the Tagalog adjective *malambing* translates very roughly as 'demonstrative' or 'loving', but there are occasions when neither translation expresses exactly what a Filipino English speaker wants to say (Bautista 1998). There is, then, a strong case for including such lexical gaps in a dictionary of Philippine English.

Similarly, given that almost all Asian-English speakers are bi- or multilingual and make extensive use of code-switching/code-mixing, it seems logical to include this phenomenon in grammars and dictionaries of Asian Englishes. The following example taken from Y. Kachru and Nelson (2006: 256) comes from the ending of an email to Y. Kachru:

> Love to all, I had better sleep and rest my legs as I am the only young *buddhi* here, or my legs will *jawab denge*.

The Hindi elements, *buddhi* and *jawab denge*, mean respectively 'old woman' and 'buckle (literally "give up")'. As the authors point out, the majority of the Hindi items embedded in the text do not cover lexical gaps in English. Instead, they are part of a bilingual's 'competence in creative use of language . . . a communicative choice which necessarily draws on linguistic structure as such, but also on the message and the speaker's intentions' (p. 261). In other words, speakers who have more than one language available to them code-switch/mix as a matter of choice and for a range of pragmatic and expressive reasons that will be alien to those who are monolingual or have only ever spoken second languages in classroom settings. (See Y. Kachru and Nelson 2006, chapter 18, for further discussion and many more examples.)

The most comprehensive attempt at codifying Asian Englishes to date is the **Macquarie Regional Asian English Dictionary** co-published with Grolier Publishers in 2000 as the *Grolier International Dictionary: World English in an Asian Context* (see Bolton 2003: 28, 209–11), which documents the Englishes of South-East and South Asia. Its aim is to meet the needs of English speakers in the region by providing up-to-date coverage of items with international currency along with local words which 'though part and parcel of everyday English in the region, have never appeared in a dictionary before' (Butler 1997: 97). In this way the dictionary recognises that Asian English speakers need English for both international communication and communication at home.

  Activity

❏   As regards local words, the Macquarie dictionary acknowledges that the Englishes of the Asian region are not monolithic, but 'function in their totality, combining a standard dialect in formal and informal register, with a nonstandard and colloquial form' (Butler 1997: 99) – just like the Inner Circle Englishes, in fact. The dictionary does not try to cover all these dialects, but for each Asian variety presents the standard form mainly in its formal style, while including some informal items. All items are selected from a corpus of English in Asia, **ASIACORP**, which is being collected from texts (e.g. newspapers, fiction and non-fiction) produced in the respective variety of English and intended for local rather than international use. These are some of the items included in the dictionary. If you are not familiar with the Englishes of South-East Asia, can you understand any of them?

1 academician
2 actsy
3 adobo
4 aggrupation
5 aircon

❏ One of the most difficult decisions for the dictionary compilers has been to decide whether items are standard informal (and thus candidates for inclusion) or non-standard colloquial (and therefore to be excluded). The following are citations of localisms taken from the corpus material under the heading 'Social organisation'. Some were accepted by the consultants for Singaporean, Malaysian and Philippine Englishes while others were discarded, mainly on the basis of the consultants' intuitions as to the boundary between standard informal and non-standard colloquial. Which do you think they accepted and discarded?

Singaporean/Malaysian English

community centre: One of the better seafood places in Sandakan is a restaurant, behind the Community Centre and the long distance Mini bus terminal.

kongsi: She could not find domestic work and had to rely on the benevolence of her *kongsi*, or sorority.

mui tsai: By the post war period, girls from as young as four or five years, pledged as *mui tsai* or bond servants by their parents or guardians were almost certainly no longer being brought in from China.

Philippine English

dalaga: 'It is generally understood that the more difficult it is to invite a *dalaga* to a feast, the higher she is in the estimation of the community. A feast is considered particularly successful if one or more well-known dalagas are persuaded to attend' (Butler 1997: 109).

Activity

Now look at the key. If you are an Asian English speaker, do you agree with the consultants' decisions?

Key

1 *noun*: an academic
2 *adjective*: conceited, proud [ACT + –SY]
3 *noun*: a Philippine dish of pork or chicken stew cooked in soy sauce, vinegar and garlic. [Spanish: pickle, sauce]
4 *noun*: a group, especially within a political party. [Spanish: *agrupación*]
5 *noun*: 1. airconditioning. –*adjective* 2. airconditioned

(Butler 1997: 96–7)

community centre: not selected
kongsi: selected
mui tsai: not selected
dalaga: not selected

The Macquarie Asian English Dictionary clearly represents a critical phase in the evolution of codified Asian Englishes. Relaying a discussion which took place at a conference in Manila in 1996 about who would use the dictionary and for what purposes, Bautista (1998: 64) reports the conclusion that 'it would be used by both Filipinos and non-Filipinos – the Filipinos would find evidence that their words have gained legitimacy . . . while the non-Filipinos would use the dictionary to know the meaning of certain local usages'. However, as she points out in relation to Philippine English, but in words which should have resonance for speakers of all Asian Englishes, 'eventually a full-blown Philippine English Dictionary should be prepared by Filipinos themselves'.

POSSIBLE FUTURE SCENARIOS   B8

Range and complexity of Englishes

In order to capture the range and complexity of all Englishes in the early twenty-first century, Mesthrie and Bhatt use the term English Language Complex (ELC) which was first suggested by McArthur (2003: 56). The ELC, they explain, 'may be said to comprise all subtypes distinguishable according to some combination of their history, status, form and functions' as follows:

a   Metropolitan standards: 'the two metropolitan standard varieties, whose formal models are those provided by the radio and television networks based largely in London and US cities like Washington, Los Angeles and (for CNN) Atlanta'.
b   Colonial standards: the 'exterritorial' Englishes that have developed in Australia, New Zealand, Canada, South Africa, Zambia and Zimbabwe. Their standards 'were, until recently, not fully accepted within the territories, since the metropolitan standards exerted a counter-influence' but are nowadays 'much more prominent as British influence recedes'.
c   Regional dialects: within the previous two subtypes, varieties that can be identified on the basis of regional variation, with regional differentiation being more evident in the (older) UK and US English settlements than in the other (younger) ones.
d   Social dialects: within regions, varieties that can be identified on the basis of social class and ethnicity, e.g. Cockney, Estuary English, and RP accents in London.

e   Pidgin Englishes.
f   Creole Englishes.
g   English as a Second Language (ESL): 'varieties that arose in countries where Eng-
    lish was introduced in the colonial era in face-to-face communication or (more
    usually) in the education system in a country in which there is, or had once been,
    a sizeable number of speakers of English. In ESL countries like Kenya, Sri Lanka
    and Nigeria English plays a key role internally in education, government and
    administration'.
h   English as a Foreign Language (EFL): 'the English used in countries in which
    its influence has been external, rather than via a body of "settlers". Mesthrie and
    Bhatt point out that in places such as China, Europe and Brazil, English 'plays a
    role for mainly *inter*-national rather than *intra*-national purposes'. However, they
    seem to interpret 'international' as referring to communication between speak-
    ers from these places and *'native' English speakers*, i.e. EFL, since they do not dis-
    tinguish between this type of communication and ELF, in which speakers from
    these places more typically communicate with *each other* rather than with 'native'
    English speakers (see strand 6).
i   Immigrant Englishes: 'in the context of migration to an English-dominant coun-
    try, second-language varieties of English which originate as EFLs may retain some
    distinctiveness or may merge with the regional English of their territory, depend-
    ing on a host of social and economic factors. Thus whilst English in Mexico is of
    the EFL variety, Chicano English of the USA shows greater affinity with general
    US English . . . though it is still a distinctive variety amongst many speakers'.
j   Language-shift Englishes: 'varieties that develop when English replaces the erst-
    while primary language(s) and culture(s) of a community', although there is 'fre-
    quently a sense of continuity with the ancestral language(s) and culture(s) in the
    shifting community'.
k   Jargon Englishes: unlike a pidgin English, a jargon English contains a great deal
    of instability and individual variation. It may or may not develop into a stable,
    expanded pidgin as did the Pacific jargon English that became Tok Pisin (see
    strand 2).
l   Hybrid Englishes: or 'bilingual mixed languages'. They 'occur in code-mixing in
    many urban centres where a local language comes into contact with English', e.g.
    Hinglish, the Hindi–English hybrid found in north Indian cities.
             (Mesthrie and Bhatt 2008: 3–6, and see also Mesthrie 2002: 112–13)

As Mesthrie and Bhatt (2008: 4–5) point out, groups (a) to (d) are often considered
to be 'special' because they relate to the ENL or Inner Circle varieties. The other eight
groupings of the ELC are, nevertheless, of just as much interest within modern sociolinguistics, and some of them possibly even more so within the field of World Englishes specifically.

Convergence or divergence?

With so many different English language groupings in existence, new varieties within these groupings continuing to emerge, and the numbers of speakers of existing varieties expanding year on year, there is a very real concern as to how long the English languages will retain the potential for mutual intelligibility. Increased diversification may be inevitable. As Crystal argues:

> The growth in diversity is noticeable at both national and international levels. Nationally, urban dialects are adapting to meet the identity needs of immigrant groups, such as the currently evolving Caribbean Scouse in Liverpool [UK]. With over 300 languages now spoken within London, for example, it would be surprising indeed if several did not produce fresh varieties as they interact with English . . . The linguistic consequences of immigrant diversity have long been noted in cities in the USA, but are now a major feature of contemporary life in the urban centres of most other countries where English is a mother-tongue, notably Australia. At an international level, the evidence is overwhelming of the emergence of a new generation of nonstandard Englishes as the global reach of English extends. . . .
>
> Because no language has ever been spoken by so many people in so many places, it is difficult to predict what will happen to English as a consequence of its global expansion; but increasing variation, extending to the point of mutual unintelligibility, is already apparent in the colloquial speech of local communities . . . such as the code-mixed varieties now found all over the world, and identified by such names as Singlish, Taglish, and Chinglish (McArthur 1998). Nor do current models yet allow for what is going to happen to English in communities where new types of social relationship have linguistic consequences – such as the thousands of children being born to parents who have only English as a foreign language in common, and who find themselves growing up with this kind of English as the norm at home. In such cases, non-native English (presumably including features which would be traditionally considered as learner errors) is being learned as a mother-tongue, and new kinds of nonstandard English must surely be the outcome.
>
> (Crystal 2002: 241–2)

Crystal also cites evidence of increasing diversity in lexis, pronunciation and grammar to demonstrate that regional distinctiveness is already increasing steadily, and he predicts that the gap between standard and non-standard Englishes will widen further. On the other hand, he points out elsewhere (1997: 134) that talk of the complete fragmentation of English is nothing new. The American Noah Webster predicted as much (in relation to American and British Englishes) in the late eighteenth century, and the British Henry Sweet (in relation to American, British and Australian Englishes) in the late nineteenth century. In Crystal's view, however, speakers of World Englishes will use their local English dialects in their own countries, but will speak a new form of English, which he labels **World Standard Spoken English** (**WSSE**) in international situations (1997: 137). Although it is too early for him to say with certainty how WSSE will evolve, he predicts that American English will be the greatest influence on its development. In other words, Crystal seems to see locally used Englishes as becoming increasingly divergent while internationally used Englishes increasingly converge to the point of merging into a single world variety based on American English.

Trudgill (1998) approaches the subject from a rather different perspective. In his view, English lexis will increasingly converge and pronunciation will increasingly diverge, while the grammatical situation is as yet unclear. He considers the lexical effect to be the result of the '**Americanisation** of the English language – **homogenisation** in the direction of North American usage' (1998: 31). For, despite the fact that some British English words find their way into American usage, 'the general trend does seem to be towards increasingly international use of originally American vocabulary items' (p. 32). Trudgill points out that this trend is easily explained in terms of widespread exposure to the American English dominated media and film industries around the world: 'We learn new words readily and constantly, and it is a simple matter to pick up new items from what one reads, and from what one hears on radio, on television, and at the cinema' (p. 32). Words cited by Trudgill as once specifically American but now in general use include 'briefcase', 'dessert', 'junk', 'peanut', 'radio', 'raincoat', 'soft drinks' and 'sweater'.

At the grammatical level, on the other hand, Trudgill does not consider developments to be as clear, partly because grammatical change takes place more slowly and is thus more difficult to document. Among the few items which Trudgill presents as potential candidates for the Americanisation of World English grammar are:

❏ 'hopefully' used in American English as a sentence adverbial, as in 'Hopefully it won't rain tomorrow', whereas in standard British English it has traditionally functioned as an adverb of manner (e.g. 'She watched the door hopefully')
❏ 'have' used dynamically as in American English 'Do you have coffee with your breakfast?', compared with standard British English where it has traditionally been used statively in such sentences (e.g. 'Have you (got) coffee in the cabinet?').

On the other hand, Trudgill identifies a feature of British English grammar that is filtering through into American use. He labels this item 'pro-predication *do*' and gives the example of 'I don't know if I'm going to the party tonight, but I might do', where American speakers have traditionally omitted the final 'do', but are now beginning to include it. He concludes that as far as grammar is concerned, 'there is no conclusive evidence as to whether convergence/homogenisation or divergence/disintegration' is taking place (Trudgill 1998: 33).

However, the situation appears much clearer in the case of phonology and here, argues Trudgill, the picture which is emerging is one of divergence. For example, **th-fronting**, the substitution of /θ/ and /ð/ with respectively /f/ and /v/ as in 'think' pronounced 'fink' and 'brother' as 'brover', is spreading rapidly in both England and New Zealand but not affecting American English. And some phonological changes are moving in opposite directions. For instance, areas of England and New Zealand which have traditionally been **rhotic** (i.e. pronounced the 'r' which is followed by a pause as in 'far' or by a consonant sound as in 'part') are steadily becoming non-rhotic, while in North America, areas which have been non-rhotic are becoming rhotic.

Trudgill concludes that

English looks set to become increasingly homogenised at the level of lexis, although there is still a long way to go, but at the level of phonology, the dominant national native-speaker varieties of the language are slowly diverging from one another. Since there is still relatively little face-to-face contact, for the vast majority of people, between speakers of American English and Australian English, or between New Zealand English and Irish English, we must expect that this trend will continue for the foreseeable future.

(Trudgill 1998: 35)

Trudgill is concerned here, of course, primarily with the Inner Circle Englishes – the first four members of Mesthrie and Bhatt's ELC. Apart from a reference to the fact that 'English . . . has more non-native than native speakers' (p. 30), he makes no mention of non-Inner Circle Englishes. We could nevertheless infer that if the phonological divergence he predicts is borne out by events, it will affect every English regardless of which type of family member it is. By the same token, if lexical convergence takes place, we could infer that all World Englishes will converge on American English lexis. Or could we? Given the small number of native compared to non-native English speakers, the spread (as opposed to concentration) of English around the globe, the switch from uni-directional (west to east) to transnational cultural flows (Pennycook 2007), the possibility of new hegemonies of English emerging in countries such as China and India, and the growing recognition that native English speakers may hinder rather than promote international communication (see Graddol 2006, and C8 below), it seems unlikely that any native speaker variety will continue for much longer to exercise such influence over the development of World Englishes. As Graddol (1999: 68) argued some time ago

At one time, the most important question regarding global English seemed to be 'will US English or British English provide the world model?' Already that question is looking dated with the emergence of 'New Englishes', and dictionaries and grammars that codify new norms.

If there is to be a world model at the lexical or any other linguistic level, the role, surely, will go to one of the other groupings outlined by Mesthrie and Bhatt (see the start of this unit).

Activity

Look back at Mesthrie and Bhatt's twelve groupings of English (at the start of this unit). Which, if any, do you think is/are most likely to exert the greatest influence on the future development of English? Or do you think, instead, that English is likely to fragment into a number of mutually unintelligible varieties?

Section C

EXPLORATION
CURRENT DEBATES IN
WORLD ENGLISHES

POSTCOLONIAL AMERICA AND AFRICA

Unit C1 presents perspectives from two particular sites of English use: firstly the English Only movement in the US, with its opposition to any form of institutional bilingualism; and secondly English in Africa and the controversy over whether or not its use serves the purposes of the large number of multilingual ethnic Africans.

'English Only' in the US

In the US census of 1990, 62 million of a total population of 251 million were found to belong to 'visible' ethnolinguistic minority groups:

- ❏ African (31 million)
- ❏ Latin American (22 million)
- ❏ Asian (7 million)
- ❏ Aboriginal, First Nations (2 million)

(Bourhis and Marshall 1999: 245)

By the time of the 2000 census, these numbers had increased substantially, although they are not directly comparable because of changes in the groupings (the figures below are rounded up or down to the nearest half million, and are followed by their percentage of the total US population in the 2000 census):

- ❏ African (34.5 million, 12.3 per cent)
- ❏ Hispanic or Latino (35 million, 12.5 per cent)
- ❏ Asian (10 million, 3.6 per cent)
- ❏ American Indian and Alaskan Native (2.5 million, 0.9 per cent)

(US Census Bureau, www.census.gov/population/www.socdemo/race.html)

The total thus increased by around 20 million over the ten-year period, representing around two-thirds of the overall US population increase to 281 million. Moving in the opposite direction, by 2001, the white population of **California** had fallen to below half the state's total population of 34 million. Although California represents an extreme example, the trend is being repeated throughout the US, with the largest overall increase being in those from Hispanic/Latino backgrounds.

With this dramatic increase in multi-ethnicity, fear of bilingualism is inevitably increasing among the largely monolingual L1 English population. It is against this backdrop that the **English Only movement** is conducted, although it has its roots in the late nineteenth century. Up until that time, although the languages of supposedly 'inferior' groups (African and Native American) were disparaged (see section B1), multilingualism was tolerated. But at this point, immigrants from southern Europe began to arrive in the US in substantial numbers. These people were regarded as racially inferior by the northern Europeans who had initially colonised the territory.

Theodore Roosevelt's response to the arrival of these immigrants was, as the Milroys point out, 'similar to the rhetoric of the contemporary English Only movement':

> we have room but for one language here and that is the English language, for we intend to see that the crucible turns our people out as Americans, of American nationality, and not as dwellers in a polyglot boarding house
>
> (quoted in Milroy and Milroy 1999: 157)

As a means of safeguarding their position, the US government began reversing the policy of allowing education for immigrants to take place in their native languages.

By the early 1920s, nearly three-quarters of the US states were insisting on English as the only language of instruction, a policy which was often executed inhumanely. For example, Native Indian children could be kidnapped from their reservations and families, and forced to live in boarding schools in order to learn the English language and the culture of its mother-tongue speakers. These children, as McCarty and Zepeda (1999: 203) point out,

> faced a system of militaristic discipline, manual labor, instruction in a trade, and abusive treatment for 'reverting' to the mother tongue. Many children fled these conditions only to be rounded up by Indian agents (called 'school police' in Navajo) and returned to school.

Tolerance for other languages increased in general through the twentieth century. In 1968, the Bilingual Education Act officially recognised the need for education to be available in immigrants' native languages, albeit as a means of enabling immigrants to progress to English-only education rather than to maintain L1 proficiency. However, from the late 1960s, when large numbers of people began to arrive in America from developing countries in Africa, the Caribbean, Latin America and Asia, the xenophobia that followed led directly to the establishing of the English Only movement. In California, the motivation to end bilingual education was especially strong. In 1998, The English Language Education for Children in Public Schools Initiative (more commonly known as Proposition 227) was passed, requiring all children for whom English is not their L1 to be placed in **immersion** programmes for a year and then to be transferred to mainstream education. Given that the language of the environment is English and the aim to subtract rather than add a language (i.e. **subtractive** rather than **additive bilingualism**), it would be more appropriate to describe these programmes as 'submersion' (Richard Watts, personal communication). Ferguson (2006: 45), on the other hand, uses the term for 'the not uncommon practice' of placing a child immediately in a mainstream classroom with no special language assistance at all. He glosses this practice 'sink or swim'.

Despite an abundance of research into SLA (second language acquisition) demonstrating the effectiveness of bilingual education as compared with that of immersion, school officials have worked hard to justify the switch in policy. For example, the Superintendent of Schools in Oceanside, California, Ken Noonan, wrote a paper titled 'Why we were wrong about bilingual education' in the *Washington Post*, concluding:

Now I am convinced that English immersion does work, and that it should begin on a student's first day of school . . . Now I believe that using all of the resources of public education to move these students into the English-speaking mainstream early and quickly is far more important than my former romantic notions that preserving the child's home language should be the ultimate goal of our schools.

Activity

Compare this official's firm conviction in the superiority of monolingual English-only education (and the underlying ethos that other languages are inferior), with the accounts of some of those bilingual students who actually experienced it. The following is a sample of the 250 language biographies collected from Asian American college students by Hinton over a number of years at the University of California at Berkeley:

1   At the age of ten, my family on my mother's side immigrated to America and this is where I learned my second language. Going to school made me feel deaf, mute and blind. I could understand nothing that was going on around me.

2   I didn't have any friends at all because nobody spoke Chinese. How I longed to go back to Taiwan and to see familiar faces and to hear my native language being spoken.

3   It was two heartless comments from a group of small boys in my 'white' neighbourhood for me to want to deny my language let alone my culture, as well. How was I to react to a racist comment of 'Ching chong chooey go back home to where you belong. You can't even speak English right.' Sixteen small words which possessed so much strength and contained so much power caused a small naïve child to lose her heritage – to lose what made her.

4   I know that I have been extremely fortunate to have been able to learn English so easily, but I have paid a dear price in exchange. I began my English education with the basics, starting in first grade. As a result, I had to end my Chinese education at that time. I have forsaken my own language in order to become 'American'. I no longer read or write Chinese. I am ashamed and feel as if I am a statistic adding a burden and lowering the status quo of the Asian community as an illiterate of the Chinese language.

5   When some of my classmates began to ridicule and throw racist remarks at Chinese people, I began to distance myself away from Chinese culture. I felt ashamed when my parents spoke to me in Cantonese at a supermarket. I got into heated arguments about why only English should be spoken at home . . . I continuously tried to fit in, even if it meant abandoning culture and identity. I was probably most hostile to my background during those years in junior high.

6   The loss of one's cultural language symbolized the loss of one's cultural identity. Many Asian Americans pride themselves for successfully

turning their kids into 'complete' Americans who speak English in flaw-less American accent. In my perspective, this actually is something that they should be ashamed of. Without doubt, fitting oneself into the main-stream is important; yet retaining one's cultural language is not at all trivial. To me, I will try my best to excel both in English and my mother tongue, Cantonese.

(Hinton 1999: 21–30)

Linked to the English Only movement is the **No Child Left Behind** (NCLB) Act (2002), which focuses on the needs of disadvantaged children, particularly language minority students. Crucially, the act links school funding to these children's fluency in the English language, which is assessed annually. The NCLB's approach is therefore deemed by some observers to emphasise immigrant children's learning of English at the expense of their mother tongues, with one scholar commenting informally that it could more accurately be called 'No Child Left Bilingual'. If you are interested in find-ing out more about the criticisms of NCLB, a useful source is James Crawford's arti-cle 'No Child Left Behind: A Diminished Vision of Civil Rights' (originally published in *Education Week*, 6 June 2007 and reproduced on his *Language Policy Website & Emporium* at: http://ourworld.compuserve.com/homepages/JWCRAWFORD/home. htm). He describes the approach as 'a misguided reform' and argues that it has a nega-tive impact on the very language minority students that it was supposedly designed to help.

Activity

❏   Bearing in mind the experiences quoted above, along with any relevant language learning experiences of your own, draw up a list of arguments that could be used to oppose the English Only movement. You might like to consult a book on SLA (e.g. Lightbown and Spada 2006), to read for yourself some of the research findings which demonstrate how L2 learners draw on their knowledge of the L1 in order to tackle the com-plexities of the L2.

If you have access to people who have learnt English by immersion, prepare a questionnaire to find out about their experiences and their reflections on them. You might want to include questions on some of the issues which Hinton's subjects raise, such as:

their parents' attitudes,

their feelings/experiences in the classroom,

any experiences of racism,

their rejection (or not) of their L1,

any effect on their L1 (degree of L1 attrition),

any effect on their communication with older generations,

effects on their identity, and

their attitude towards bilingualism.

❑ If you learnt English by immersion yourself, reflect on the experience and discuss it. With hindsight, to what extent do you think you benefited or otherwise?

❑ The English Only movement claims that mastery of English by marginalised minority-language speakers is the single most important factor in improving their economic position. According to May (2008/2001: 216), on the other hand, '[a]rguments asserting that English is the key to social mobility, and conversely that its lack is the principal cause of social and economic marginalisation . . . conveniently overlook the central question of the wider structural disadvantages facing minority-language speakers'.

He goes on to argue that while mastery of English is important, 'it is only *one* variable in the equation', and to point out that 'African Americans have been speaking English for two hundred years and yet many still find themselves relegated to urban ghettos'. How far do you agree with English Only, and what other factors do you think may be involved?

English in Africa

African English is normally taken to refer to the English spoken in sub-Saharan Africa by the indigenous population. As discussed in A1, the history of English in Africa is complex and has led to the evolution of three distinct strands: West African, East African and South African English. There is a debate over whether they should employ their own local (**endonormative**) standards or continue to look outside to Britain for (**exonormative**) standards. There is as yet little agreement on which items constitute features of the various new African Englishes, and which are simply examples of 'learnerese' – incorrectly learned English containing errors (see, for example, de Klerk 1999 and Titlestad 1998).

A still more fundamental issue is that of whether the use of English in fact serves the interests of the indigenous peoples of Africa. In his influential book, *Linguistic Imperialism*, Phillipson (1992: 49) argues that 'the dominance of English is asserted and maintained by the establishment and continuous reconstitution of structural and cultural inequalities between English and other languages'. He believes that the spread of English serves to promote the interests of the British and American 'Centre' at the expense of the countries of the 'Periphery'. On the other hand, Brutt-Griffler argues that linguistic imperialism was not responsible for the spread of English, that 'no distinctive ideology existed concerned with spreading English in the colonial dependencies for cultural or linguistic reasons' (2002: 29), and that second language users were themselves agents in its spread.

The rest of this section presents the reaction of a Nigerian linguist, Bisong (1995), to the **linguistic imperialism** claim, followed by a number of counter-arguments, including Phillipson's own response. Although focused on Nigeria, Bisong believes his arguments have wider relevance, providing insights into the role of English in other

African contexts. This debate is thus a critical one for the future of English as a world language.

Bisong asks and answers three questions:

1   Has English succeeded in displacing or replacing other languages in **Nigeria**?

> Although English is the official language of Nigeria, it has not succeeded in displacing or replacing any of the indigenous languages. It performs a useful function in a multilingual society and will continue to do so, since no nation can escape its history. But attitudes to the language have changed since colonial times. It is no longer perceived as the Imperial tongue that must be mastered at all costs. Reasons for learning English now are more pragmatic in nature, and run counter to Phillipson's argument that those who acquire the language in a situation where it plays a dominant role are victims of linguistic imperialism. I would want to maintain that Nigerians are sophisticated enough to know what is in their interest, and that their interest includes the ability to operate with two or more linguistic codes in a multilingual situation. Phillipson's argument shows a failure to appreciate fully the complexities of this situation.
>
> (Bisong 1995: 131)

2   Has the dominance of English caused Nigerian culture to be undervalued and marginalised?

> Because Nigeria is a multicultural society, the Euro-Christian culture embodied in the English language is only one of a number of cultures that function to shape the consciousness of Nigerian people. To maintain that one of the foreign cultures must play a dominant role since the language that embodies it is widely used is again to fail to come to grips with the reality of the situation.
>
> (Bisong 1995: 131)

3   Why did writers like Chinua Achebe, Wole Soyinka and Ngũgĩ wa Thiong'o, all of them literate and fluent in their mother tongues, write in English?

> It would be naïve to assume that creative writers like Achebe, Soyinka, and Ngũgĩ chose to write in English because they were victims of Centre linguistic and cultural imperialism. Because of the peculiar history of countries in the Periphery, English has become *one* of the languages available for use by the creative writer. This sociolinguistic reality has to be accepted for what it is. Arguments that carry the implication that the users of this language do not know what is in their interest should not be seen simply as patronizing. They reveal a monolingual failure to grasp the complex nature of a multilingual and multicultural society
>
> (Bisong 1995: 131)

Activity ✪

❏   Phillipson (1996) responded to Bisong by taking up four central issues. Consider his counter-arguments to Bisong's claims and decide where you position yourself in this debate.

1   *African multilingualism and stigmatisation*: Phillipson cites evidence showing the degree to which African languages are marginalised in favour of English.

2   *The Centre and Periphery*: he points out that his 1992 book 'does not attribute responsibility for what happens exclusively to people in the Centre', but that local governments, such as that of the newly independent Nigeria, have also played a part in promoting English over local languages in order to 'de-emphasize "ethnicity" and build up a sense of nationhood' (Phillipson 1996: 161–2). He also points out that his approach is not monolingual as he does not recommend replacing English with a single (indigenous) African language in each country.

3   *Literature*: he points out that ninety per cent of the African population do not speak English, and therefore do not have access to literature in English. Phillipson (1996: 164) argues here that writing in English in Africa is a form of elitism and that choosing to write in an African language is 'a political choice to reach a particular community and assist it to resist a repressive government'.

4   *Language choice at school*: he maintains that parents select English-medium schools because of 'the appalling neglect of state schools' which 'generally use the dominant local language as a medium and are starved of funds by politicians who send their children to private English-medium schools' (Phillipson 1996: 165). He then counters Bisong's claim that three or four hours of exposure to English at school cannot threaten competence in the mother tongue, with the argument that 'if success in education through the medium of English is the primary route to the upper sections of the education system and positions in the modern sector of the economy, and if the rich wealth of Nigerian oral culture has little place in this scheme of things, then the three or four hours are presumably the most important ones of the day. Parents are doubtless acutely conscious of this' (Phillipson 1996: 166).

❏   Bisong claims that 'no nation can escape its history'. You might choose to disagree with him, as the Sri Lankan scholar, Canagarajah, does implicitly in his book, *Resisting Linguistic Imperialism in English Teaching*. Canagarajah argues, as the title of his book suggests, for a policy of resistance to colonialism as manifested in the present-day teaching of (British) English in Sri Lanka. On the other hand, if you tend to agree with Bisong, then it is important to be clear about which 'history' cannot be escaped. For, as Omoniyi points out, before the era of colonialism, African kingdoms like Zulu, Shona, Yoruba, Berber, Hausa, Igbo, and so on, were in fact monolingual ethnic states. It was only when the African continent was arbitrarily divided up in the nineteenth century that their structure was no longer ethnically determined, so that they were transformed into the multi-ethnic, multilingual African societies of the present day (Omoniyi 1999: 373). At the other extreme, however, there are, today, children of elite families in Nigeria who are being brought up as monolingual speakers of English .

❏ Obeng and Adegbija (1999: 365) argue that 'infighting and sociopolitical rancor among major language groups have stifled the emergence of bona fide national languages that could be symbols of identity in most African countries. In Nigeria, for instance, although the constitution recognises Hausa, Yoruba, and Igbo as cooffical with English, it is very obvious that the English language performs most official and quasinational roles. However, being bereft of any Nigerian cultural or ethnic flavoring has made it difficult for English to effectively perform the role of a national language'. And they ask: 'If you were asked to advise a sub-Saharan African government on the selection of a national language, would you recommend an African language of wider communication or a European language?' How would you answer this, and to what extent does their argument contradict that of Bisong?

❏ Bisong cites the authors Achebe, Soyinka and Ngũgĩ in support of his claim. While he is right in respect of Achebe and Soyinka, the same cannot be said of Ngũgĩ, who has written about his own experience of colonialism and, in particular, his enforced learning of English in Kenya with disgust. If you want to pursue this point now, look ahead to the extract from Ngũgĩ in D4. Having read it, how would you respond to Bisong's claim about this author? For a more extreme view, see Ebunlola Adamo (2005), who argues that 'the "imposition" of the English language on the world, Africa, and in particular Nigeria (through the media, information technology, and other means of propaganda, and under the guise of globalization) is a form of linguistic terrorism' (p. 21), and that '[t]he English have terrorized Nigeria with their language for about five centuries' (p. 23). And for a less extreme, but still critical, view of English in Africa, and particularly Tanzania, see Rubagumya (2004), who argues that at present, learning English is both 'at the expense of indigenous African languages' and 'at the expense of getting a meaningful education' (p. 141).

❏ If you want to explore the subject of linguistic imperialism in greater depth, you might like to read Brutt-Griffler's (2002) challenge to Phillipson's (1992) theory and Phillipson's (2003b) critique of her position (both are in the journal *World Englishes*), and decide which position you find more convincing.

CREOLE DEVELOPMENTS IN THE UK AND US

In B2 the examples were taken mainly from the Pacific pidgin, Tok Pisin. In C2, the focus is on two varieties of English that originated in the Atlantic in the creoles of West Africa and the Caribbean: London Jamaican and Ebonics.

London Jamaican

In recent years, interest has grown in this creole, or **patois** (also spelt **patwa**) as it is usually known by its users, who may also refer to it as 'Black Talk', 'Nation Language' and 'Black Slang' (Sebba 2007). As Sebba (2007: 279) points out, 'Jamaican Creole emerged as the "heritage language" used among the second generation [of migrants from the Caribbean], even those whose parents were *not* Jamaican Creole speakers' and is 'used as a symbol of group identity by "Black British" children and adolescents – as well as by some White adolescents in friendship groups with Black peers'. (See Rampton 1995/2005 on the use of minority language varieties by members of ethnic outgroups, a phenomenon known as **language crossing**.) For its black British speakers, then, Jamaican Creole reflects the process of recreolisation, where a creole that has moved further along the Creole Continuum in the direction of the standard language, shifts back towards earlier creole forms (see Romaine 1988: 188–203, Sebba 1997: 225–7, 233, Todd 1990: 61–5).

London Jamaican, a combination of creole and a local form of non-standard English, is spoken, as its name suggests, particularly (though not exclusively) in the London area.

Since most of its speakers are also fluent in British English, they do not need creole for communicative functions and use it, rather, as a powerful marker of group identity. It serves this function even for speakers who have limited fluency in creole, and who are only able to smatter their conversation with token creole features such as sterotypical creole words and pronunciations (Sebba 2007: 281). In other words, as Sebba goes on to say, 'Creole in the London context is a speech style, defined by the participants of an interaction in contrast with 'English', and marked by a selection of salient 'non-English' features'. He points out the cultural attraction that creole holds for its speakers and its value as a 'non-legitimated variety', arguing that this accounts for the fact that London Jamaican focuses on Jamaican Creole instead of the many other mother-tongue creoles of its speakers, and adding that 'it is often not learnt in the family home, but at school and from the peer group' (1997: 233).

The most comprehensive account of London Jamaican is that of Sebba (1993). He examines in detail the features of **Jamaican Creole** in Britain and shows how the speech code-switches between London Jamaican and **London English (Cockney)**. In this section, many of the details are taken from a master's dissertation by Graham (2000), which contributes to this work. Graham was convinced that the patois of the black youth living in her part of Brixton (South London) differed in striking ways from the London English of the local white youth, and that these black adolescents were engaging in acts of identity by looking to their Jamaican roots for some aspects of their speech style. She set out to find out precisely which features of Jamaican Creole they did and did not adopt.

Jamaican Creole grammatical features in the London Jamaican data:

❏ interchangeable use of pronouns, e.g. 'mi' and 'I' both used for 'I' and 'me'; 'im', 'i' both used for he, she, it, him, her, its, his, hers, its,
❏ use of present tense for both present and past, e.g. 'an I se' meaning 'and I said',
❏ elimination of tense suffixes –s, –ed,––t and participle endings –ing,
❏ –ed, –en, –t, e.g. 'yu bret stink' for 'your breath stinks',
❏ negation with 'no', often with phonological changes, as in 'no bret stink' for standard English 'my breath doesn't stink'.

Jamaican Creole phonological features in the London Jamaican data:

❏ substitution of /θ/ and /ð/ with /t/ and /d/ e.g. 'bret' for 'breath' and 'dis' for 'this' (whereas speakers of London English substitute these sounds with /f/ and /v/),
❏ labialisation when the sound /b/ is followed by certain vowels, e.g. 'boys' is pronounced 'bwoys',
❏ dropping of word-final consonants, e.g. 'bulleh' for 'bullet',
❏ realisation of the vowel sounds /ɒ/ and /ɔ:/ as /a:/ so that 'cloth' becomes 'klaat',
❏ lack of weak vowels especially schwa, so that, e.g. the word 'rapper' is pronounced [rapa] rather than [rapə] and the article 'the' is regularly pronounced [da] and [di].

Jamaican Creole lexical features in the London Jamaican:

❏ Graham quotes from Hewitt (1986: 129–30) including *mash-up* ('destroy'), *picky-picky* (*frizzy*, of hair) and *duppy* ('ghost'). However, she repeats Hewitt's (1986) caution that words of Jamaican Creole origin may also be used by speakers from other groups including whites and non-Caribbean blacks.
❏ Examples in Graham's own data include the taboo Jamaican Creole words *bomb-klaat* ('toilet paper') and *blodklaat* ('sanitary towel').

Features of the London Jamaican data which are also markers of London English but *do not* occur in Jamaican Creole are as follows:

❏ the glottal stop (represented by ʔ), e.g. 'ghetto' pronounced [geʔo] and 'gotta' as [goʔa]'
❏ the vocalisation of dark 'l' (the RP /l/ sound when it is followed by a pause or a consonant) e.g. 'bill' as 'biw', and 'help' as 'hewp', whereas in Jamaican Creole, this 'l' is pronounced as clear 'l' (the RP 'l' sound when it is followed by a vowel)', and
❏ the substitution of /θ/ and /ð/ with /f/ and /v/ alongside /t/ and /d/.

These are some other features of Jamaican Creole (from Sebba 1993). The first two also occur in London Jamaican, but the third and fourth do not:

❏ lack of inversion in question forms, as in 'im did phone you?',
❏ absence of the copula, as in 'dis party well rude',
❏ the addition of the sound /h/ to the beginnings of words which start with vowel sounds, e.g. 'accent' pronounced 'haccent', and
❏ use of the suffix 'dem' added to a noun to indicate plurality, e.g. *man-dem* meaning 'men', or a large quantity as in *kaan-dem* ('a lot of corn').

Activity ✪

❏ How do you account for the fact that London Jamaican speakers have in their repertoires features of both London English and Jamaican Creole? Can you see any reason for their selection of features in each case? For example, why do they use the London English glottal stop? Why do they not use Jamaican Creole /h/ before a vowel? If they are engaging in acts of identity, how fluid is this identity?

❏ If you have access to adolescent speakers of Black English, ask them questions based on the features set out above to find out whether they think they use (or do not use):
    the linguistic items identified above as being exclusive to London Jamaican,
    those items identified as featuring also in London English,
    other features not mentioned.
If possible, record the speakers talking to each other to see how far their intuitions agree with what they do in practice.

❏ If you do not have access to young speakers of Black English, you could devise a similar small-scale research project for another adolescent group that you have identified as speaking a variety of English which differs in interesting ways from that of their local peer group.

❏ Sebba (2007: 292) observes that the trend for crossing into black speech has increased over the past few years, and describes how the White British comedian, Sacha Baron Cohen, in the role of the spoof chat-show host, Ali G, uses a number of creole-based London Jamaican features in his speech. Sebba argues that the popularity of Ali G 'demonstrates that creole has made its mark on the consciousness of speakers of British English' and that this 'suggests that even if creole is largely relinquished as a main medium of communication in the Caribbean in succeeding generations, it will continue to exist as a language of youth and adolescence, well beyond the confines of its original ethnic roots'. How far do you agree?

Ebonics

As Pandey (2000: 1) comments, '[f]or many Americans, the variety referred to as "Ebonics" or **African-American Vernacular English [AAVE]** is simply "improper speech" that they neither respect nor recognize'. Wolfram (2006: 328) points out that despite the popular use of the term Ebonics, many linguists prefer terms such as AAVE 'because of the strong emotional reactions and racist parodies sometimes engendered by the use of the term Ebonics'. But what is this variety, and why does it elicit such strong emotions?

Wolfram (2006: 330) lists a number of distinguishing features of AAE (African American English), his preferred term. These include:

❑ habitual 'be' for intermittent activity, as in *Sometimes my ears be itching*.
❑ absence of copula for contracted forms of 'is' and 'are', e.g. *She nice*.
❑ present tense, third-person *–s* absence, as in *She walk*.
❑ *ain't* for *didn't*, as in He *ain't* do it.
❑ reduction of final consonant clusters when followed by a word beginning with a vowel, as in *lif' up* for 'lift up'.
❑ use of [f] and [v] for final 'th', as in *toof* for 'tooth', *smoov* for 'smooth'.

As you will have noticed, some of these features occur in other commonly stigmatised varieties of British and American English (see unit B5) including London Jamaican (above) and Estuary English (unit C4). But as Wolfram points out, the uniqueness of AAE lies 'in the particular combination of structures that make up the dialect', and to this day, there is still no agreement about how Ebonics developed. It is, nevertheless, 'a distinct, robust, and stable socio-ethnic dialect of English that is maintaining itself', and whose 'growing sense of linguistic solidarity and identity among African Americans' is unifying the dialect across different localities, while its 'everyday uses of language . . . encompass the full range of communicative functions' (Wolfram 2006: 340). But we turn now to the debate that has surrounded this English variety since the mid-1990s.

The debate

On 18 December 1996, the school board in Oakland, California, passed a resolution regarding its policy in relation to the language skills of African American pupils. Despite the various attempts that had been made by the board up until that point, these pupils had continued to exhibit far higher levels of illiteracy than their peer group. The board decided on a novel approach: to treat African American pupils in the same way that they had treated Asians and Hispanics. In other words, they proposed teaching them standard English through their mother tongue, African American Vernacular English (AAVE), also commonly known as **Ebonics** (from 'ebony' and 'phonics'). As the pupils' English skills improved, the teaching of other subjects through the medium of English would then be phased in.

The Oakland board's resolution included the following claims:

❏   Many African Americans speak Ebonics.
❏   Ebonics is not a debased dialect or jargon but a valid linguistic system influ-
    enced by the West and Niger-Congo languages spoken by their ancestors.
❏   African Language Systems are genetically based.
❏   Ebonics could and should be used as a medium for the children who were
    being failed by the current education system
❏   Funds would be set aside for the devising and implementing of a teaching
    programme in Ebonics.

(Todd 1997: 13–14)

There was an immediate and highly polarised outcry. These are some of the responses
(taken from McArthur 1998: 217–19):

From the San Francisco Chronicle, 21 December 1996

Tatum Willoughby, a fifth-grade student at Prescott Elementary on Campbell
Street in West Oakland, used to cry because she had trouble 'speaking the
right language,' as she calls it. The bright African American child tried hard to
translate the phrases and words she uses at home – black English – into the
standard English her teacher said would help her excel. But after months of
being taught through a program that recognizes that African American children
may come into the classroom using Ebonics . . . Tatum reads her essays with
pride. Occasionally, the 10-year-old slips into black English, such as saying 'dis'
for 'this.' But she quickly corrects herself. 'Most people won't understand you if
you speak (black English),' Tatum said.

(front page: Thaai Walker and Nanette Asimov)

I think it's tragic. Here we have young black kids who are incapable in far too
many cases of negotiating even the most basic transactions in our society
because of their inability to communicate . . . We're going to legitimize what
they're doing. To me it's just ass backwards.

(editorial section: quoted comment by Ward Connerly,
a University of California regent)

If people are not willing to accept ebonics as a second language, then they
should at least accept that African American students are not achieving at the
level they need to, and we need to do something about that.

(editorial section: quoted comment by Alan Young, director of state
and federal programs, Oakland school board)

Editor – I am absolutely thrilled at the Oakland school district's choice of ebonics
as the language of choice in the classroom. I expect that very shortly we will see
New York punks being taught in Brooklonics, Georgia rednecks in Ya'allonics,
Valley girls in Bimbonics, chronic nerds in Siliconics and farm boys in Rubiconics.
But what most of us need to keep up with the bureaucrats is a thorough
understanding of Moronics.

(letter section: Richard Ogar of Berkeley)

Editor – The real goal of those backing this move is multiculturalism, as opposed to the melting pot society which is what made this nation so successful. If the US is to remain a leading economic and social force as we enter the 21st century, we must not allow the PC crowd to have its way in imposing multiculturalism on the nation. The action of the Oakland school board does a tremendous disservice to black students, and I hope it is soundly rebuked by higher authorities, without whose funding it cannot succeed.

(letter section: from Jack D. Bernal in San Francisco)

From The Oakland Tribune, 21 December 1996

The [board's] report offers sound goals – African-American students will become proficient in reading, speaking and writing standard English. It recommends greater involvement of parents and incentives for teachers who tackle these challenges. The Ebonics approach would presumably make African-American students eligible for state and federal bilingual funds, giving the district more resources to provide additional help for them. District officials deny the approach is a strategy to get more funding. There's nothing wrong with looking for additional ways to help a population that is struggling in the public school system. But making non-standard English a language undermines the very goals the board has embraced. It sends a wrong and confusing message to students. If what they are speaking is a language, what's the urgency of learning another language?

(front page: Brenda Payton)

From The International Herald Tribune, 24–25 December 1996

The Reverend Jesse Jackson said Sunday that the school board in Oakland, California, was both foolish and insulting to black students throughout the United States when it declared that many of its black students speak a language distinct from traditional English . . . 'I understand the attempt to reach out to these children, but this is an unacceptable surrender, borderlining on disgrace,' he said. 'It's teaching down to our children'. . . Mr Jackson said the Oakland board had become a laughingstock, and he urged its members to reverse their decision.

('Jesse Jackson ridicules acceptance of Black English' by Neil A. Lewis)

From The New York Times, 26 December 1996

To the Editor: The California State Board of Education endorsed ebonics in 1991, and the State Department of Education has financed research institutes and conferences that have studied the subject exclusively. I spoke at two such conferences this year alone. Oakland's school board is not the first district to apply this policy. Los Angeles and San Diego have used it for years . . . Those like the Rev. Jesse Jackson, who seek the quick headline will find themselves out of step with the legitimate demands for cutting-edge education.

(letter by John W. Templeton, Executive Editor, Aspire Books, San Francisco)

From The New York Times, 14 January 1997

Hoping to quell the uproar set off by its resolution to treat black English as a second language in its classrooms, the Oakland school board will scratch part of a plan that suggested it would offer instruction in the tongue that some linguists call ebonics, school officials said today. After almost a month of national debate and a weekend of sometimes tense meetings here, the Oakland schools task force that introduced the black English policy . . . produced a new resolution on Sunday that calls only for the recognition of language differences among black students in order to improve their proficiency in English. 'The debate is over,' the head of the task force, Sylvester Hodges, said. 'We are hoping that people will understand that and will join us' . . . The many writers, educators and politicians who have attacked the school board's original plan have tended to agree that the issue is perhaps more about the symbolism than the specifics of what black children in Oakland might be taught.

('Oakland scratches plan to teach Black English' by Tim Golden)

From **The Economist** *(UK)* **4 January 1997**

The school board thought it might help if the slang these children used at home were recognized as a distinct primary language, separate from English, and if teachers showed respect for this language and used it in the classroom, as a means to bridge the gap between standard English and the speech of the ghetto . . . The quasi-language in question has been christened 'Ebonics', a lumpish blend of 'ebony' and 'phonics'. Supporters of Ebonics say it derives from the structures of Niger-Congo African languages and marks the persistent legacy of slavery. Other linguistic scholars note that some usages have appeared only recently, as the ghettos have become more isolated from mainstream American life.

Activity

❑ Todd (1997: 16) says 'the Oakland debate revealed more about the attitudes of the partakers than it did about Ebonics or about educational problems'. What do you think she means? How do you account for the fact that opposition to the resolution was voiced by both members of the black population and members of the conservative white population?

❑ Which side, if either, do you support, and why?

❑ How does the Oakland board's approach to the education of its blacks fit in with the ethos of the English Only movement which you looked at in unit C1?

❑ Why do you think so much importance, not to mention emotional investment, is attached to the variety of English used for educational purposes? You may like to read the article on pidgin English in Cameroon (in unit D2) before you think about this issue.

❑ Finally, a challenge for those of you who would like to examine the Ebonics debate in detail. In her introduction to a symposium on the Ebonics debate in the journal *World Englishes* 19/1, Pandey (2000: 4) asks:

1   Why should discussions on World Englishes focus on Ebonics?

2   What language(s) are monodialectal speakers of Ebonics speakers

of? Are they *native speakers* of English? What is their first language or *mother tongue*?

3   What prompted the Oakland school board's resolution on Ebonics and its subsequent modification? Was it altered by the same board members who worded the initial resolution?

4   What lessons can be gleaned from a focus on the Ebonics debate?

Pandey recommends that students read through the six articles that form the Ebonics symposium in order to find answers to these questions and to stimulate discussion. If you are studying this book in class and have access to the journal *World Englishes*, you might like to divide the six articles among yourselves and then return to the four questions above to compare notes.

TEACHING AND TESTING WORLD ENGLISHES

The Englishes that are revered, and are the goal of teaching and testing in many parts of the world are still native speaker varieties, particularly British and North American; the methodologies and materials that are promoted are still those favoured by the ENL centres – communicative approaches with an emphasis on 'learner autonomy' and monolingual (English-only) textbooks; the teachers who are most highly sought after are native speakers of English; and the tests which are taken most seriously measure learners' competence in relation to native-speaker norms. And it seems that at least one major exporter of native English envisages no early change of direction: as recently as March 2008, the British Council's director, Bhaskar Chakravarti, was reported as saying 'the star by which we steer our British Council work is our published ambition that "every teacher and learner of English in the world should have access to the skills, ideas and materials they require from Britain"' (*Guardian Weekly, Learning English Supplement*, 7 March 2008).

Unit B3 was concerned with the English language itself and the legitimacy of its non-native varieties. In this unit we go on to consider issues concerned with, firstly, the teaching and, secondly, the testing of English.

Teaching English today

Given the fact that native speakers are widely held to make better teachers of English than non-native speakers, we will start by asking why this should be so. Is it really a question of their being better teachers, or simply one of knowing English (as a native language) better? Firstly, two scholars who argue against the 'native-is-best' premise:

> [T]eachers of English are required to teach not English as a general linguistic phenomenon but English as a subject – a subject which keeps company with others

on the curriculum – history, physics, geography and so on. Now nobody, I think, would suppose that somebody who lived through a particular period of history was especially well qualified to teach it as a subject – that the best teachers of the history of the Second World War, for example, are a diminishing group of octogenarian old soldiers who have actually lived the experience. Similarly, it would surely be odd to argue that the best teachers of the geography of, say, the Austrian alps are Tyrolean shepherds because they have a unique intimacy with the landscape . . . Of course these people have a wealth of intimate experience which can be drawn upon as data, and so they can serve as expert *informants* on certain aspects of the subjects concerned. But this does not make them expert *instructors*.

(Widdowson 1994a: 1.10–1.13)

Widdowson goes on to observe that there has been 'persistent confusion' between the phenomenon of ENL and the teaching of English as a second language, and that this confusion has led to the misguided belief that a native English speaker automatically has the expertise to *teach* English. This, he points out, ignores not only the fact that native speakers of English 'are not noted for their ready acquisition of any language other than their own', but also the need for teachers to have substantial education in pedagogy. In other words, it is not enough to simply '[s]tart with native speaker ability, add on a little common sense, or perhaps a brief rudimentary training in technique, [and] get hold of a course book'.

Seidlhofer approaches the issue from another perspective, that of the shared experience of non-native teachers of English and their students:

[T]he non-native teacher has been through the process of learning the same language, often through the same L1 'filter', and she knows what it is like to have made the foreign language, in some sense, her own, to have appropriated it for particular purposes. This is an experience which is shared only between non-native teachers and their students. One could say that native speakers know the destination, but not the terrain that has to be crossed to get there: they themselves have not travelled the same route. Non-native teachers, on the other hand, know the target language as a foreign language. Paradoxically, it is precisely this which is often perceived as a weakness, although it can be understood and drawn upon as an important resource. This shared language learning experience should thus constitute the basis for non-native teachers' confidence, not for their insecurity.

(Seidlhofer 1999: 238)

Despite the fact that linguists have been making observations of these kinds for many years, there appears still to be little change in practice. For, as Kirkpatrick points out, native speaker English teachers are in great demand around the world:

The demand for native speakers is so high in many places that being a native speaker is the only qualification that many teachers require. Thus native speakers who have no specialist training in English language teaching are routinely employed by schools, institutions and universities all over the world. I know from personal experience that many Chinese universities currently employ native speakers to teach English to a wide range of students and that only a small minority of these teachers have teacher training qualifications. That teachers only need to be native speakers is often explicitly stated in advertisements.

(Kirkpatrick 2007a: 185)

It seems, then, that the position articulated over ten years ago by Nayar, still holds true:

The discourse of Applied Linguistics as well as the vast amount of supporting material brought out by the ESL/EFL enterprise have created and perpetuated the image of the native speaker as the unquestionable authority of not just language ability but also of expertise in its teaching. Native speaker status is often seen as the *sine qua non*, automatically bestowing authenticity and credibility on a teacher, as an English Language expert or even a teacher trainer. As an initial gate-keeping shibboleth, nativeness can assume primacy over pedagogic expertise or actual language competence in the ELT enterprise.

(Nayar 1998: 287)

❏ If you are or have been a learner of English as a second language, or a native or non-native teacher of English to second language learners, to what extent does/did your experience resonate with the comments made above by Kirkpatrick and Nayar?

❏ This is Kirkpatrick's (2007a: 195) 'checklist' for teachers who wish to work in Outer and Expanding Circle Countries. How far do you agree with it? Would you add or remove any of the criteria? Which of them (if any) do you think could/should be applied to teachers of L2 English learners in Inner Circle countries?

  Teachers should

a be multilingual and multicultural and ideally know the language of their students and understand the educational, social and cultural contexts in which they are working;

b either be able to provide an appropriate and attainable [i.e. local] model for their students or, if they speak another variety, understand that the local variety is . . . not inferior to their own;

c understand how different varieties of English have developed linguistically, and the ways in which they differ phonologically, lexically, grammatically, rhetorically and culturally;

d understand how English has developed in specific contexts and how it has spread across the world;

e understand the role(s) of English in the community and how these interrelate with other local languages;

f be able to evaluate ELT materials critically to ensure that these do not, either explicitly or implicitly, promote a particuar variety of English or culture at the expense of others;

g   be able to evaluate the specific needs of their students and teach towards those needs;

h   be prepared to contribute to the extra-curricular life of the institution in which they are working.

❏   Prepare a short questionnaire to enable you to find out whether people believe native speakers or non-native speakers make better teachers of English, or if they think there is no difference, along with the reasons for their answer. Give the questionnaire to as many people as possible, both native and non-native speakers of English and, if you can, both students of English and non-students. Analyse your results: what is the consensus? If they favour native speaker teachers, do the reasons they give focus entirely on linguistic competence (e.g. accent, knowledge of grammar and idioms) or do they also refer to teaching ability? What do the responses tell you about attitudes to non-native teachers? How much do these attitudes seem to depend on whether or not the respondent is him/herself a native or non-native speaker? Finally, do you detect among your non-native speaker respondents any feeling of linguistic insecurity (a term coined by the sociolinguist Labov to describe how people feel about their language variety when it is constantly denigrated, and their acceptance of the negative stereotyping of their English by the dominant native speaker community)?

❏   Looking back at Kirkpatrick's 'checklist', one conclusion that can be drawn is the need for prospective teachers of English to be educated extensively about World English varieties and their implications, rather than, as is often the case, receiving a cursory training in British and/ or American English (e.g. see Jenkins 2007: 246 in respect of the Cambridge ESOL (English for Speakers of Other Languages) teacher training programmes). Have a look at the way World Englishes has been introduced into programmes at Portland State University (Brown and Peterson 1997) and/or the Open Cyber University of Korea (Baik and Shim 2002). Both had highly successful outcomes, with students gaining a much increased awareness of the sociolinguistic realities of English, and far more positive attitudes towards non-native Englishes. Do you think an education programme of this kind would have a similar effect on prospective teachers of English in your own context?

❏   Kirkpatrick (2007a: 196) argues that '[g]overnments, ministries and employers, particularly those in outer and expanding circle countries, need to recognise the advantages associated with multilingual local teachers who are expert users of English' instead of classifying them as 'inferior'. He believes that '[i]t is these teachers upon whom governments and institutions should be spending their resources to ensure that they receive training and opportunities for professional development' rather than spending on importing large numbers of native English teachers. Do you agree with him?

Testing English today

No matter how much effort is put into making the teaching of English more appropriate to the contexts of teaching, if the examination boards continue to measure students' success in English against native speaker norms, then little is likely to change. It is well known that tests have a **washback** effect on classroom teaching: that is, the language and skills that are tested in examinations are the ones that teachers choose to teach and learners desire to learn, otherwise they have nothing to show for the efforts they have made.

So far, however, there are few signs that the testing of English is embracing non-native speaker variation and innovation. As Lowenberg (2000: 67) points out, little consideration has as yet been given to

> the linguistic norms for English against which proficiency in English is generally assessed, that is, the norms of standard English. Rather, an implicit, and frequently explicit, assumption has been that the universal target for proficiency in standard English around the world is the set of norms which are accepted and used by highly educated native speakers of English.

He goes on to demonstrate how many of these NS norms do not reflect the norms of non-native speaker varieties in a large number of World English (Outer Circle) settings such as Bangladesh, Kenya, Nigeria, Sierra Leone and Singapore.

Lowenberg (2000, 2002) provides several examples of the sort of English usage which is considered standard in its local (Outer and/or Expanding Circle) context, but which diverges from Inner Circle use and would therefore be regarded as deviant in international tests of English. For example:

❑ The use of 'would' rather than 'will' in Malaysian and Indian English as in 'We accept the verdict of the Kelantan people and we hope they *would* accept the verdict of the rest of the country'.

❑ The use of uncountable nouns as countable in a number of countries including the Philippines, Nigeria and Malaysia and much of the Expanding Circle, as in 'Thank you for upkeeping the *equipments* and facilities provided on this train'.

❑ Similarly, 'West said they used *a digital equipment* that was capable of transmitting both video and still images' (Malaysian English) and 'Although it is *a hard work*, I enjoy it' (Korean English).

❑ Prepositional collocations such as (Singaporean English) 'I live in an apartment *at* Belmont Road'.

❑ Use of prepositions considered to be redundant in standard British and American English, such as in the phrase 'discuss *about*' which is attested as standard use in a number of non-native speaker varieties of English such as Nigerian, Malaysian, Zambian and Singaporean, and also found widely in Expanding Circle Englishes.

The testing of English around the world, then, still reflects very strongly the 'deficit linguistics' view that was discussed in unit B3 and gives a clear impression that what is being tested is not proficiency per se, but proximity to certain native speaker norms.

The difficulty nevertheless remains of establishing precisely which features exemplify difference and which deficiencies. It cannot be assumed that all differences from native speaker norms represent developing varietal norms: they could be errors (but in relation to the L2 norm) or even nonce words (words invented for a specific purpose and used only once).

Activity

❑ As regards the Outer Circle, Lowenberg (2000: 81) describes as 'almost neo-colonial' the 'assumption held by many who design English proficiency tests . . . that the native speakers still should determine the norms for standard English around the world'. He later (2002: 433–4) extends this position to the Expanding Circle, arguing that items in tests such as TOEIC do not reflect the fact that 'normative features in Expanding Circle varieties sometimes diverge from Inner Circle norms'. In his view, the existence of these Expanding Circle norms casts serious doubt on the validity of tests for Expanding Circle countries that are based only on Inner Circle norms. Do you agree with Lowenberg in relation to testing in either or both circles?

❑ Y. Kachru and Nelson (2006: 131) argue that '[t]he many contexts and norms of world Englishes preclude any simple limitation of "correctness" and make professional test-writers' tasks more difficult the more they come to understand about world Englishes'. Take a look at some English language tests that are used on a worldwide basis, e.g. TOEIC, TOEFL, IELTS, and any of the University of Cambridge (Cambridge ESOL, formerly UCLES) tests. Or better still, look at the practice books produced by one of the examination boards, as then you will be able to check the key to find out which answers are considered acceptable. How strictly do their writers limit correctness to native English norms? How far do they demonstrate an awareness of World Englishes by accepting non-native speaker variation of the kind Lowenberg describes and the complex situation to which Y. Kachru and Nelson refer?

❑ If you live in an Outer or Expanding Circle setting, design a short grammar test that takes account of its local norms. To what extent do you need to break away from Inner Circle norms in order to do this?

❑ Kachru (1992: 361) considers that the only solution to the current inappropriateness of English language teaching and testing around the world is for a 'paradigm shift' in which, for example, a clear distinction is made between the use of English in monolingual and multilingual societies, there is mutual exposure to the major native and non-native varieties of English, and while one variety may be the focus of teaching, emphasis is given to the 'awareness and functional validity' of the others. Think about the ways in which such a paradigm shift could be implemented, for example, how could awareness of a range of non-native varieties of English be raised in ELT classrooms?

❏ In a 'Point and Counterpoint' debate in *ELT Journal*, vol. 60, no. 1, Jenkins argues that 'recent changes in both users and uses of English have become so far-reaching that a major rethink of English language teaching goals is called for', and that 'this will first require a substantial overhaul of English language testing, given that teachers and learners alike will be reluctant to embrace any curriculum change that is not reflected in the targets set by the major examination boards' (Jenkins 2006a: 43). Taylor responds by arguing in favour of the status quo, claiming *inter alia* '[t]he need to acknowledge the expectations and preferences of test-takers and other test users (for example, teachers, parents, employers, admissions officers)', who currently favour native English norms (Taylor 2006: 58). Which point of view do you agree with? If possible, read the two parts of the debate before you decide.

EMERGING 'SUB'-VARIETIES   C4

In this unit, we will look at two varieties of English, Singlish and Estuary English, which are generally stigmatised by non-linguists as sub-standard (i.e. inferior) versions of the related standard variety. To linguists, on the other hand, Singlish and Estuary English are more likely to be regarded as *non-* rather than *sub*-standard Englishes.

Singlish

The variety popularly called Singlish by Singaporeans and others, though more often known by linguists as **Colloquial Singapore English** (**CSE**), differs in certain respects from the related standard variety, **Standard Singapore English** (**SSE**). However, as Deterding (2007: 6) points out, it is not clear whether these two varieties 'exist along a continuum' (Deterding's preferred explanation, with frequency of occurrence of non-standard features as the main distinction between them), or whether 'a diglossic situation exists between them, involving a clear switch between two styles of speech'. Either way, as you will see in the third example below, young people are often able to move easily from one to the other. And regardless of how Singlish is explained, the issue of whether it should be banned is currently exercising the minds of educationalists, government officials and journalists alike. Some are concerned that the use of Singlish among the young is likely to affect their literacy. Another fear is that if young people grow up speaking only Singlish, they will not be able to speak an internationally acceptable or understandable form of English, something which many Singaporeans regard as crucial to the continuing success of a country with a total population of little over four million.

Gupta (1999: 62) defines Singlish as a contact variety rather than a 'semi-institutionalised codemix variety' such as Spanglish or Hindlish. She points out that 'the Sing- of Singlish is Singapore, not a language' and that 'the main difference from StdE [standard English] is syntactic, and the lexis is dominated by English'. She adds that 'it is Singapore Colloquial English (*sic*) which is the most usual ENL of those who learn English at home'.

Activity

The following utterances (from Gupta, 1994: 71–2) are by a 4-year-old child, who is pleading with her mother to go and see a Care Bear film (for which she believes you must first buy a Care Bear), something which may only be feasible if they attend a church near where the film is being shown.

> Mummy, you must buy Care Bear first leh.
> Then you got ticket go and see.
> You didn't buy Care Bear hor, then ah, you cannot.
> Can to the church there.
> Church there got Care Bear cartoon.
> Tomorrow then go lah.
> Tomorrow go church lah.
> Sunday then go lah.

❏   Try to describe some of the linguistic features of Singlish based only on this evidence.

The second example, from Gupta (1999: 62) also features a child, this time one of almost 6 years old, who is a native speaker of English. The conversation is between Gupta herself (AG) and the child (R). They are looking at a photograph of a crowd of people in a performance:

> R   Then this is the Jesus son.
> AG   Jesus's son!
> R   No, this is Jesus son.
> *[1 sec]*
>   Hah?
> AG   Jesus son?
> R   Yah
> AG   Jesus didn't have any children.
> R   That one – ah – because ah, like us hor, /is/ Jesus daughter and son ah. Acting only lah.

❏   What can you add to your list of Singlish features from this extra evidence?

The third example comes from Pakir (1995: 7). In this school, while Mandarin is the normal language used by the girls for informal interaction, in this particular class they regularly use English even informally. Here, the girls are engaged in group-work. The formality level has dropped from the standard spoken English which tends to characterise these students' speech, and, as Pakir points out, their language includes a number of colloquial features:

S1 On the way to Damascus, saw bright lights, heard Jesus . . .
     Conversation with Jesus, Jesus gives him instructions . . .
S3 Got instructions. Can lah.
S1 OK, so what . . . Then Saul is blinded, right?
S2 He was instructed to go into the city; but he was going into the city
     anyway!
S1 Ya woh.
S3 Saul was baffled. Mystified. He heard the sound but did not see
     anyone.
S2 But '. . . did not see anyone' indicates that Saul must have seen
     something.
S3 He saw a bright light!
S2 Sorry, I'm sorry. So cheem.
     (cheem = Hokkien, meaning 'deep')

❑   Once again, identify features which seem to you to signal Singlish usage, then compare your notes with the following account.

Grammar

The following is adapted from the list of grammatical features of CSE offered by Bautista and Gonzalez (2006: 135) which they obtained from Alsagoff and Ho (1998). Wherever possible, the features are illustrated with genuine data from Deterding (2007) ('D'), and elsewhere with constructed examples from Alsagoff and Ho ('AH'):

Features associated with the verb
❑   past tense not morphologically marked: 'She eat here yesterday' (AH: 137),
❑   present tense with no –s suffix: 'nowadays she . . . she look after my niece and nephews' (D: 45),
❑   copula dropped to describe states: 'This coffee house very cheap.' (AH: 139), 'the young ones . . . all all right also lah' (D: 52), and
❑   adverbials such as *already* preferred to morphological marking of aspect: 'My baby speak already' (AH: 140), 'the rest of them um . . . um already completed their studying' (D: 52).

Features associated with the noun
❑   non-count nouns treated as count: 'I bought a lot of furnitures from IKEA' (D: 42), 'reading some fictions' (D: 43),
❑   indefinite article dropped: 'yah, sat on elephant's back' (D: 109), and
❑   relative clause with different word order and *one*: 'That boy pinch my sister one very naughty' (AH: 147).

Features of sentence structure

❏ subject and sometimes object dropping: 'so in the end . . . didn't try out the rides so initially want to take the ferris wheel' (D: 58), 'Every year, must buy for Chinese New Year.' (AH: 147),

❏ conjunction dropping: 'so only tried one or two dishes, didn't really do much cooking' (D: 107),

❏ use of *or not* in questions: 'You can eat pork or not?' (A + H: 150),

❏ use of *is it?* tag question: 'he think I want to listen to his story is it?' (D: 56), and

❏ use of pragmatic particles *lah* (often to create solidarity), and *ah* (to mark off the topic or to indicate that more is to follow): 'shopping-wise, nothing much to buy there lah' (D: 69), 'which subject ah . . . I guess I have no preference now' (D: 72).

Pronunciation

The following pronunciation items are from Deterding (2007):

❏ Avoidance of the sounds [θ] and [ð]. In initial positions [t] and [d] are often used, so that e.g. 'thing' is pronounced 'ting', and 'then' is pronounced 'den'. In final positions, [f] is often used instead of [θ] and [ð] so that 'birth' is 'birf' and 'with' is 'wif'.

❏ Replacement of final plosive (stop) consonants i.e. [p] [t] [k], but especially [t] and [k] with a glottal stop [ʔ], so that 'quite' is pronounced [kwaɪʔ] and 'not' is [nɔʔ].

❏ Less distinction between long and short vowels than in many other accents of English, with typically long vowels being shortened and diphthongs being pronounced as monophthongs, e.g. 'taught' as [tɔʔ], 'staff' as 'stuff', 'days' as [des], and 'know' as [no].

❏ Rhythm very syllable-timed, sometimes described as having a 'staccato effect'.

❏ Because of the evenly timed rhythm, words often have equal stress on their syllables, but in some words that have an audible stress pattern, this may differ from the pattern in other English varieties, e.g. 'biographies' as bio**gra**phies, 'opportunity' as o**ppor**tunity, 'colleague' as co**llea**gue.

Lexis

These lexical items are from Deterding (2007) ('D'), supplemented with some from Brown (1999) ('B'):

❏ Borrowings: many words from the other Singaporean languages are borrowed into English, e.g. *kiasu* (fear of losing out, Hokkien), *chim* (profound, Hokkien), *makan* (to eat, Malay), *kampung* (rural village, Malay), *pasar malam* (night market, Malay), *siau* (crazy, Hokkien), *buaya* (womaniser, literally 'crocodile', Malay), *ulu* (rustic, unsophisticated, Malay), *rojak* (all mixed together, Malay), *obiang* (vulgar, tasteless dressing or display of wealth, origin unclear).

❏ Shifted meaning: e.g. 'bring' is used where 'take' is more common in other varieties, and 'stay' is used to mean 'long-term residence: 'my dad will have to help up . . . by erm bringing my niece to school in the morning' (D: 80), 'my grandmother, my aunt and uncle also stay next door' (D: 81).

❏ The tendency to extend the grammatical functions of verbs to adjectives and of nouns to verbs: e.g. the verb 'blur' is an adjective meaning 'confused' as in 'You so blur like sotong' (where 'sotong' is the Malay for 'squid'). [Note that 'blur' with this meaning has an entry in the 1999 *Encarta Dictionary*.]

❏ Idiomatic forms peculiar to Singlish, e.g. 'love letters' (flaky, tube-shaped biscuits): 'I would bake pineapple tarts and love letters for my neighbours' (B: 133); 'havoc' (wild and unruly): 'young women today are more havoc' (B: 103); '4-D' (four digit, a form of gambling): 'a major illegal 4-D syndicate' (B: 88).

The politics of Singlish

As mentioned earlier, the use of Singlish is causing concern among some members of Singapore society, particularly the government. These concerns led, in 2000, to the launch of the Speak Good English Movement (SGEM), the main purpose of which has been to promote the use of SSE and discourage the use of Singlish. According to the official view, Singlish is 'not English' but 'English corrupted by Singaporeans . . . broken, ungrammatical English sprinkled with words and phrases from local dialects and Malay which English speakers outside Singapore have difficulties in understanding' (quoted in Rubdy 2001: 348). In other words, the prime motivation behind the SGEM is an economic imperative: the need for Singaporeans to maintain international intelligibility in English in order to be able to compete in the world's financial markets rather than develop '[their] own type of pidgin English . . . which the rest of the world will find quaint but incomprehensible' (Prime Minister Goh Chok Tong, quoted in Rubdy 2001: 345).

Sociolinguists see Singlish rather differently. Schneider (2007) observes that concerns about falling standards of English are a common feature of many emergent postcolonial Englishes. And Mugglestone (2003) reports that worries over pronunciation have been expressed at various times in Britain during the past 300 years – yet I doubt any reader of this book, whether in favour of Singlish or not, would recommend a return to the British English current during the reign of King George I (1714–27).

As Rubdy points out, Singlish has become a symbol of cultural identity and social cohesion for many Singaporeans, arguing that '[i]n recent years, an increasing number of young and middle-aged Singaporeans have begun to accept and even expect the use of vernacular English in the in-group' (2001: 345). She accepts, on the one hand, that a language has to have an economic basis in order to survive, but argues on the other, that

> while realizing that Singlish is the glue that binds Singaporeans into a distinct group that can be identified as a unique speech community in its own right, what is clear is that the authorities would rather Singaporeans used a different 'brand' of glue – one that is closer to either British or American standard English.
>
> (Rubdy 2001: 352)

Wee (2002) takes great exception to the Singapore government's insistence on linking English with its Inner Circle users and their English norms. He argues that Singaporeans have ownership of their English, and that they therefore have the right to determine their own English norms. And Wee (2005) takes things even further with his contention that the Singapore government's SGEM, which, like others, he sees as an attempt to eliminate Singlish completely, is not only an example of linguistic discrimination but, more seriously, a breach of linguistic human rights.

Both Rubdy (2001) and Deterding (2007) suggest that the Singapore government may well be successful in eliminating Singlish. They compare the SGEM with the Speak Mandarin Campaign, also launched for economic reasons (communication with China). As Deterding (2007: 91) notes, the Speak Mandarin Campaign 'has been extraordinarily successful, to the extent that Mandarin Chinese, a language that almost nobody in Singapore spoke as a home language thirty years ago, is now the common language among young Chinese Singaporeans'. He ponders whether the SGEM will meet with equal success, and suggests that, on the basis of the Speak Mandarin Campaign and also the government's success in non-linguistic areas (e.g. persuading people to flush public toilets and not to chew gum), 'it is quite possible that the popular use of Singlish will indeed be eliminated'. On the other hand, maybe Singaporeans nowadays have become less willing to follow government exhortations. We shall see.

 Activity ✪

> ❑ To what extent do you believe that the use of Singlish in Singapore is a potential threat to Singapore's economy and the financial stability of its population? Or do you believe that Singlish can operate harmlessly alongside SSE?
> ❑ Either way, do you agree with the view that financial considerations are so vital that they should always influence language policy, or do you believe that cultural factors should take precedence? Why?

Estuary English

The English variety known by many as **Estuary English** (**EE**) has, in its relatively short life, proved as controversial as Singlish. For example, the UK Education Secretary in 1994 launched a campaign to stop the spread of EE among schoolchildren.

The term 'Estuary English' was originally coined by Rosewarne, a pronunciation specialist, in 1983. This is how he described EE some thirteen years later, in 1996:

> Estuary English, a new accent variety I first described in 1984, is neither Cockney nor RP, but in the middle between these two. 'Estuary English . . . is to be found in its purest form along the seaward banks of the Thames, whither it has drifted from the eastern end of the capital' (leader article in the *Independent on Sunday* of 18 June 1995). The heartland still lies by the banks of the Thames and its estuary, but it has spread to other areas, as the *Sunday Times* announced on 14 March 1993 in a front-page headline 'Estuary English sweeps Britain'. Experts on British English agree that it is currently the strongest influence on the standard spoken

form and that it could replace RP as the most influential accent in the British Isles.

(Rosewarne 1996: 15)

The following is a summary of the main EE pronunciation features that Rosewarne (1996: 16–18) has observed:

❑ The sound 't' in word final position is replaced with a glottal stop [ʔ], so that 'there's a lot of it about' may be pronounced as 'there's a loʔ of iʔ abouʔ'.

❑ The dark 'l' of RP (the 'l' sound before another consonant sound or a pause) is vocalised. In other words, it is substituted with the sound /ʊ/, so that 'milk' sounds like 'miwk', and and 'bill' like 'biw'. (This is known as *l*-vocalisation).

❑ The final vowel sounds in words such as 'very funny' are longer than they are in RP and can be represented by the symbol [iː].

❑ The yod (the 'y' sound immediately after the 'p' in 'pure'), represented as [j], is dropped in EE pronunciations of words such as 'assume' and 'pursuit'.

❑ The sound combinations [tj] and [dj] in words such as 'duty' and 'tune' are realised as [tʃ] and [dʒ].

❑ EE avoids the syllabic consonants that occur in RP in the final syllables of words such as 'middle' pronounced [mɪdl] and 'button' pronounced [bʌtn], and instead places a schwa between the [d] and [l] in 'middle, and the [t] and [n] of 'button'.

❑ Finally, although Rosewarne (1996) does not mention this, other sources on EE also refer to *th*-fronting, i.e. the substitution of the sound [θ] with [f] as in 'fink' for 'think' and 'birf' for 'birth'.

Rosewarne (1996: 20) concludes 'It will be interesting to see the direction of change in the future, whether RP will change so as to absorb EE, or if EE replaces RP as the standard form of British English'. However, his claim that EE is a 'new accent variety' has not gone unquestioned. A number of linguists have argued that the EE phenomenon documented by Rosewarne is neither new, nor a variety in the terms that he describes it. These are some of their counter-claims:

Maidment considers that Rosewarne's description of EE suffers from naïvety because it fails to take account of the sociolinguistic fact of **intraspeaker variation**. In other words, 'a speaker of a given accent within his or her competence a range of styles from informal to formal' and will adjust their accent according to contextual factors such as location, addressee and topic of conversation. He goes on, '[i]f this is the case, then the boundary between Cockney and EE becomes extremely fuzzy unless style of speech is controlled for', and concludes:

> All this leads to the possibility that EE is no more than slightly poshed up Cockney or RP which has gone 'down market' in appropriate situations and that rather than there being a newly developed accent which we should call EE, all that has happened over recent years is that there has been a redefinition of the appropriateness of differing styles of pronunciation to differing speech situations. For example, the perception may be that it is now more acceptable to use informal style in broadcasting.
>
> (Maidment 1994)

Wells (1998), from a similar standpoint, proposes that EE be (re-)defined as 'standard English spoken with a non-RP, London-influenced accent'. He argues that it 'differs from Cockney (i) in using standard grammar and (ii) in lacking stigmatized characteristics such as h-dropping . . . and intervocalic T-glottaling within a word'. Trudgill (2002: 177–9) describes EE as 'an inaccurate myth':

> It is inaccurate because it suggests that we are talking about a new variety, which we are not; and because it suggests that it is a variety of English confined to the banks of the Thames Estuary, which it is not.

He argues that EE is a lower middle-class accent of the south-east of England that has become more widespread as the use of RP declines, and some of whose features are influenced by those of the London area. He goes on to dispute Rosewarne's claim that EE 'could replace RP as the most influential accent in the British Isles':

> The sociolinguistic conditions are not such that it could turn into the new RP. There is no parallel here to the nationwide network of residential Public Schools which gave rise to RP. What we know about the geographical diffusion of linguistic innovations, moreover, indicates that there is no way in which the influence of London is going to be able to counteract the influence of large centres such as Liverpool and Newcastle which are at some distance from London. And we also know that linguistic innovations are not spread by radio and television.

Kerswill (2007: 50–1), like Trudgill, believes that EE 'spans a very wide range of accents, from near-Cockney . . . to near-RP'. For this reason, he questions whether it can actually be called 'a variety' at all. Instead, he suggests, it would be more realistic to see it 'as referring to a set of levelled (relatively homogeneous) regional – as opposed to local – accents or dialects spoken in the south-east of England'. These, he goes on to argue, 'are a result of greatly heightened mobility since the period just after the Second World War, coupled with a change in ideology allowing non-RP users to occupy a range of professions, especially in broadcasting, from which they were formerly effectively barred'.

But the most far-reaching critique of EE is that of Przedlacka (2001, 2002). Her careful empirical study of teenage speech in the Home Counties was carried out in order to answer these two questions:

a   Is there a coherent and uniform variety, frequently referrred to as Estuary English?

b   Can we legitimately call it a newly emerging accent?

(Przedlacka 2002: 97)

The conclusions that she draws from her extensive data are that 'we are dealing with a number of distinct accents, not a single and definable variety', that 'what is known as "Estuary English" appears to be part of more general changes' such as *l*-vocalisation and *th*-fronting, and that some of the features presented as EE innovations, e.g. increased glottaling and *l*-vocalisation, 'are not exclusive to the British Isles'. And like some of the linguists quoted above, Przedlacka argues that the speech of the Home Counties is subject to influence from the London Cockney accent, and that when Cockney variants occur in Home Counties speech, 'they are no longer uniquely Cockney or "Estuary English"' (2002: 97–8).

Activity

❏ Why do you think the notion of a completely new variety, Estuary English, has been so easily accepted by the general public, whereas linguists question its existence and explain it as merely an extension of existing varieties of English? Do you think the general public would have been as convinced about EE's existence if it had not had a 'catchy' name – if it had been called, for example, 'London-influenced Home Counties speech'?

❏ The media, as well as many members of the general public in the UK and elsewhere, seem to have a very low opinion of EE. Read through these media reactions to EE (in Maidment 1994), and consider why these views might be held, and why they are so extreme:

> It is not an accent . . . just lazy speaking that grates on the ear and is an extremely bad example to our children.

> The spread of Estuary English can only be described as horrifying. We are plagued with idiots on radio and television who speak English like the dregs of humanity.

> God forbid that it becomes standard English. Are standards not meant to be upheld? We must not slip into slovenliness because of a lack of respect for the language. Ours is a lovely language, a rich language, which has a huge vocabulary. We have to safeguard it.

> It is slobspeak, limp and flaccid: the mouths uttering it deserve to be stuffed with broken glass.

❏ Make a list of some of the most typical features of Estuary English (depending on your local context) and interview a range of people in different age groups to elicit their views of these features. How do you account for any differences of opinion?

❏ Why do you think it is young people who are currently the main users of both Singlish and EE? Do you anticipate that these varieties will spread to other age groups over time?

❏ Look back at the pronunciation features of Singlish and EE. How might you account for the fact that despite the very different linguistic backgrounds of their speakers, they have certain features in common, e.g. glottal stops, substitutions of 'th', and vocalising of dark 'l'?

C5 STANDARDS ACROSS CHANNELS

In this unit, we will explore the notion of standard usage across the different channels of speech and writing, and the recent third channel of e-discourse, focusing mainly, though not exclusively, on British English.

Speech and writing

When people talk about 'standard English', they generally have the written channel in mind. However, the inappropriacy of evaluating English speech on the basis of writing has become increasingly apparent with the growth in the past decade in the number and size of corpora containing authentic speech, such as the British National Corpus, COBUILD and CANCODE (Cambridge and Nottingham Corpus of Discourse in English).

Baron (2000: 21–2) discusses three different approaches to speech/writing differences, the Opposition View, the Continuum View and the Cross-over View. According to the **Opposition View**, speech and writing have dichotomous characteristics as shown in Table C5.1.

Table C5.1 Characteristics of speech and writing (source: Baron 2000)

Writing is:	Speech is:
objective	interpersonal
a monologue	a dialogue
durable	ephemeral
scannable	only linearly accessible
planned	spontaneous
highly structured	loosely structured
syntactically complex	syntactically simple
concerned with past and future	concerned with the present
formal	informal
expository	narrative
argument-oriented	event-oriented
decontextualised	contextualised
abstract	concrete

The **Continuum View**, on the other hand, looks at speech and writing in real-world contexts and regards them as being located at various points on a continuum, depending on the specific context of use (see Figure C5.1).

Figure C5.1 Continuum view of speech and writing.

The **Cross-over View**, meanwhile, takes into account the fact that 'merely because a linguistic message looks as if it's designed to be spoken or written hardly ensures that will be the medium through which everyone experiences it' (Baron 2000: 22). For example, it is common nowadays to find 'talking books' (books that are read aloud on cassettes rather than with our eyes), or for lectures to be posted on websites where students who cannot attend in person are able to read them. Can you think of further examples to demonstrate the Cross-over View, as well as examples which support or contradict the Opposition View?

Leech et al. (1982: 139–40) reconcile the differences in the Opposition and Continuum approaches by talking of **typical speech** and **typical writing**. They categorise the typical features of the two channels as follows:

Table C5.2 Features of typical speech and writing (source: Leech et al. 1982: 139–40)

	Typical speech	*Typical writing*
1	Inexplicitness	Explicitness
2	Lack of clear sentence boundaries	Clear sentence boundaries
3	Simple structure	More complex structure
4	Repetitiveness	Non-repetitiveness
5	Normal non-fluency	Fluency
6	Monitoring features	No monitoring features
7	Interaction features	No interaction features
8	Features reflecting informality	Features reflecting formality

In Table C5.1, non-fluency (5) refers to features which reflect the fact that speech tends to be unprepared and therefore includes phenomena such as hesitations, false starts, grammatical blends and unfinished sentences. **Monitoring features** (6) and interaction (7) features relate to the dialogic nature of speech. Speakers monitor the effect their speech is having on the addressee(s) with words and phrases such as 'well', 'I mean', 'sort of' and 'you know', and they use **interaction features** to invite participation, particularly by means of second-person pronouns, questions, and imperatives. By characterising typical speech and writing in this way, Leech et al. are then able to demonstrate how they operate on a continuum rather than in direct opposition (see Figure C5.2).

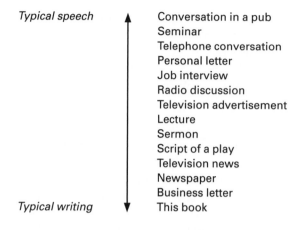

Typical speech

Conversation in a pub
Seminar
Telephone conversation
Personal letter
Job interview
Radio discussion
Television advertisement
Lecture
Sermon
Script of a play
Television news
Newspaper
Business letter

Typical writing

This book

Figure C5.2 Typical speech and writing continuum.

Activity

❑ Do you agree with the order in which Leech et al. have placed the speech/writing contexts on their continuum? If not, what changes would you suggest? Do you think any of these result from the fact that their continuum dates from 1982? Why might this be so? And where on the continuum would you place the following: work-related email, social email, internet chat room conversation, text message?

❑ Here is a transcribed conversation (from Crystal and Davy 1975, reproduced in Leech et al. 1982). Speaker A is describing the family holiday to speaker B. Look back to Leech et al.'s lists of features of typical speech and typical writing and see how many of them are exemplified in the transcript. For example, inexplicitness (1) occurs in lines 8/9 ('and all this'), non-fluency (5) occurs in line 4 ('er'), and monitoring (6) in line 4 ('sort of'). Because this is a transcript, there is no punctuation, but vertical lines are used to indicate units of intonation (tone units or 'word groups') and dashes to indicate pauses. The items in brackets are B's responses to A.

B:	so what how did you map out your day | you had your	1
	breakfast in the kitchen |	2
A:	we have our breakfast | (laughs) in the kitchen | – and	3
	then we sort of did what we liked | and er got ready to	4
	go out | (m |) we usually went out quite soon after	5
	that | – erm the children were always up | at the crack of	6
	dawn | (m |) with the farmer | – and they went in the	7

milking sheds | and helped him feed the pigs | and all	8
this | you know we didn't see the children | – and er	9
then we used to go out | we – we had super weather | -	10
absolutely super | – and so we went to a beach | usually	11
for er but by about four o'clock it we were hot and we	12
had to come off the beach (m | m |) – so we'd generally	13
go for a tea somewhere | just in case supper was delayed	14
you know | (laughs) laughs and then we'd get back | and	15
the children would go straight back on to the farm | . . .	16

❏ Now imagine that you are speaker A and that you are describing your farm holiday, not in a conversation, but in a letter. Write the letter retaining as much of the information provided in A's speech as possible. Then compare your written version with the spoken original above and see how many differences there are to illustrate Leech et al.'s distinctions between typical speech and typical writing. Are there any other differences which are not covered in their lists of characteristics? And how far can any similarities be accounted for by the fact that conversations and personal letters are fairly close together at the 'Typical speech' end of their continuum?

This is Leech et al.'s (1982: 141–2) own version of the imaginary letter:

Dear B,
    I thought I would write and tell you about our summer holiday, which we spent on a farm.
    Every day, the children were up at the crack of dawn with the farmer. They went to the milking sheds with him and helped him feed the pigs, so that we barely saw them at all.
    Then we would have our breakfast in the kitchen. After breakfast, we usually did what we liked for a short while, and then went out.
    We had absolutely super weather, and so we usually went to a beach. But by about four o'clock we were hot and had to come off the beach. Then we'd generally go and have tea somewhere just in case supper was delayed. When we got back, the children would go straight back on the farm . . .

❏ Finally, both the original recording and the imaginary letter are around three decades old. Which spoken and/or written features might nowadays be produced differently in British English?

Since the late 1980s, computerised database **corpora** have been demonstrating in increasing detail the way in which speech operates according to its own grammatical rules, with writing tending 'to reflect earlier norms while speech commonly embodies innovation' (Baron 2000: 95). The work of Carter and McCarthy for CANCODE, for example, has provided useful evidence of the **grammar of spoken (British) English**. These are some of the phenomena they found in their data (see e.g Carter and McCarthy 1995). Try to identify the feature of spoken English exemplified in each set of examples before reading on for the technical names and details:

1   a   Jamie, normally you put him in his cot and he's . . .

     b   That chap over there, he said it was okay . . .

     c   The women in the audience, they all shouted.

2   a   'Cos otherwise they tend to go cold don't they pasta?

     b   They do, I suppose, take up a lot of time, don't they, kids?

     c   It's not actually very good is it that wine?

3   Y   What's the matter?

     Z   Got an awful cold.

     Y   Just seen Paco.

     Z   Did he say anything?

     Y   Nothing.

     Z   Interesting isn't it?

4   a   Why I rang you was that I needed to check something.

     b   Where we always go wrong is that we forget it's a one-way street.

     c   What fascinates me with that is the way it's rolled.

Brief notes

1 Heads (or 'left dislocation')

Heads are nouns or noun phrases which are brought to the front of a clause to identify them for the listener as the most important part of the message. They are then repeated with a pronoun in the clause which follows. In the above examples, the heads are (a) 'Jamie', (b) 'That chap over there' and (c) 'The women in the audience'.

2 Tails (or 'reinforcement')

Tails parallel heads by repeating the subject of the preceding clause in order to amplify and reinforce what has been said. They thus tend to serve an affective function by showing the speaker's attitude towards his or her subject. The tails in the above examples are (a) 'pasta', (b) 'kids' and (c) 'that wine'.

3 Ellipsis

Ellipsis simply means omission. It refers specifically to the omission of items in a grammatical structure which go unnoticed in speech but which would be required in a written text. The items which are omitted are those which are retrievable from either the immediate situation or from the surrounding text (i.e. the 'cotext'). In the example dialogue, the ellipted items are: I've (got an awful cold); I've (just seen Paco); He said (nothing); It's (interesting, isn't it?).

4 Word order

The **word order** varies considerably across speech and writing. One area in which this is particularly so is that of reported speech. The examples above all demonstrate **wh-clefting**, which CANCODE has shown to be far more widespread in spoken than in written English. These *wh-* clauses are brought to the front of the clause often, as with heads, for emphasis, though they can also serve to contradict an anticipated response. The <u>wh</u>-clefts in the above examples are: 'Why I rang you', 'Where we always go wrong' and 'What fascinates me with that'.

Can you think of further examples of the grammar of speech? One fairly recent phenomenon, for instance, is the use of quotative *like* as in 'I walked into the house and it was like "Where on earth have you been?" As recently as the year 2000, quotative *like* was used only by younger speakers of English, but over the following two years was adopted by older age groups, demonstrating the relative speed with which speech innovations spread through the speech community.

E-discourse

Look at the following examples of authentic emails (all sent to me) and identify features that are typical of written and spoken English (see C5), and features which do not occur in either and, instead, seem to be emerging features of e-style:

> **1** change of plan, im going to stay in leeds instead, all trains are booked up for coming back up, and none of my m8s are coming back to london like i thought they would. ive got 4 essays to write and i want to get them done before xmas so i think i will spend this weekend working! plus im going to be coming back on the 12/13th anyway so its hardly anytime anyway. sorry to disapoint, and give my luv to the the wrinklies!
> nick

> **2** Alessia and Martin,
> The book I mentioned at our last meeting is:
> Kelly Hall, J. and Eggington, W. G. (eds) (2000) *The sociopolitics of English language teaching*. Clevedon: Multilingual Matters.
> I spoke to Jenny today and she said that she might have referred this title already.
> If you have difficulties in accessing this book in the near future, let me know.
> Constant

> **3** How are you? do you have travel plans for the summer? We are now here for the summer – sort of – and celebrated C's 60th last weekend. Do give me a ring for chat when you have a moment.
> Rx

4 Hi JJ, yes I got both msgs (and sorry your English she be so bad because you're a NS!!) The attachmts came through too, but I've deleted them. They don't seem to be sth you want to keep on your computer/flash drive!
Have a good week!
B

5 Dear Dr. Jenkins,
Thank you for your quick response. I'm afraid I can't send you my IELTS certificate right now, because I won't take it until March, 2002. But before that, I'll send my application form and two references to you as soon as possible. Will that be OK?
And if there's anything else I should do, please let know.
Thank you very much.
Sincerely,
(first name + family name)

6 Dear Professor Jenkins,
Thank you very much for your kind assistance. The pertinent materials will be couriered to your office at due course.
Yours sincerely,
(first name + family name)

7 Dear Jenny,
I am writing regarding my decision to change courses from the MA in Applied Language Studies in Education to Applied Linguistics and ELT.
    In the conversation I had this morning with Dermot, he said that you had authorized the late change and that I should get in touch with you. I have been unable to contact you by phone. My phone number at work is (. . .) and at home is (. . .).
    I will keep trying to call you this week.
Thank you very much for allowing me to change at such a late stage.
Kind regards,
(first name + family name)

8 It might be worth bearing in mind that (in spite of what Metrical Phonologists and others might claim) it is not universally accepted that 'knowing the stress pattern' is necessary for recognizing English words.
    There's a good (and short) review of the question by James McQueen and Anne Cutler in W. Hardcastle and J. Laver *The Handbook of Phonetic Sciences* (Blackwell, 1997), pp. 579–82. On p. 580 they say 'stress information does not facilitate human word recognition'. I find the section on Prosodic Information in their chapter (Cognitive Processes in Speech Perception) very useful reading for my final year students.
Peter

Despite the fact that emails seem to make use of conventions drawn from both speech and writing, there is, as Baron (2000: 193) points out, 'evidence for an increasingly oral basis to written language' in **e-style**. She outlines the linguistic profile of email at the end of the 1990s as follows:

❏ *Social dynamics* (predominantly like writing):
   – interlocutors are physically separated,
   – physical separation fosters personal disclosure and helps level the conversational playing field.

❏ *Format* ((mixed) writing and speech):
   – like writing, email is durable,
   – like speech, email is typically unedited.

❏ *Grammar*:
   – lexicon (predominantly like speech),
   – heavy use of first- and second-person pronouns,
   – syntax: (mixed) writing and speech,
   – like writing, email has high type/token ration, high use of adverbial subordinate clauses, high use of disjunctions,
   – like speech, email commonly uses present tense, contractions.

❏ *Style* (predominantly like speech):
   – low level of formality,
   – expression of emotion not always self-monitored (flaming).
                                                      (Baron 2000: 251)

Baron concludes that 'email is largely speech by other means'. Nevertheless, just as with speech and writing, there will always be differences in email style depending on who is emailing whom and on the age, sex and L1 of the emailer. Younger emailers, for example, tend to use fewer apostrophes and contractions and more features of telephone texting (see the final activity below). Five of the above eight messages were from emailers for whom English is not their L1. Although in one case (5), the content of the message clarifies this, I am not convinced that it would otherwise be possible to identify this emailer as an L2 speaker. And are you able to identify the four who did not reveal themselves in this way? Perhaps, as Baron argues, 'email is beginning to develop a group of "native users" who are learning email as a primary and distinct avenue for creating many types of messages, rather than transferring to email prior assumptions from face-to-face speech or traditional writing' (2000 258). If this is so, it may be that differences across the native and non-native Englishes are being lost in the process.

❑ Find the following examples: an extract from your recent academic writing, a piece of your own informal writing, and an email and a text message you have sent recently. In addition make a recording of yourself in conversation and transcribe one to two minutes. Compare and contrast the language used across the different channels. What conclusions are you able to reach in relation to your own context(s) of language use?

❑ Alternatively, if you are a regular emailer, or have (permitted) access to someone else's emails, print out or copy down a sample of the emails received over a period of a week. Analyse them for their language and style. If these are very different from the messages that were sent to me and are reproduced above, how do you account for the differences? Could they be connected with age, sex, first language, professional status, type of email list subscribed to, or something else?

❑ Most readers will be familiar with the use of **texting**, the sending of short written messages from one mobile phone to another. Some items in the above emails are typical of texting, e.g. 'm8' for 'mate' and 'sth' for 'something'. Other examples from Crystal (2008b: 19) include:

what R U sayin?

c u in 5 min x

U miss me? ;-)

let me know if u want me 2 pick u up

Crystal's view of texting is that people do it because it is easy and fun, and that it is 'the latest manifestation of the human ability to be linguistically creative and to adapt language to suit the demands of diverse settings' (2008b: 175). However, some see it as harmful to the English language and harmful to children's developing literacy. For example, Crystal (2008b: 13) quotes from an article in *The Guardian* newspaper in which texting was described as 'bleak, bald, sad shorthand' that 'masks dyslexia, poor spelling and mental laziness' and is 'penmanship for illiterates'. What is your view, and why? And do you see any connections between negative attitudes towards texting and similar attitudes towards Singlish and Estuary English (see C4)?

THE NATURE OF ENGLISH AS A LINGUA FRANCA

C6

ELF beginnings

Of all the themes covered in this book, English as a Lingua Franca (ELF) has seen the most dramatic developments in the years following the writing of the first edition. Since then, there has been a vast amount of research into ELF, the first international conference dedicated to it (Helsinki 2008), and a large number of publications on the subject. PhD theses on ELF have been written (e.g. Cogo 2007, Dewey 2007a, Kaur 2008, Pölzl 2005), and many more are underway. Even more importantly, there have been major developments in ELF corpora, in particular, the Vienna-Oxford International Corpus of English (VOICE) (see Seidlhofer 2002), the corpus of English as a Lingua Franca in Academic Settings (ELFA) (see Mauranen 2003), and the corpus of South-East Asian ELF (see Deterding and Kirkpatrick 2006). Corpora of this kind have made it possible for researchers around the world to explore the ELF phenomenon at all linguistic levels, in different geographical regions (e.g. Seidlhofer et al. 2006 on ELF in Europe), and in a wide range of domains, both professional and social.

While research into communication in which English is used as the common language, or lingua franca, had been conducted since the 1990s (see e.g. Firth 1996, James 2000, Meierkord 1996), the focus of that research was on how, *despite its deficiencies* (when compared with 'correct' English, i.e. ENL) and the low proficiency levels of some of its speakers, this communication was often successful. ELF research proper is of a different nature. It takes as its starting point a position similar to that held by researchers of Outer Circle Englishes: that just because a language item differs from the way it is produced by Inner Circle speakers, it is not automatically an error. In the case of ELF, it may, instead, be an example of an emerging ELF variety.

In a seminal article published in late 2001, Seidlhofer pointed out that despite the fact that 'ELF is the most extensive contemporary use of English worldwide . . . what constitutes a target is still determined with virtually exclusive reference to native-speaker norms'. Thus, there was, she noted, 'a conceptual gap' which could only be remedied by according ELF 'a central place in description alongside English as a native language' (2001: 133–5). Hence the urgent need for ELF corpora to be collected in addition to corpora of ENL. Although ELF research based on this same premise had already been published (e.g. Jenkins 2000), it was Seidlhofer's 2001 article that acted as a clarion call and from which widespread interest in ELF can be dated.

Defining ELF

The term ELF has already been used several times in strand 6. But what exactly is ELF? Very roughly, it is English as it is used as a contact language among speakers from different first languages. The following five points present its main characteristics more precisely:

1 *It is used in contexts in which speakers with different L1s (mostly, but not exclusively, from the Expanding Circle) need it as their means to communicate with each other.*

In the past, some ELF researchers used the term 'English as an international language' (EIL) to refer to communication that included native speakers of English, and reserved ELF exclusively for non-native communication. However, researchers found the distinction unworkable in practice. How, for example, should you refer to an ELF interaction in which the participants are joined midway by a native English speaker? Does it then become EIL? Do the target norms suddenly change to the native speaker's ENL norms? Put like this, it sounds ridiculous. If ELF is to be seen as a kind of English in its own right, then in such situations, it would be for the native speaker to orient to the ELF norms of the other speakers rather than vice versa. For reasons of this kind, ELF researchers do not exclude Inner or Outer Circle speakers from their definition of ELF, and researchers who still use the term 'EIL' use it interchangeably with ELF. Having said this, it is undoubtedly true that the majority of ELF communication consists of Expanding Circle speakers interacting with each other, often with no native English speakers present.

2 ELF is an alternative to EFL rather than a replacement for it, and depends on the speaker's (or learner's) potential needs and preferences.
A common myth about ELF is that it is promoted to replace EFL as a learning target. This is not so. There will always be learners and users of English who need to blend in with native English speakers, or who wish to aspire to a native English accent. For such people, English as a foreign language (EFL) will be more realistic. The important point is that learners should be made aware of the differences between EFL and ELF so that they are in a position to make an informed choice. The differences between EFL and ELF are summarised in Table C6.1, which shows on the left-hand side the characteristics of the paradigm to which their English will belong if they choose to learn/use EFL, and on the right-hand side, the characteristics if they choose ELF.

Table C6.1 EFL and ELF (source: Kirkpatrick 2007b adapted from Jenkins 2006c).

EFL	ELF
Part of modern foreign languages	Part of World Englishes
Deficit perspective	Difference perspective
Metaphors of transfer/ interference/ fossilisation	Metaphor of contact/evolution
Code-mixing and -switching are seen as interference errors	Code-mixing and -switching are seen as bilingual resources

3 Linguistically ELF involves innovations that differ from ENL and which, in some cases, are shared by most ELF speakers.
However, this is *not* to suggest that ELF speakers do not also have features that characterise their own *local* varieties of English. While many ELF researchers are investigating the features that are common to all or most ELF speakers regardless of their L1, it

is clear that ELF speakers also use features that are particular to their own ELF variety, and/or to the English of the broader regional area from which they come. Shim (1999), for example, presents a large number of features of South Korean English of which some are used by ELF speakers from other areas, while others are specific to South Korean English speakers. And Deterding and Kirkpatrick (2006) present features that typify ELF use among a number of different L1 groups in the South-East Asian region, of which some are specific to that region while others are shared with ELF speakers elsewhere.

4 Pragmatically, it involves the use of certain communication strategies, particularly accommodation and code-switching. This is because ELF forms depend crucially on the specific communication context rather than being an 'all-purpose' English.

It should by now be clear that ELF is not a single, 'all-purpose' English but depends, like any natural language use, on who is speaking with whom, where, about what, and so on. In this respect, accommodation and code-switching are crucial features of ELF, and are used extensively by skilled ELF speakers (see Cogo 2007, Cogo and Dewey 2006, and Klimpfinger 2007 for illustrated discussions of both phenomena). We will return briefly to this point when we look at accommodation later in the unit.

5 Descriptions of ELF that may lead to codification are drawn from communication involving proficient ELF speakers.

As far as proficiency level is concerned, while ELF communication can, of course, involve participants of any level of proficiency, this is not the same as saying that the output of lower-proficiency ELF users could become an alternative *target* to ENL. Some people nevertheless believe, like Mesthrie and Bhatt (2008: 214), that ELF is entirely a 'basilectal' kind of English that is 'created "on-line" for immediate communication purposes' by speakers 'who are still in the process of mastering the language'. This is not the case. ELF communication undoubtedly includes lower-proficiency speakers who use English like this, along with the full proficiency range from beginner to expert user (see Jenkins 2006c). However, only the output of proficient ELF users (and there are many of these) is being collected for the purposes of possible later codification.

ELF features

We will now look at some features of ELF, focusing on the two areas where most has so far been published: lexicogrammar and pronunciation.

Lexicogrammatical features

The following features (taken from Seidlhofer 2004: 220) have been identified in ELF corpora as being used frequently and systematically, and being communicatively effective:

- ❏ 'dropping' the third person present tense –*s*,
- ❏ 'confusing' the relative pronouns 'who' and 'which',
- ❏ 'omitting' definite and indefinite articles where they are obligatory in ENL, and inserting them where they do not occur in ENL,

❏ 'failing' to use correct forms in tag questions, e.g. 'isn't it?' or 'no?' instead of 'shouldn't they?',

❏ inserting 'redundant' prepositions, as in 'We have to study about . . ',

❏ 'overusing' certain verbs of high semantic generality, such as 'do', 'have', 'make', 'put', 'take',

❏ 'replacing' infinitive constructions with that-clauses, as in 'I want that . . ', and

❏ 'overdoing' explicitness, e.g. 'black colour' rather than just 'black' (similarly, from Dewey 2007a, 'How long time . . .?' rather than just 'How long . . .?').

As Seidlhofer points out, these items would all be considered 'deadly grammatical sins' if compared with ENL forms. In fact, they would be described in the very terms used above, e.g. 'failing', 'overusing', 'confusing', and so on. Seidlhofer always inserts scare quotes around such words to indicate that they are not relevant to ELF, which, unlike EFL, should be considered *in its own right* and not by comparison with an ENL yardstick. Unfortunately, the publisher of Seidlhofer (2004) removed the scare quotes in error, so they have been reinstated above.

Activity

Let us now explore some of these ELF features in use. The following is a short piece of ELF data in which two speakers, R (German L1, male) and S (French L1, female) are choosing a picture for the front of a charity calendar. Read through the dialogue and as you do so, identify the features that make it a successful and collaborative discussion, such as supportive interruptions, positive minimal responses (e.g. 'yeah'), repetition of the interlocutor's words, completion of the interlocutor's sentence and the like.

1	R	I think on the front xx on the front page should be a picture who-
2		which animates p-people to er spend money, to the charity
3	S	yes
4	R	and I think er yeah maybe
5	S	I think a picture with child
6	R	Yeah, child are always good to
7	S	Yes
8	–R	to trap people spend money
9	S	Yes. I think, erm, let me see, erm . . .
10	R	I don't know . . . but maybe we should er choose a picture who
11		gives the impression that this child needs needs the money or
12	S	So I think, then that's my, this one, no
12	R	Yeah it's quite happy
14	S	Yeah, she's happy er. Maybe this one
15	R	Yeah.
16	S	He look very sad . . . and he has to carry heavier vase
17	R	Mm, that's right.
18	S	Too heavy for him, or . . .
19	R	Hm hm

20	S	But also this one, even if he's smiling

20 S But also this one, even if he's smiling
21 R Yeah, that's right . . . And maybe this one can show that the that
22   the chari-er charity can really help
23 S Uh huh
24 R and that the charity can er make a smile on a on a chil –on on a
25   child's face
26 S Yes
27 R Yeah I think this one would be
28 S A good one
29 R It would be good

. . . long pause
–   self-correction
–R   continuation
xx   unintelligible

❏ If we were to take parts of this dialogue out of context (e.g. 'He look very sad'), it might appear that the speaker has very low proficiency, but in fact both R and S have high proficiency ('Advanced' according to Cambridge ESOL's criteria). How could you demonstrate that such items, when used by Expanding Circle speakers, are not necessarily signs of low proficiency, and should be classified as examples of ELF rather than as errors? To what extent should it depend, for example, on how frequently and systematically they are used, or whether they do/do not cause intelligibility problems? What other criteria would you suggest?

❏ Which of the non-ENL features in the above dialogue, in your view, have the potential to become legitimate features of ELF lexicogrammar? Why not the others?

Pronunciation features

A number of pronunciation features were found in Jenkins's (2000) ELF research to be important contributors to mutual intelligibility in ELF communication. They were collectively labelled the 'lingua franca core' (LFC), and are summarised as follows:

❏ all the consonant sounds except voiceless 'th' /θ/, voiced 'th' /ð/, and dark 'l' [ɫ],

❏ vowel length contrasts (e.g. the difference between the vowel sounds in 'pitch' and peach'),

❏ avoidance of consonant deletion at the beginnings of words (e.g. the *cri-* in 'crisp'), and only certain deletions intelligible in word-medial and final position (e.g. 'factsheet' as 'facsheet' but not 'fatsheet' or 'facteet'; 'scripts' as 'scrips' but not 'scrits' or script'); on the other hand, the avoidance of consonant clusters by means of the addition of vowels, such as 'film' pronounced [fɪləm], seems not to be a problem in ELF, and

❏ production and placement of nuclear (tonic) stress, e.g. in Ian McEwan's novel

Amsterdam, one character sends a postcard to another, on which he has written 'You deserve to be sacked'. This can be interpreted either as 'You deserve to be **sacked**' (but you have not been) or 'You de**serve** to be sacked' (and you have been).

This is not by any means to suggest that the LFC features are needed *all the time*. Use of these features depends crucially on who is talking with whom. Obviously, if conversation partners both come from L1s that have e.g. one sound for /r/ and /l/, or use /v/ where other varieties use /w/, it is unnecessary for them to produce these sounds for intelligibility between themselves. Quite the opposite in fact: use of their shared variant would signal solidarity between them. Accommodation is key here, and successful ELF pronunciation (like any other linguistic level) will depend on speakers' ability to 'shuttle between communities' (Canagarajah 2005: xxiii), adjusting their English as they do so, for the benefit of their addressees, rather than conforming to any preset notions of correctness (as is the case with EFL).

The following features of ENL pronunciation were not found to contribute to intelligibility in ELF, and did not lead to communication problems when they were substituted with a feature influenced by the speaker's L1 pronunciation:

❏ these consonant sounds: voiceless 'th' /θ/, voiced 'th' /ð/, and dark 'l' [ɫ],
❏ vowel quality (e.g. in the above conversation between R and S, R pronounces the word 'ch<u>a</u>rity' as 'ch<u>e</u>rity', and 'fr<u>o</u>nt' as [frɒnt] with the vowel like that in RP 'song',
❏ weak forms (e.g. the vowel sound in 'to', 'from' and 'of' when replaced with a schwa,
❏ other features of connected speech such as assimilation (adjusting one sound to become like the next, e.g. 're<u>d</u> paint' to 'reb paint') and elision (leaving sounds out, e.g. 'prob<u>a</u>bly' as 'probly', 'frien<u>d</u>ship' as 'frienship'),
❏ the direction of pitch movements,
❏ the placement of wordstress, which varies considerably even across L1 Englishes, and
❏ stress-timed rhythm.

As far as these items are concerned, the ELF pronunciation position is that when ELF speakers replace these 'non-core' features of ENL with forms influenced by their own L1s, the results should be regarded as instances of legitimate regional variation rather than errors. In other words, supporters of ELF believe that Expanding Circle ELF speakers should have the same rights as Inner and Outer Circle speakers in terms of their regional accents being accepted, rather than having their local pronunciation features described as 'errors'.

ELF processes

We have looked in detail at some of the observed features of ELF. What is striking is how much their evolution has in common with changes that have occurred – and are still occurring – in ENL. English, like any living language, evolves over time through natural processes such as regularisation. For example, the six Old English present tense verb endings from the eighth century have, over the years, been reduced to two endings, –s on the third person singular and zero marking on the others. So we might expect this process to continue and the –s to be replaced with zero eventually. Another reason why language evolves in particular ways is physiological. Certain sounds, for example, are more 'marked' than others, i.e. less frequent in the world's languages, mainly because they are more difficult to articulate. An example of a very marked sound is the voiceless dental fricative /θ/, so it would be logical to expect this sound to die out. A further factor is 'recoverability'. According to the notion of recoverability (Weinberger 1987), ambiguity is far more likely to result from the removal of phonological information than from its addition. This may help explain why native English speakers replace weak forms with strong forms when intelligibility is critical, and why some ENL varieties have no weak forms at all. It may also explain why the addition of vowels did not cause problems in the ELF pronunciation data, whereas the removal of sounds often did.

Many of the features described earlier as potential lexicogrammatical and pronunciation features of ELF have resulted from natural processes similar to those that have been affecting ENL down the ages, and, more recently, the Outer Circle Englishes. The difference is that a crucial new factor has entered the equation: language contact on a massive scale among Expanding Circle speakers. So not only is there the usual contact involved in bilingual creativity, that is, contact between the local language(s) and English, resulting in new local forms such as German speakers' preference for 'handy' rather than ENL 'mobile phone'/'cell phone', or South Korean speakers' use of 'on life' in preference to ENL 'alive' (Shim 1999: 252). Now there is also the vast amount of intercultural communication via ELF. What seems to be happening, as Lowenberg (2002) demonstrates, is that ELF speakers in many cases, through the mutual reinforcement that arises from contact among them, are simply accelerating the processes that have already been taking place more slowly in ENL. The problem for ELF speakers is that when they innovate in such ways (e.g. by using ENL uncountable nouns as count nouns – 'informations', 'advices', etc.), the outcome is inevitably described as 'error' until it has been 'sanctioned' by native English speaker use.

Attitudes towards ELF

The previous point leads us to the issue of attitudes towards ELF. The notion that ELF speakers should have the right to innovate in ways such as these, and that the outcome of their innovations should be considered legitimate forms of English rather than errors, has been controversial, to say the least. While some have seen ELF as common sense, even democratic, others have been outraged by the notion that there could be any challenge to the authority of British and American English standards in the Expanding Circle. This is an example of the more negative kinds of comment: '. . . giving up on this high objective [RP] – and the LFC boils down to this exactly – will easily bring the ideal down into the gutter with no checkpoint along the way' (Sobkowiak 2005: 141). Another commentator dismisses ELF as nothing more than political correctness, 'a PC-based stance' (Waters 2007: 358). And a well-known ELT materials writer devoted his entire talk at the 2008 IATEFL (International Association of Teachers of English as a Foreign Language) conference to attacking the notion of ELF, giving his talk the title 'ELF and other fairy stories'.

There are even sociolinguists who share such perceptions, e.g. Görlach (2002: 12–13) refers to ELF forms as 'broken, deficient forms of English', adding that '[t]here is no danger of such deviant uses "polluting" the standards of native speakers'. Trudgill (2002: 150–1) makes a similar point, arguing that such forms are 'interesting and amusing' but that '[t]he true repository of English is its native speakers, and there are so many of them that they can afford to let non-native speakers do what they like with it so long as what they do is confined to a few words here and there'. The reading in D6 responds in detail to perceptions of these kinds. For now, the most it is possible to say about ELF is that it is at a relatively early stage in its development and thus, despite its current impact, positive as well as negative, its future is as yet unclear.

Activity

❏ Coleman (2006: 3) believes that '[o]nce ELF has been objectively described and has lost its stigma, and once the previously assumed target of native speaker proficiency is set aside as unrealistic and unnecessary, then new and less inequitable conceptions of global English and its learning and teaching become possible'. Do you agree or disagree? Why?

❏ What is your response to the following claim?

There really is no justification for doggedly persisting in referring to an item as 'an error' if the vast majority of the world's L2 English speakers produce and understand it. Instead, it is for L1 speakers to move their own receptive goal posts and adjust their own expectations as far as *international* (but not *intranational*) uses of English are concerned.

(Jenkins 2000: 160)

❏ Do you see any similarities in the negative attitudes towards ELF, Singlish and Estuary English (see C4)? If so, how do you account for them?

❏ If ELF does become accepted and widespread in intercultural communication, do you predict any problems for native English speakers?

C7 **ASIAN ENGLISHES IN THE OUTER AND EXPANDING CIRCLES**

In this unit we explore in greater detail recent developments in English use in three Asian settings: India, Hong Kong and China. In particular we will consider roles of and attitudes towards the local variety. These three settings have been selected because while they have a certain amount in common, there are important differences both in the ways in which English functions in each context and in the attitudes of their users towards their own English. In particular, whereas Indian English is a firmly established and widely accepted variety, the status of Hong Kong English is still ambivalent, while China English is in the early stages of its development and is not considered a variety of English by the majority, either inside or outside the region.

Indian English

According to Crystal, India has approximately 200 million L2 and 350,000 L1 English speakers, in other words, almost as many as the number of L1 and L2 English speakers in the US (around 241 million). On the other hand, if Kachru (2006: 453) is correct, then the figure for English users in India is nearer 333 million, well above that for the US. Either way, this means that India, at least for now, has one of the two highest populations of English speakers, even if China may take over at some point in the not too distant future.

The earliest English language policy for India was enshrined in Macaulay's famous Minute of 1835, passed shortly after he arrived in Calcutta to take his seat on the Supreme Council of India:

> We must at present do our best to form a class who may be interpreters between us and the millions whom we govern; a class of persons, Indian in blood and colour, but English in taste, in opinions, in morals, and in intellect. To that class we may leave it to refine the vernacular dialects of the country, to enrich those dialects with terms of science borrowed from Western nomenclature, and to render them by degrees fit vehicles for conveying knowledge to the great mass of the population.
>
> (quoted in Bailey 1991: 138)

This became the British government's official language policy in India, giving the English language priority in Indian administration, education and society. English-medium universities and schools and an English press were established in India, and contributed to the gradual encroachment of English on Indian languages and its role as the official language and primary lingua franca of the country.

In the post-independence era from 1947, in an attempt to acknowledge the strength of nationalist feeling, especially in the pro-Hindi camp, the 1950 Constitution of India declared Hindi the official national language, but allowed English to continue to be used for official purposes for a further fifteen years, after which it was gradually to be replaced by Hindi. This policy proved unsuccessful in part because of anti-Hindi feeling in southern India, and in 1967 the Official Languages (Amendment) Act provided that English would be the 'associate' official language and could continue to be used alongside Hindi in all official matters at the national level. In addition, the Constitution recognised eighteen regional languages as having the right to function as the official languages of individual states.

In practice, however, there is something of a contradiction between government policy and language use, as English continues to be used as the primary de facto official national language and is also the official language of many of the states in the south and north-east. In fact, in the post-independence period there has been a steady growth in the use of English in the country, with English nowadays being used primarily for communication among Indians rather than with native speakers of English. This is not primarily on account of anti-Hindi feeling in these parts of the country, although the role of English as a *neutral* language of wider communication certainly plays a part. More important are its perceived usefulness both within India and internationally; the fact that English has not killed off India's indigenous languages but functions in a complementary relationship with them; and the steady growth of an Indian English identity which finds expression in a linguistic variety with its own grammatical, lexical, phonological and discoursal norms.

In adapting to local cultural norms, Indian English has developed its own varietal characteristics through the interaction of Indian languages and social behaviours with those of English. These characteristics differ in quite major ways from British English and would still be considered 'deviant' by those who take an interlanguage/ fossilisation view of the indigenised varieties of English (see B7). The Indianisation of English essentially involves on the one hand adaptations of existing features of British English and on the other, the use of transferred mother-tongue items where British English lacks the scope to express a particular concept – or, to put it another way, where British English is 'deficient'. At the discoursal level, Indian English also makes considerable use of code-switching and code-mixing.

Activity

❏   Here are some examples of Indian English (all taken from Parasher 2001). What are the lexical, grammatical, discoursal and any other features which identify these as specifically Indian English usage? (The key is at the end of the section.)

1 Newspaper advertisement
Brahmin girl, divorcee kashyapa, 35, B.Com. H, 5' 3″, very fair, respectable family, issueless, Govt. employee UDC Hyderbad Rs.5,000/-p.m., required well settled broad-minded life partner from same caste.
Write Box no. . . .

                                          Deccan Chronicle, 5 October 1997

2 Politeness formulae
(a)   It will not be out of place to request you to send us the details of chemicals, etc.
(b)   Kindly please advise me.
(c)   I invite your kind attention.
(d)   I respectfully submit the following few lines for favour of your kind consideration.

3 Honorifics
Helloji
Thank youji
Doctorji
Doctor Sahib

4 Code-switching and code-mixing

A: Good morning.

B: Good morning

A: Kya haal hen. (How are you?)
    Kayi din se aap dikhai nahin diye. (I haven't seen you for a long time.)

B: Men Dilli gaya hua tha, ek selection committee ki meeting thi. (I was away in Delhi. There was a Selection Committee meeting.)

❏ Finally, growing acceptance of English as an Indian language is not universal and is still the subject of considerable debate. Below is a letter to the editor of the *Maharashtra Herald*, an English daily newspaper published in Pune which responds to an interview published a few days earlier. It is followed by a second letter sent to the editor four days later in reply to the first. Read the two letters and decide firstly which writer you support and why, and secondly, how you would have answered the writer of the first letter, bearing in mind what you have read in this unit.

Mother Tongue Supreme

This refers to writer Ruchira Mukherjee's assertion that, 'People are beginning to think in English' (*Maharashtra Herald*, 5 October).

Well, the question is: Can an Indian really think in English? As far as thinking is concerned, one can only think in one's mother tongue.

Since English is an alien tongue to every Indian, no Indian can claim to think in English. Because it is linguistically next to impossible to be equally at ease with a target language, which English is, for every Indian.

I've been speaking Persian right from my childhood. In fact Persian was the first language I picked up. My Persian is as good as that of a native speaker of Iran and Central Asia and it's replete with typical native idiosyncracies and idioms of written and colloquial Persian.

Yet Persian is not the language of my consciousness, though I do my written work mostly in this language.

My mother tongue, which is Bengali, always comes to me naturally and it predominates my thinking process. Likewise, however good one may be at English, he can't have that native sensibility.

You can never iron out the ingrained impressions of your respective mother tongue which at times prevail over English or for that matter, any language learnt at a relatively later stage. English will always play second fiddle to an Indian's linguistic mental make up.

(*Maharashtra Herald*, 13 October 1998, quoted in D'Souza 2001: 148)

What's Mother Tongue?

Sumit Paul's letter 'Mother Tongue Supreme' of October 13 is not correct. He wonders if an Indian can 'really think in English'.

First of all, I would like to define mother tongue. The mother tongue of an Indian can be French or English or anything. One's mother tongue is that which one learns from infancy. (For example, a language learnt from one's parents.)

Secondly, if one's parents are, let us say, Bengali, but never spoke to the child in Bengali but only in English, then the mother tongue of the child would be English and not Bengali. A language cannot be inherited, it is taught and learnt.

How can Sumit Paul claim that English is 'an alien tongue to every Indian'? Sumit is not a spokesman for Indians. I personally know many Indians whose parents' language is Hindi or Malayalam or so on, but whose own mother tongue is English, or rather family language is English.

They excel in English above anything else. Many times, even when neither the mother tongue nor family language is English, the person excels in English above all else. Many service officers' families are good examples.

Paul assumes that every Indian first learns his parents' language and then English. And that an Indian has to be better at the parents' language than English. He further assumed that everybody learns first the language of his parents' race, and that it is the same as the language spoken by the parents, and that it is called the mother tongue!

(*MH*, 17 October 1998, quoted in D'Souza 2001: 149)

Activity

❏ In your view, is Indian English a new language? If so, would you describe it as a single language, a mixed or hybrid language, a new variety, or something else?

❏ What are the implications of linguistic varieties such as Indian English for the study of languages in isolation and for the study of bi- and multi-lingualism? Has the time come when Englishes should be studied primarily as they are used in bilingual and multilingual societies or is it still helpful to study them in monolingual use?

Key/comments

1 Newspaper advertisement

This sort of text is commonly found in contemporary Indian newspapers among educated middle/upper-middle-class families, where marriages are 'arranged'. Two items are transferred directly from the mother tongue (*kashyapa*, and *issueless* meaning 'childless'). Otherwise the lexis is not unlike British English, although the information is more densely packed than would typically be found in a British advertisement, and the sociocultural assumptions are very different.

2 Politeness formulae

Parasher, from whom the examples are taken, notes a tendency for Indian English to use indirect, roundabout expressions rather than direct, specific ones in requests such as (a) (2001: 27). He also notes the preference for 'please', 'request', and 'kindly' over syntactic devices such as the modal 'could' which are common in British English. The four exponents are all examples of formulae used by Indian English speakers.

3 Honorifics

These are borrowed from Indian languages and then added to British English lexical items to mark a polite style. In three of the exponents, the suffix '-ji' is tacked on to the end of a greeting (a), politeness expression (b) and professional title (c), whereas in the fourth, the word 'Sahib' ('sir') follows the title.

Hong Kong English

Hong Kong has a population of over seven million, of whom almost two-and-a-half million speak English (Crystal 2003a), though this assumes there has been no major change in the figures since Hong Kong ceased to be a British crown colony and became a Special Administrative Region in 1997. It was a British colony from 1842 up until this point, and for the first hundred years of colonial rule, the British and Chinese communities led separate lives as a result of language barriers, racial prejudice and cultural differences. On those occasions when they did make contact, it was mainly for business purposes, and communication was for the most part conducted in pidgin English (Evans 2000: 198).

During the years of British sovereignty up to the First World War, English was largely restricted in Hong Kong to colonial use and, in particular, to the domains of government, the law, the professions, and education. Then, during the period between the two world wars, a Western-educated Chinese elite started to become involved in business and the professions, and by the 1960s, English had metamorphosed from a colonial language used only by a small Chinese elite to an important language of wider communication in the region. This was primarily the result of 'the transformation of Hong Kong from a colonial backwater into a leading centre of business and finance' (Evans 2000: 198). And because English had, during the same period, emerged as the international lingua franca, a much larger number of ethnic Chinese needed to be proficient in the language.

English is now spoken in Hong Kong by over seven million people, of whom almost a third are L2 speakers (see A2). This means that it is spoken by a similar percentage to that for the highest estimate of the number of L2 speakers of Indian English, and a considerably larger percentage of the more common estimate of 200 million L2 Indian English speakers. Despite this, the position of Hong Kong English as an accepted variety is far less secure. While its existence is often acknowledged, it is apparently not the variety to which many L2 Hong Kong English speakers aspire. Instead, they remain attached to British English norms of correctness, and, despite the fact that Hong Kong English is often categorised as an Outer Circle English (see Figure A7.2), some see it as belonging in the Expanding Circle.

Whether it is the cause or result of such factors, unlike Indian English, there are few reference works such as dictionaries and pedagogic grammars that acknowledge the existence of a legitimate Hong Kong English. Meanwhile, attitudes among Hong Kong's teachers of English suggest that it could be some time before the local English is used as a pedagogic model. In a study into attitudes, teachers were asked where they looked for models of correctness and acceptability (Tsui and Bunton 2000). The vast majority who responded (of whom two-thirds were native speakers of English) cited native speaking countries, particularly Britain, and tended to be cautious or even critical of local Hong Kong sources. The term 'Hong Kong English' did not occur in any of the (1,234) responses, and there were no favourable references to deviations from native speaker norms. This may, of course, be connected to the fact that so many of the respondents were themselves L1 English speakers. However, there was no evidence of the existence of a Hong Kong English identity among the L2 English respondents. And as Joseph (2004: 160) points out:

> only if and when teachers come to recognise that the 'errors' in Hong Kong English (at least the regularly occurring ones) are precisely the points at which a distinct Hong Kong identity is expressed in the language, will a Hong Kong English genuinely begin to emerge, and to be taken as a version of standard English rather than as a departure from it.

This recognition may not be feasible while such a large proportion of English teachers in Hong Kong are native speakers of English, who are imported along with high-stakes Anglo English tests such as TOEFL, IELTS and LPAT, as Luk and Lin (2006) point out.

Nevertheless, Bolton (2000: 267) asks, is it not the case that 'conditions now exist for a recognition of the autonomy of Hong Kong English, on a par with other Englishes in the Asian region?'. He goes on to provide evidence of both a Hong Kong accent (as do Hung 2000 and Deterding 2006) and a Hong Kong English lexis.

Activity

As regards vocabulary, a number of Hong Kong English items are included in the Macquarie dictionary (see B7 for a description of the dictionary). The following are examples of entries cited by Bolton (2000: 280). If you are not familiar with Hong Kong English, can you guess their meanings (the key is at the end of this section)?

1 ABC
2 Ah
3 astronaut
4 BBC
5 big brother
6 black hand
7 black society
8 bo lei
9 Buddha's delight
10 Canto-speak
11 Canto star
12 char siew
13 China doll
14 Chinglish
15 chit

Bolton (2003: 90) also points out that '[a]mong the non-Chinese minorities of Hong Kong there is much greater linguistic and ethnic diversity than has previously been recognised', while Kirkpatrick (2007a: 140) observes that there is also 'greater linguistic diversity among the Chinese community' than generally realised. Clearly, then, in a multilingual society of this kind, there is scope for a local English to develop into an established variety and serve as a local lingua franca. To this, Kirkpatrick (2007a) adds the effect of the 1997 hand-back of Hong Kong to the People's Republic of China, arguing that it may be creating a sense of Hong Kong identity among the Hong Kong Chinese. This identity may also involve a growing attachment towards English, with people looking back to the time of British rule as a time of 'a benevolent, non-intrusive government and a politically stable shelter offering security and promising prosperity' (Li 2002: 40).

According to Schneider's dynamic model of the evolution of New Englishes (2003: 243–54), a postcolonial English goes through five stages in its development: foundation, exonormative stabilisation, nativisation, endonormative stabilisation, and differentiation. Hong Kong, argues Schneider, is at stage three, in light of evidence that 'Hong Kong English has developed a distinct vocabulary segment of its own', and that 'it cannot be disputed any longer that there exists a Hong Kong English accent' that is 'developing distinct rules and features of its own (Peng and Setter 2000)'. Like Bolton, he believes that this accent 'is beginning to be regarded as a positively evaluated source of identification' for Hong Kong students (Schneider 2003: 260). Perhaps, then, as is so often the case, language change is being led by the young, and through them, Hong Kong English will soon move on to Schneider's fourth stage and become an endonormative English instead of looking outside to Britain for its norms (to the extent that it still does so). A final possibility, suggested by Deterding (2006: 172), is that now that there is pressure on children in Hong Kong schools to learn Mandarin, 'it may indeed happen that Hong Kong English will be further influenced by both Cantonese and Mandarin'.

 Activity

> If you are familiar with the Hong Kong setting, how do you see the future of English there? Do you agree with any of those who believe that Hong Kong has already developed, or is in the process of developing, its own variety of English? Or do you agree with those who think it will remain dependent on British English norms? Or do you believe the outcome will be something else entirely?

Key

1 an Australian-born Chinese/American-born Chinese
2 an informal term of address: *Ah Sam/Ah Chan*
3 a public servant in the most senior career grade in the Hong Kong Civil Service
4 a British-born Chinese
5 a Chinese kinship term referring to the eldest male sibling in a family, or a recruiter or protector in a Chinese secret society or triad
6 a behind-the-scenes mastermind who plans political or criminal activities
7 a Chinese secret society or triad
8 a variety of strong black tea
9 a vegetarian dish of bean curd, nuts, tiger lilies and a hair-like seaweed which is particularly popular at Chinese New Year, as the Cantonese name of the seaweed (*fat choi* or 'hair vegetable') sounds very similar to the New Year greeting wishing prosperity
10 the Cantonese language
11 a singer of Cantonese pop songs
12 Chinese-style roast pork
13 a pretty young Chinese woman of submissive demeanour
14 any variety of English strongly influenced by Chinese, or any variety of Chinese featuring a high proportion of English loanwords
15 bill

See Bolton (2003: 288–97) for many more examples of Hong Kong English vocabulary.

China English

We turn now to China, whose English is very clearly an Expanding Circle variety, at least for the time being. As Bolton (2003: 228) points out, 'there has been a dramatic and rapid spread of English throughout China in the last forty years or so'. In 1957, he tells us, there were only 850 secondary school English teachers, whereas by 2000, the number had risen to over 500,000, with numbers due to rise as the learning of English is extended to primary schools. There are now in excess of 200 million English speakers in China, and the number is rising fast with around 50 million secondary school children learning the language. If this development continues, there will soon be more speakers of China English in the world than of any other English variety.

But to what extent can we yet call China English a 'variety'? Kirkpatrick and Xu (2002) present evidence of the existence of certain discourse and rhetorical norms derived from Chinese in the English of speakers of L1 Chinese languages. And Kirkpatrick (2007a) presents lexical, grammatical and phonological features of Chinese English speakers' English, while Deterding et al. (2006) provide a detailed analysis of their English phonology. Lexical examples include nativised words such as *pu-ke* for card games in general (from ENL 'poker'), and direct translation of Chinese metaphors such as 'a flowered pillowcase' meaning 'someone who is good-looking but otherwise useless' (see Kirkpatrick 2007a: 146–51 for many more examples). The most salient and widespread features of China English pronunciation appear to be: 'replacement of /θ/ and /ð/ with [s], insertion of a final [ə], avoidance of weak forms for function words, and stressing of final pronouns' (Deterding et al. 2006: 194). Other features, they note, are less widespread as they depend on the specific L1 Chinese language of the speaker.

Kirkpatrick and Xu (2002: 269) argue that such features

> should not be seen as 'deviations' from Anglo norms, but that, as Chinese speakers are more likely to use the language with other English speakers in the East Asian region rather than with speakers of inner circle varieties of English, the Chinese variety of English is actually a more culturally appropriate model of English than any superimposed 'Anglo' norm.

And Kirkpatrick (2007a: 151) implies that China English already meets sufficient criteria to be considered an emerging new variety of English. He finds this 'quite remarkable given the relatively short time in which the Chinese have embraced the learning of English'. As he also points out, recent studies such as Hu 2005 (and see Hu 2004 in unit D7) show that Chinese English speakers themselves are already moving towards accepting China English as a variety. Deterding et al. (2006: 195) hold a similar view, although they are slightly more reticent about the current status of China English:

> As an ever-expanding number of speakers of English in China become proficient in the language, it is likely that distinctive styles of Chinese English will continue to emerge, and one day a new variety may become established with its own independent identity.

On the other hand, they all believe it is likely that China English is destined to grow in importance: that it will become the most common variety of English spoken in Asia (Kirkpatrick), and have more speakers than the total for North America and Britain (Deterding et al.). And at the point when this happens, argue Deterding et al. (2006: 195), 'it may start to have a major impact on the way the [English] language evolves'. Nevertheless, as Kirkpatrick and Xu (2002) point out, it is not yet clear that educators and government officials in China will accept China English as a classroom model.

| What do you predict will happen to China English over the next ten years? | Activity |

LANGUAGE KILLER OR LANGUAGE PROMOTER?   C8

In this final unit of section C, we will consider two very different perspectives on the effects of the global spread of English: firstly, its potential to cause the deaths of other languages; and secondly, its role within a framework of bilingualism.

English as a killer language

Crystal begins his book *Language Death* (2000) by asking some key questions. Try to answer them before looking at Crystal's answers below:

1   How many languages are there in the world today?
2   At what rate are they dying off?
3   How many of the world's languages are spoken by fewer than 1,000 people?
4   How many indigenous languages are there in North America?

Recent estimates of the number of languages in the world vary between 3,000 and 10,000, but by most definitions of a 'language' the figure lies between 6,000 and 7,000.

Over the next century, something like two languages will die each month. A quarter of the world's languages are spoken by fewer than 1,000 people. Though estimates vary, there may still be close to two hundred indigenous languages in use in North America.

Trudgill points this out in his review of another book on the subject, Grenoble and Whaley's *Endangered Languages* (1998):

> One of the greatest cultural tragedies ever to befall the human race is taking place before our eyes but no one is paying attention. There are members of the British intelligentsia who profess to be concerned about language and who agonise over utter trivialities such as the failure of the nation to use *hopefully* or to place *only* 'correctly'. Here is what they should be worrying about: of the world's 6,000 or so languages, as many as 3,000 are in the process of dying out, and another 2,400 are endangered.
>
> (*Times Higher Education Supplement*, 8 May 1998: 26; emphasis in original)

The first stage in the process of reversing **language death** is to identify the cause. Although no one factor is likely to prove singly responsible for the dramatic loss of languages which we are currently witnessing, one cause is frequently named by endangered language experts as bearing the greatest share of responsibility: the English language. The English language, of course, does not exist in a vacuum, but must be considered within the framework of globalisation as a whole. That is, English operates in a global context in which the most politically and economically powerful English speakers – those in the Inner Circle countries – have now benefited massively and disproportionately from the spread of the language.

Activity

> ❏ To what extent has exploitation by the countries of the 'centre' been responsible for causing speakers of other languages, especially the smaller languages, to replace their mother tongues with English for some or even all important language functions?
> ❏ How far has the endemic monolingualism of the Inner Circle countries played a part in the process?

❏ Here are some quotations taken from various writings on endangered languages. Read them and decide – with the help of first-hand knowledge if you speak or are familiar with an endangered language yourself – how far you agree or disagree with them. You might also like to refer back to the discussion in C1 of the English Only campaign in the USA.

Europeans who came from polities with a history of standardizing and promoting just one high-prestige speech form carried their 'ideology of contempt' for subordinate languages with them when they conquered far-flung territories, to the serious detriment of indigenous languages. And in addition . . . Europeans . . . seriously confounded technological and linguistic development . . . Unable to conceive that a people who lacked a rich material culture might possess a highly developed, richly complex language, they wrongly assumed that primitive technological means implied primitive linguistic means . . .

Two other European beliefs about language are also likely to have had an unfavorable impact on the survival of indigenous languages in the very considerable portions of the globe where a standardized European language became the language of the dominant social strata . . . Particularly widespread and well established is a belief in a linguistic survival of the fittest, a social Darwinism of language. This belief encourages people of European background to assume a correlation between adaptive and expressive capacity in a language and that language's survival and spread. Since their own languages are prominent among those which have both survived and spread, this is of course a self-serving belief . . .

The second of the additional beliefs disadvantageous to indigenous languages in regions dominated by speakers of European languages may actually be more characteristic of Anglophones than of speakers of other European languages. Anglophones however are particularly thickly distributed in regions that once had large numbers of indigenous languages, so English single-handedly threatens a disproportionate number of other languages. The belief in question is that bilingualism (and by extension multilingualism, all the more so) is onerous, even on the individual level. This belief is so widespread, in fact, that it can be detected even among linguists.

(Dorian 1998: 9–11)

Most Western countries participate in murdering the chances that they might have to increase the linguistic diversity in their countries, because they do not give immigrants and refugees much chance of maintaining and developing their languages. Development co-operation also participates, with very few exceptions, in murdering small languages and supporting subtractive spread of the big killer languages, especially English. 'Subtractive spread' means that new languages are not learned in addition to the language(s) people already have, but instead of them, at the cost of the mother tongue(s), The whole homogenisation process that globalisation is made to 'demand' has to be problematised and nuanced before it is too late.

(Skuttnab-Kangas 1999: 6–7)

Those who control particular linguistic resources are in a position of power over others. Linguistic capital, like all other forms of capital, is unequally distributed in society. The higher the profit to be achieved through knowledge of a particular language, the more it will be viewed as worthy of acquisition. The language of the global village (or McWorld, as some have called it) is English: not to use it is to risk ostracization from the benefits of the global economy

(Nettle and Romaine 2000: 30–1)

Educational policy is another striking example of misguided strategies imported from the West into developing countries. Believing that tribal languages stood in the way of unity and were not suitable as languages of education and technology essential for western-style development, most newly independent countries did not develop their own languages, but continued using the languages of their former colonisers even when most of their citizens did not know them. Western policies and practices have generally reinforced European languages . . . Development agents sent into the field rarely bother to learn the local languages, which leads to communication problems. The World Bank and International Monetary Fund seldom make reference to the possible role indigenous languages might play in development. The use of western school curricula in developing countries tends to devalue traditional culture and excludes formal study of traditional knowledge systems. Younger members of the culture are educated to believe that traditional knowledge is not worth learning because it will not lead to a job.

(Nettle and Romaine 2000: 160–4)

'Globalisation is the wave of the future', more than one recent newspaper headline (not to mention the received popular wisdom) has announced, and, to some extent, this is so. But globalisation is both a constructive and a destructive phenomenon, both a unifying and a divisive one, and it is definitely not a culturally neutral or impartial one. In our day and age, it is definitely the globalisation of pan-Western culture (and pop-consumer culture in particular) that is the motor of language shift. And since America-dominated globalisation has become the major economic, technological and cultural thrust of worldwide modernisation and Westernisation, efforts to safeguard threatened languages (and, therefore, inevitably, contextually weaker languages) must oppose the very strongest processes and powers that the world knows today. That, in a word, is exactly why it is so hard to save threatened languages.

(Fishman 2001: 6)

English-knowing bilingualism

Bilingualism and multilingualism, though threatened to some extent by language death, and though regarded as aberrations by English mother-tongue speakers in the UK and US, are the de facto norm throughout the rest of the world. Speakers of 'big' languages, particularly English, meanwhile, have long been reluctant to acquire other languages, have expected others to make the effort to learn 'their' language, and have viewed code-switching as a sign of linguistic incompetence. However, bilingualism will by definition play a critical role in the prevention of language death so long as efforts are made to persuade learners of English that they should become practition-ers of **English-knowing bilingualism** (see Pakir 1991, 2002; Kachru 1982/1992): that is, they are made aware of the value of maintaining within their linguistic repertoires their indigenous language(s) for local identity functions alongside their English.

If English-knowing bilingualism is to become the recognised rather than begrudgingly tolerated world norm, however, it will be crucial for the (largely mono-lingual) mother-tongue English speech communities to embrace the concept – and not merely as an acceptable practice for non-English mother tongue 'others', but as one in which they themselves engage. Such an engagement will enable 'citizens of the UK, the USA, Canada, Australia, New Zealand, and other largely English-speaking coun-tries . . . to avoid being the monolingual dinosaurs in a multilingual world' (Brumfit 2002: 11). Moreover, with bilingualism will come flexibility and accommodation skills of the sort these citizens have always expected of English-speaking 'others' whenever English is spoken in cross-cultural contexts.

As was clear in the quotation from Hilary Footitt in unit A6, people need to speak second languages in order to develop intercultural competence. This is not to say that people need necessarily to *acquire* these cultural practices along with the languages: it will depend on whether they will be speaking a particular language with its native speakers. In the case of learners of English for local (Outer Circle) or international (Expanding Circle) use this is generally not so, and there is rarely an imperative for them to learn British, American or Australian culture along with the English lan-guage. Indeed, it would be counterproductive for them to make a one-to-one cultural link between the English language and the cultural practices of any one of its minority groups of mother-tongue speakers, when their goal is to use English in predominantly non-English mother-tongue contexts. But awareness of the existence of difference is another matter and this is an area in which English mother-tongue speakers have much catching up to do.

English monolingualism is not only a problem for intercultural communica-tion at the international level, however. Within the Inner Circle countries there are, through immigration, increasingly large numbers of non-L1 English speakers. In Brit-ain, around one person in fourteen is now from an ethnic minority group and this trend is predicted to continue. In the US, the numbers are far greater, as a result of both more extensive immigration and the existence of the indigenous population. But in both communities, the learning of another language – any language – would help to reduce that fear of the 'other' which is bred out of ignorance of difference, and which often leads to racist attitudes and behaviours, and to campaigns such as Eng-lish Only. Better still would be the learning of one of the community languages of the immigrant population, or one of the heritage languages of the indigenous peoples, a practice which began a few years ago in New Zealand, where the Maori language is being taught in some **Pakeha** (New Zealander of European origin) schools. Despite the latter example, though, the expectation is overwhelmingly that immigrant and indigenous minorities (which in some cases are very large minorities) should learn the lingua-cultural practices of the L1 English population.

The monolingual emphasis among English L1 speakers can cause problems in international contexts, where English is used as a medium for communication that does not relate to intranational (either Inner or Outer Circle) functions. The problem is hierarchical. That is, educated (but monolingual!) L1 English speakers, unaware of the superiority of the bilingual's linguistic repertoire and skills, assume the right to the senior position in the English language hierarchy. English for international use thus has at its pinnacle, and serving as global models, the varieties of English used by a small minority of (L1) English speakers. Yet many of these are among the least linguistically able speakers of English as an international lingua franca in the world, the least able to exercise accommodation skills (adjusting their language to facilitate communication), and the most biased against other varieties of the English language whether non-standard L1 or standard/non-standard L2 (see Figure C8.1).

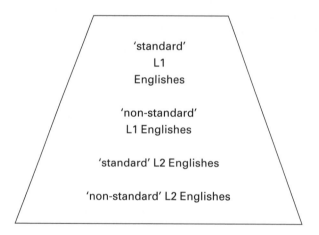

Figure C8.1 Traditional hierarchy of Englishes.

On the other hand, if we reconceptualise the hierarchy by taking into account the advantages of English-knowing bilingualism and of what is involved in being an English-using bilingual, we come up with a very different hierarchy. This time, we prioritise the varieties of English spoken by its bilingual speakers, be they L2 or (though less likely) L1 speakers (see Figure C8.2). In addition, we put intranational (local) varieties at the equivalent level in the hierarchy, be they ENL or ESL varieties, rather than adopting the traditional practice of placing Inner Circle standard Englishes above Outer Circle ones.

One final point to make about English-using bilinguals is that the code-switching of those who speak Expanding rather than Outer Circle varieties of English does

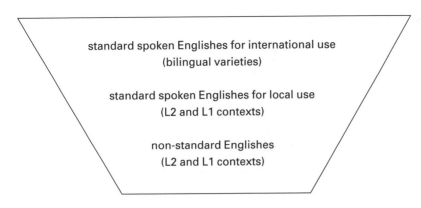

Figure C8.2 Reconceptualised hierarchy of Englishes.

not, as is sometimes claimed, serve purely communicative functions. Rather, it is also frequently used as a means of promoting identity and self-expression. Matsuda (2000: 52–3), for example, reports the following comments from participants in her study of Japanese–English bilinguals:

❏ I use Japanese when I request something. Japanese is softer . . . don't you think so? And when I apologize . . . well, I might use English if I don't really feel like apologizing. A Japanese apology sounds more sincere (Keiko).
❏ I think my personality differs in English and Japanese. I'm more *wild* when I speak English . . . I mean, more outgoing and not so *conservative*. Yeah, I'm more *conservative* in Japanese. I feel '*this is me*' when I can say something in English (Chikako).
❏ My personality changes from Japanese mode to English mode. I'm more sarcastic and joking all the time and outgoing and, well, that's when I'm speaking English. In Japanese, I'm quieter (Eriko).

Again, it is the monolingual mindset which is unable to grasp the fact that a language does not have to be a mother tongue in order to be capable of expressing aspects of a speaker's social identity. And if English remains the world's primary international language, the expressive function is likely to become increasingly central to its international use.

Activity

❏ In the year 2000, a Conservative member of the (then) UK parliament, the shadow health secretary Liam Fox, launched a verbal attack on overseas doctors in the UK, arguing that 'Their English language skills are not up to scratch and patients are suffering as a result' (*The Guardian*, 28 August 2000, p. 2). He announced that a Conservative government, if elected, would introduce 'a tough English language test that might apply to overseas doctors already working in Britain'. The ensuing debate was heated, with some arguing that overseas doctors from outside the EU already had to pass stringent English language tests, and that the charge amounted to racism. On the other hand, others claimed, for example, that overseas doctors 'cannot communicate with patients because they cannot understand the everyday language' (letter to the editor, *The Guardian*, 4 September 2000), or called into question the overseas doctors' English accents. To what extent do you believe that racism was involved? And do you think that if the British nation was not so predominantly monolingual, the same charges would have been made? Can you think of any more recent examples of this kind? Do you consider, for instance, that the current Labour government's ruling that all non-EU immigrants must pass a high-level English language test in order to be allowed to stay in the country is similar?

❑ Look back to the two hierarchies of English as an international language. Do you agree with the way in which the traditional hierarchy has been recast? What advantages and disadvantages do you see in each case, and what implications does the second hierarchy have for the future development of English?

Section D

EXTENSION
READINGS IN WORLD ENGLISHES

How to use the readings

The readings in this final section of the book have been selected in order to provide a range of perspectives on the themes of the individual units. You will not necessarily agree with their conclusions, but the purpose of the readings is to engage you critically and encourage you to read still further, so that you are able to develop your own informed views on the subject in hand. After each reading there are suggestions of issues to consider and prompts for discussion, though you are recommended to look through them *before* you read the text itself.

The numbering of the readings corresponds to the numbering of the sections in the previous three parts of the book. Thus, the reading which follows this introduction in D1 relates to the material in A1, B1 and C1, the reading in D2 to the material in A2, B2 and C2, and so on.

D1 ## THE DISCOURSES OF POSTCOLONIALISM

In his earlier book, *The Cultural Politics of English as an International Language* (1994), Alastair Pennycook charted the colonial background underlying the contemporary place of English as the world's primary international language. His 1998 book, *English and the Discourses of Colonialism*, starts with the British departure from Hong Kong in 1997 which, in theory, signalled the ending of mainstream British colonialism. Pennycook demonstrates in this book, however, the extent to which he believes colonialism still permeates both British discourses and those of the postcolonial territories. In the following extract, he looks critically at some of the arguments that are often put forward to justify why the English language 'deserves' its place as the global lingua franca.

Our marvellous tongue

Alastair Pennycook

Alastair Pennycook (reprinted from *English and the Discourses of Colonialism*, London: Routledge, 1998: 133–44)

The wondrous spread of English

The nineteenth century was a time of immense British confidence in their own greatness, and writing on English abounded with glorifications of English and its global spread. [. . .] Although the fervent triumphalism that appears so evident in [. . .] earlier descriptions of the spread of Empire and English is a less acceptable aspect of more recent discourses on the spread of English, I would like to suggest that the same celebratory tone seems to underlie recent, supposedly neutral descriptions of English. Thus, it is interesting to compare Rolleston's (1911) description of the spread of English with Crystal's (1987) from the *Cambridge Encyclopedia of Language*:

Alastair Pennycook

> The British flag waves over more than one-fifth of the habitable globe, one-fourth of the human race acknowledges the sway of the British Monarch, more than one hundred princes render him allegiance. The English language is spoken by more people than that of any other race, it bids fair to become at some time the speech of the globe, and about one-half of the world's ocean shipping trade is yet in British hands.
>
> (Rolleston 1911: 75)

> English is used as an official or semi-official language in over 60 countries, and has a prominent place in a further 20. It is either dominant or well established in all six continents. It is the main language of books, newspapers, airports and air-traffic control, international business and academic conferences, science, technology, medicine, diplomacy, sports, international competitions, pop music, and advertising. Over two-thirds of the world's scientists write in English. Of all the information in the world's electronic retrieval systems, 80 per cent is stored in English. English radio programmes are received by over 150 million in 120 countries.
>
> (Crystal 1987: 358)

The similarities become more obvious when we turn to other books and articles on English. Bryson's (1990) book *Mother Tongue: The English Language* starts: 'More than 300 million people in the world speak English and the rest, it sometimes seems, try to' (p. 1). [. . .] Claiborne (1983) opens his book *The Life and Times of the English Language: The History of Our Marvellous Tongue* with:

> By any standard, English is a remarkable language. It is, to begin with, the native tongue of some 300,000,000 people – the largest speech community in the world except for Mandarin Chinese. Even more remarkable is its geographical spread, in which it is second to none; its speakers range from Point Barrow, Alaska, to the Falkland Islands; from Hong Kong to Tasmania . . . English is also by far the most important 'second language' in the world. It is spoken by tens of millions of educated Europeans and Japanese, is the most widely studied foreign tongue in both the USSR and China, and serves as an 'official' language in more than a dozen other countries whose populations total more than a thousand million . . . English is the lingua franca of scientists, of air pilots and traffic controllers around the world, of students hitch-hiking around Europe, and of dropouts meditating in India and Nepal.
>
> (Claiborne 1983: 1–2)

and so on and so on.

[. . .]

According to Simon Jenkins (1995), attempts to introduce artificial languages have failed because 'English has triumphed. Those who do not speak it are at a universal disadvantage against those who do. Those who deny this supremacy merely seek to keep the disadvantaged deprived.' As we shall see later, this notion of 'linguistic deprivation' for those who do not speak English and even for those who do not speak it as a native language starts to have very particular significance within this discourse.

At times, too, the descriptions of this global spread start to use terms even more reminiscent of the prose of George (1867) or de Quincey (1862) and their

**Alastair
Pennycook**

talk of 'destiny' and the inevitable spread of English being like a mighty river flowing towards the sea. An editorial in *The Sunday Times* (UK) (10 July 1994), responding to the attempts in France to limit the use of English in various public domains, thunders against the French for opposing the 'European lingua franca which will inevitably be English'. To oppose English is pointless, the editorial warns, since 'English fulfils its own destiny as Churchill's "ever-conquering language". With every shift in international politics, every turn of the world's economies, every media development and every technological revolution, English marches on'. The editorial then returns to slightly more sober language:

> No other country in Europe works itself into such a frenzy about the way English eases the paths of multi-national discussion and assumes an ever-growing role as the language of power and convenience. The Germans, Spanish and Italians have accepted the inevitable. So, further afield, have the Russians, Chinese and Japanese. If you want to get ahead, you have to speak English. Two billion people around the world are believed to have made it their second language. Add that to 350m native English speakers in the United States, Britain and the Commonwealth, and you have an unstoppable force.

After these remarkable claims for the global spread of English and its inevitable path towards ascendancy, the editorial goes on to reassert that France must acknowledge 'the dominance of Anglo-American English as the universal language in a shrinking world', and that 'no amount of protectionist legislation and subsidies can shut out the free market in the expression of ideas'. 'Britain,' it asserts, 'must press ahead with the propagation of English and the British values which stand behind it' with the British Council ('Once a target for those unable to see no further than the end of their nose, it now runs a successful global network with teaching as its core activity in 108 countries'), the BBC (which 'is told to exploit its reputation and products abroad as never before') helping with 'the onward march of the English language'. As we shall see, this juxtaposition of the spread of English with the protectionism of the *Académie Française* is a frequently repeated trope of these discourses.

An article in *US News & World Report* (18 February 1985) called 'English: out to conquer the world' starts with the usual cataloguing of the spread of English:

> When an Argentine pilot lands his airliner in Turkey, he and the ground controller talk in English. When German physicists want to alert the international scientific community to a new discovery, they publish their findings in English-language journals. When Japanese executives cut deals with Scandinavian entrepreneurs in Bangkok, they communicate in English.
>
> (p. 49)

and so on and so on. The article also derides those who would oppose the 'inevitable' spread of English, for 'English marches on. "If you need it, you learn it", says one expert'. Despite various attempts to counter the spread of English, 'the world's latest lingua franca will keep spreading. "It's like the primordial ooze," contends James Alatis, . . . "its growth is ineluctable, inexorable and inevitable"' (p. 52).

[...]

Clearly, there is quite a remarkable continuity in the writing on the global spread of English. Bailey (1991) comments that 'the linguistic ideas that evolved at the acme of empires led by Britain and the United States have not changed as economic colonialism has replaced the direct, political management of third-world nations. English is still believed to be the inevitable world language' (p. 121).

Alastair
Pennycook

[...]

In praise of English

If there are many similarities in the ways the spread of English has been both exhorted and applauded over the last hundred years, there are also interesting similarities in the way the language itself has been praised as a great language. Nineteenth-century writing on English abounded with glorifications of the language, suggesting that on the one hand the undeniable excellence of British institutions, ideas and culture must be reflected in the language and, on the other, that the undeniable superior qualities of English must reflect a people and a culture of superior quality. Thus, the Reverend James George, for example, arguing that Britain had been 'commissioned to teach a noble language embodying the richest scientific and literary treasures,' asserted that 'As the mind grows, language grows, and adapts itself to the thinking of the people. Hence, a highly civilized race, will ever have, a highly accomplished language. The English tongue, is in all senses a very noble one. I apply the term noble with a rigorous exactness' (George 1867, p. 4).

[...]

A key argument in the demonstration of the superior qualities of English was in the breadth of its vocabulary, an argument which, as we shall see, is still used widely today.

The article 'English out to conquer the world' asks how English differs from other languages: 'First, it is bigger. Its vocabulary numbers at least 750,000 words. Second-ranked French is only two thirds that size . . . English has been growing fast for 1,000 years, promiscuously borrowing words from other lands' (1985, p. 53). According to Bryson (1990), the numbers of words listed in *Webster's Third New International Dictionary* (450,000) and the *Oxford English Dictionary* (615,000) are only part of the total number of English words since 'technical and scientific terms would add millions more'. Looking at which terms are actually commonly made use of, Bryson suggests that about '200,000 English words are in common use, more than in German (184,000) and far more than in French (a mere 100,000)' (p. 3). Claiborne (1983) asserts that 'for centuries, the English-speaking peoples have plundered the world for words, even as their military and industrial empire builders have plundered it for more tangible goods'. This plundering has given English

> the largest, most variegated and most expressive vocabulary in the world. The total number of English words lies somewhere between 400,000 – the number of current entries in the largest English dictionaries – and 600,000 – the largest figure that any expert is willing to be quoted on. By comparison, the biggest French dictionaries have only about 150,000 entries, the biggest Russian ones a mere 130,000.
>
> (p. 3)

**Alastair
Pennycook**

Simon Jenkins (1995) explains that:

> English has not won the battle to be the world's language through a trial of imperial
> strength. As the American linguist Braj Kachru points out, English has achieved its
> hegemony through its inherent qualities, by 'its propensity for acquiring new iden-
> tities . . . its range of varieties and above all its suitability as a flexible medium for
> literary and other types of creativity'.

The subtitle to Jenkins' article ('The triumph of English') is 'Our infinitely adaptable
mother tongue is now the world's lingua franca – and not before time.'

Apart from clearly supporting a simple argument about the superiority of English,
this view of the richness of English puts into play several other images of English that
are extremely important: the notion of English as some pure Anglo-Saxon language,
the idea that English and English speakers have always been open, flexible and integra-
tionist, and the belief that because of their vast vocabulary, speakers of English are the
ablest thinkers. The first of these emerges in 'English out to conquer the world' when the
article suggests that 'All-told, 80 percent of the word stock is foreign-born' (p. 53). The
implications of this statement seem to be that 'English' refers to a language of Anglo-
Saxon purity, a language that despite all its borrowings and enrichments is, at heart, an
Anglo-Saxon affair. This effort to construct some clear Anglo-Saxon lineage for English
has a long history. [. . .] Writing in 1901, Earle argued that:

> We do not want to discard the rich furniture of words which we have inherited
> from our French and classic eras; but we wish to wear them as trophies, as the his-
> toric blazon of a great career, for the demarcation and amplification of an imperial
> language whose thews and sinews and vital energies are essentially English.
>
> (cited in Crowley 1989: 74)

According to Burnett (1962), 'the long process of creating the historic seedbed of the
English language actually began with the arrival of the first Indo-European elements
from the continent' (p. 75). Claiborne (1983) goes further and claims that 'the story of
the life and times of English' can be traced from 'eight thousand years ago to the present'
(p. 5). Although both these claims – that 80 per cent of English could be foreign and
that the language can be traced back over 8,000 years – seem perhaps most remarkable
for the bizarreness of their views, they also need to be taken very seriously in terms
of the cultural constructions they produce, namely a view of English as some ethnically pure Anglo-Saxon or Aryan language. Bailey (1991) comments that '"Restoring" a
racially pure language to suit a racially "primitive" nation is an idea that reached its most
extreme and dreadful consequence in Hitler's Reich, and its appearance in images of
English has not been sufficiently acknowledged' (p. 270).

The second image that emerges here is that to this core of Anglo-Saxon has been
added – like tributaries to the great river of English, as many writers like to describe
this – words from languages around the world, suggesting that English and British people have always been flexible and keen to borrow from elsewhere to enrich the
language. This image of English is then used to deride other languages for their lack
of breadth and, especially when people have sought to safeguard languages from the

incursions of English, to claim that English is democratic while other languages are not. Most commonly this argument is used against the French for their attempts to legislate against the use of English words.

[...]

Thus, the image of English as a great borrowing language is used against any attempts to oppose the spread of English, the argument being that the diverse vocabulary of English is a reflection of the democratic and open nature of the British people, and that reactions against English are nothing but evidence that other people are less open and democratic. 'English need not be protected by French Academies, Canadian constitutions or Flemish language rioters,' Simon Jenkins (1995) tells us. 'The world must just take a deep breath and admit that it has a universal language at last.' But Jenkins is of course merely repeating an old image of English, one that the linguist Jespersen was quite happy with: 'The English language would not have been what it is if the English had not been for centuries great respecters of the liberties of each individual and if everybody had not been free to strike out new paths for himself.' (Jespersen, 1938/1982). And this linguistic democracy is, as ever, far superior to the narrow-minded protectionism of the French:

> the English have never suffered an Academy to be instituted among them like the French or Italian Academies . . . In England every writer is, and has always been, free to take his words where he chooses, whether from the ordinary stock of everyday words, from native dialects, from old authors, or from other languages, dead or living.
>
> (Jespersen 1938/1982: 15)

The notion of English as a great borrowing language also seems to suggest a view of colonial relations in which the British intermingled with colonised people, enriching English as they communed with the locals. Such a view, however, is hardly supported by colonial history. Kiernan (1969) mentions Macartney's observation of the British 'besetting sin of contempt for the rest of mankind' and that 'while other foreigners at Canton mingled socially with the Chinese, the British kept aloof' (p. 148). Kiernan goes on to suggest that 'the *apartheid* firmly established in India was transferred in a great measure to China. Everyone has heard of the "Dogs and Chinese not admitted" notice in the park' (p. 156). In Hong Kong, he points out, 'the position of the Chinese as subjects under British rule increased British haughtiness'. He quotes from Bowring in 1858 as observing that 'the separation of the native population from the European is nearly absolute: social intercourse between the races wholly unknown' (Kiernan 1969: 156). As Metcalf (1995) shows with respect to India, this apartheid policy extended to the division of cities, with railway lines often built to separate the 'native areas' from the white preserves, and houses built with extensive verandahs, gardens and gateways in order to keep the colonised at bay. These observations are backed up by Wesley-Smith's (1994) analysis of 'anti-Chinese legislation' in Hong Kong. Looking at the 'considerable body of race-based discriminatory legislation' in Hong Kong, Wesley-Smith points to one of the central aims of much of this legislation: the separation of Chinese and Europeans. In 1917, Governor May [...] wrote to the secretary of state about the importance of maintaining the Peak area as an all-European reserve: 'It would be little short of a calamity if an alien and, by European standards, semi-civilised race were allowed to drive the white

Alastair
Pennycook

man from the one area in Hong Kong, in which he can live with his wife and children in a white man's healthy surroundings' (cited in Wesley-Smith 1994: 100).

If, then, the British tended to mingle with colonised or other people far less than did other Europeans, it is unlikely that the English language was in fact such an open, borrowing language as is claimed. Indeed, Bailey (1991) argues that the British 'sense of racial superiority made English voyagers less receptive to borrowings that had not already been, in part, authenticated by other European travelers' (p. 61). Thus, he goes on:

> Far from its conventional image as a language congenial to borrowing from remote languages, English displays a tendency to accept exotic loanwords mainly when they have first been adopted by other European languages or when presented with marginal social practices or trivial objects. Anglophones who have ventured abroad have done so confident of the superiority of their culture and persuaded of their capacity for adaptation, usually without accepting the obligations of adapting. Extensive linguistic borrowing and language mixing arise only when there is some degree of equality between or among languages (and their speakers) in a multilingual setting. For the English abroad, this sense of equality was rare.
>
> (Bailey 1991: 91)

There are, therefore, serious questions to be asked about the image of democratic English put into play by the construction of English as a borrowing language. Indeed, the constant replaying of this image of English as an open and borrowing language, reflecting an open and borrowing people, is a cultural construct of colonialism that is in direct conflict with the colonial evidence.

The third, and probably most insidious, view produced by the insistence on English having a far larger vocabulary than other languages relates to thought. Having stated that English has far more words than German or French, Bryson (1990) goes on to argue that:

> The richness of the English vocabulary, and the wealth of available synonyms, means that English speakers can often draw shades of distinction unavailable to non-English speakers. The French, for example, cannot distinguish between house and home, between mind and brain, between man and gentleman, between 'I wrote' and 'I have written'. The Spanish cannot differentiate a chairman from a president, and the Italians have no equivalent of wishful thinking. In Russia there are no native words for efficiency, challenge, engagement ring, have fun, or take care.
>
> (Bryson 1990: 3–4)

Now it is important to note here that this is not merely an argument that different languages cut the world up differently but rather that English, with its larger vocabulary, cuts the world up better. Claiborne (1983), having also claimed a larger vocabulary for English than for other languages, goes on to suggest that 'Like the wandering minstrel in *The Mikado*, with songs for any and every occasion, English has the right word for it — whatever "it" may be' (p. 4). Thus:

> It is the enormous and variegated lexicon of English, far more than the mere numbers and geographical spread of its speakers, that truly makes our native tongue

marvellous – makes it, in fact, a medium for the precise, vivid and subtle expression of thought and emotion that has no equal, past or present.

(Claiborne 1983: 4)

Alastair Pennycook

In case the implications of this are not clear, Claiborne goes on to claim that English is indeed 'not merely a great language but the greatest' (p. 4) and that 'Nearly all of us do our thinking in words, which symbolize objects and events (real or imagined) . . .' (p. 6). Clearly, then, in this view, if you are a speaker of English, you are better equipped than speakers of other languages to think about the world. In this view, English is a window on the world. According to Burnett (1962), 'not only in Asia and Africa, but in Europe, crisscrossed by linguistic frontiers and dissected by deep-rooted cultural loyalties, people of all classes now look to English as a window, a magic casement opening on every horizon of loquacious men' (pp. 20–1).

[. . .]

Issues to consider

❑ The journalist Simon Jenkins quotes Kachru in the extract above. Given that Kachru is, himself, far from being a glorifier of British colonialism but is, rather, a pioneer of language rights for the descendents of those whom the British colonised, how do you interpret his words? Do you agree with him? If you want to follow up Kachru's views on this subject, see, for example, his 1996 article 'The paradigms of marginality'. Bamgboṣe (1998) also deals with this theme.

❑ Pennycook is critical of the view that when people speak English as an L2 they dissect the world through the filter of the English language. If you speak English as an L2, do you believe that your view of the world and perhaps also your identity alter according to which language you are speaking, or do you use English to reflect your L1 world view and identity? Most of the evidence in this book would suggest that Pennycook is right, at least in the sense that L2 speakers adapt English to their own world view and identity, rather than vice versa. But take a look at what is said by the Japanese English speakers quoted in C8. Their comments suggest that the opposite may sometimes be true. How might you explain this? Do you think it depends, for example, on whether a local variety of English has been codified? This is a point that Pennycook (2007: 97) himself discusses in relation to Japanese English and identity.

❑ Pennycook is also critical of the notion that the English language and its native speakers are particularly flexible and adaptable. What is your view on this subject? Do you have any evidence of this flexibility and adaptability or the lack of it?

❑ If your reading of this extract has inspired you to read the entire book from which it is taken, you might also like to read two highly contrasting reviews of the book, a positive one by Filmer and a negative one by Nelson (*World Englishes*, vol. 22, no. 3: 326–30) and compare your views with theirs. You might also like to read Pennycook's much more recent book, *Global Englishes and Transcultural Flows* (2007) and explore the extent to which his position on the spread of English has/ has not altered over the intervening period.

D2 ## THE STATUS OF PIDGINS AND CREOLES IN EDUCATION

D1 presented Pennycook's views on the way postcolonial discourses continue to repro-
duce colonial perspectives on the way English is (or 'should be') used around the world.
In the next reading, we see how this perspective is not by any means restricted to the
dominant (L1) English-speaking countries, but has been adopted by the countries
once colonised by them. In other words, these ex-colonies are in a sense colluding in
the degrading and marginalisation of their own varieties of English. Whether this is
the result of 'linguistic insecurity', or whether it is simply a case of pragmatism, to the
extent that speakers of standard English varieties reap better financial rewards, is not at
all clear. As you read the article by Charles Alobwede d'Epie, bear this issue in mind.

'Banning pidgin English in Cameroon?'

Charles Alobwede d'Epie (reprinted from *English Today*, vol. 14, no. 1, 1998: 54–60)

**Charles
Alobwede
d'Epie**

At least one household, gathering or educational institution is banning pidgin English
(PE) in Cameroon every passing minute. This banning ranges from the mild hushing
down of PE users, through stern verbal orders, to written 'decrees'. This may explain
why there is a rapidly growing number of children whose first language (what would
have been known as mother tongue) is English.

Mbassi-Manga's 1973 survey of language acquisition among Anglophone children
revealed two macro-patterns – the rural and the urban. The rural pattern was characterised by what he called Home Language dominance. In other words, in rural areas,
children acquired the Home Language (HL) first, then PE and finally educated English
(EdE), thus giving the pattern HL → PE → EdE. The urban areas on their part had a
pattern marked by PE dominance, giving the formula PE → HL → EdE or PE → EdE
→ HL. The micro-pattern involved a reversal of the basic order of the macro-patterns
or/and a revelation of distinctive linguistic features in pockets of given urban centres
like Bamenda up-station, Buea GRA, and Limbe Bota.

The Koenig, Chia and Povey socio-linguistic survey of the major urban centres of
Cameroon (1977–8) led to the discovery of the following percentages of children who
acquired English and PE as their first languages respectively [see Table D2.1].

Table D2.1 Percentages of children who acquire English/pidgin English as L1 (source:
Koenig et al. 1983).

	English	Pidgin English
Bamenda	1%	22%
Mamfe	0%	25%
Kumba	1%	19%
Buea	7%	26%
Limbe	4%	31%

In this current survey, I have used the principles used in the 1977–8 survey and Table D2.2 shows the figures I have come out with.

Charles Alobwede d'Epie

Table D2.2 Percentages of children who acquire English/pidgin English as L1 (source: Alobwede d'Epie 1998).

	English	Pidgin English
Bamenda	3.5%	24%
Mamfe	1%	25%
Kumba	3%	22%
Buea	13%	28%
Limbe	9%	30%
Douala	6%	10%
Yaounde	8%	15%

These figures contrast the geometrical progression of the acquisition of EdE as a first language, with the arithmetical progression of the acquisition of PE as a first language. The dynamics of EdE therefore show that the unofficial banning of PE is steadily gaining ground.

Who bans pidgin English?

The Cameroon government does not encourage the use of PE in schools. Yet, there is no official text banning it anywhere. The Koenig et al. survey revealed that where children acquired EdE as their first language, the pattern of language acquisition was EdE → (PE) + (HL). In other words, PE and HL were optional. In such cases, some children ended up being monolingual in English especially if they were whizzed off to Britain before making contact with other children in post-primary school institutions.

Most of the children in the survey were the children of ministers and high civil servants married to educated wives. The educated wife is of paramount significance in the acquisition of EdE as a first language. I have not used the label mother tongue because EdE as a child's first language may not fit the description of mother tongue. I shall rather use the term Status Mother Tongue (SMT) to describe a situation in which a well-educated top brass family with a sound HL and PE background shuns both languages in preference to English. This imposes English on the child even though neither of his parents calls it his/her mother tongue.

SMT is no longer the monopoly of the top brass of society. The growing number of single-mother graduates (and their likes) is a major force in SMT acquisition. This explains why SMT percentages are high in Buea, Limbe, Douala and Yaounde – cities with a high concentration of single-mother graduates who are either employed or are engaged in petty business. They rent enclosed studios or houses, have SMT-speaking babysitters and because of the economic crisis, live secluded lives – conditions suitable for imposing an SMT on children. Single-mother graduates are a very conscious group. Those doing petty business see it as a temporary measure for survival and hope for a better tomorrow. They reinforce their SMT by sending their children to expensive private schools where PE and HL are banned.

Another group that bans PE is that of the New Found Status – uneducated men married to uneducated wives – people who because of their noble birth, wealth or

Charles
Alobwede
d'Epie

position at work commune with the top brass of society. This is the most dogmatic group in the banning process. Although they try to counterpoise their handicap by banning PE and HL in their homes, their children are usually bilingual in either PE and EdE or HL and EdE, since they themselves are incapable of SMT. This group spends heavily on their children's education in expensive private schools, sometimes schools meant for the children of ministers and diplomats.

Bonny Kfua [1996] of Bamenda issues the following decree in 'Time is up for pidgin English':

> Anyone reading through an essay or letter written by a class seven pupil will admit that the cry of fallen standards in our schools is a reality. Whatever might have pushed the British and Catholic Church to use pidgin as a vehicle of communication, it is high time someone courageously put an end to the widespread use of pidgin English in Cameroon

[...]

The relationship between PE and EdE

[...]

Mbassi-Manga traces the history of PE right back to 1400 when the Portuguese traders, employing the services of English servants, traded with the coastal regions of Cameroon. The English servants spoke or introduced a workaday language that was later known as PE, because of the origins of its speakers and the heavy presence of English words in the language.

Baptist missionaries came to Cameroon in 1841 and opened the first English school in 1844. Thus, from 1400 to 1844, Cameroon coastal regions were under the sway of PE. Within this time, the language was establishing its grammar, structure and lexis, and developing its synchronic and diachronic varieties as any other native language (since the traders were not settlers who could have influenced its evolution otherwise). Any language that has survived the turbulence of linguistic evolution and has co-existed with another for 444 years cannot be considered an appendix of the newcomer. This paper therefore considers PE in the light of Ngome's views [Ngome sees PE as having a greater affinity with African languages than with English]. PE is not a type of English as American or Australian Englishes are types of English, nor does it have a diglossia relationship with English as High and Low Arabic have to Arabic. It is simply a hybrid African language – a language which English speaking missionaries had to learn, as they learnt Douala, Ewondo, and other HLs in Cameroon for evangelical purposes.

PE enjoyed unchallenged leverage during the Portuguese trade (1400–1600) and the slave trade (1600–1800). The abolition of these trades triggered the opening up of free trade. This coincided with the opening up of plantations and the subsequent annexation of Cameroon by Germany (1884) and thus the colonial epoch. The Germans found both PE and English well in place but since PE was the workaday language (the language of the labourers) and their immediate concern was labour, they used it. Upon their defeat in the Second World War and the institution of British administration, the English language came in again in full force.

The co-existence of PE and EdE at these epochs had great sociolinguistic consequences. From 1400 to 1800, PE operated in an unmarked society, but, with the

Charles
Alobwede
d'Epie

introduction of EdE, the society became stratified, and that engendered the phenomenon of 'who spoke what language to whom?' in multilingual situations. This dichotomy
became more marked in the plantations where the few whites and blacks who spoke and
wrote English used it as an order-giving language and the masses who spoke PE used it
as an order-obeying language. Furthermore, plantation society was stratified into white
overlords and black underdogs. The blacks were further classified (according to their
English language competence) into Senior Service, Intermediate Service, and General
Labour. Each group had salary scales, and was assigned living quarters with facilities
commensurate to it.

[…]

These attributes stigmatised the PE speaker as he found himself quarantined not
only because he spoke PE but also because it exposed him to a lifestyle and morals associated with slovenliness, vulgarity and debasement. He found himself split between
maintaining his language (PE) loyalty, and aspiring to belong to the EdE group. He
unconsciously transferred the latter to his progeny and as such, openly or privately, individually or collectively banned PE.

Is PE the cause of fallen standards?

Talk of fallen standards presupposes that there were once high standards. Respondents
cite the performance of educational institutions between 1945 and 1960 and those
between 1960 and 1996. These two periods, they say, indicate colonial stability and educational growth after the war, as well as the relative calm and educational expansion
after independence. According to the respondents, the Standard Six pupils (end of primary school) of 1945–60 spoke and wrote better English than their 1960–96 counterparts (and even secondary school students). One thing no respondent has stated
categorically is whether PE was spoken less at that time (1945–60) than today.

There is, however, a consensus that the 1945–60 period was characterised by a
British-styled, better planned and administered educational policy, better textbooks,
limited enrolment, advanced school age and duty-conscious teaching staff. The 1960–96
period was characterized by an educational policy restrained by political constraints.
This, coupled with unrestricted enrolment, tender school age and general laxity in
administration, produced adverse results.

[…]

Substandard English in Cameroon has had different names – Broken English, Poor
English, Bush English, Joinjoin English, Bad English. Each reflects the fluidity of the bor-
derline between levels of competence. [. . .]

Bad English has nothing to do with native/non-native, educated/non-educated and
monolingual/multilingual dichotomies. It is simply a reality with the English language.

The English language reality

Norman Fairclough [1989] claims that what is today known as standard English developed from the East Midland dialect associated with the merchant class in London at the
end of the medieval epoch. According to him, its beginnings were modest – it was used
in very few places for very few purposes by very few people. This humble beginning
gave it its cult characteristic – the language of the few for the few by the few. Associated
with commerce, and therefore power, it gradually 'took over' major social institutions,

Charles
Alobwede
d'Epie

pushing out Latin and French, vastly extending the purposes it was used for and its formal resources as a result, and coming to be accepted (if not always widely used) by more and more people.

A language that was capable of sacking Latin and French at the time was a no-nonsense language. It was this language that the British used in conquering the world and establishing the greatest empire man has ever known. As it spread, it subjugated native languages and took over their major social, judiciary, administrative and economic institutions. It spread vertically rather than horizontally – thus remaining the language of the few by the few for the few, and in spite of British colonial policy of indirect rule, its intrinsic power acculturated its non-native speakers, depersonalised them and made them think and reason like Englishmen. Fishman [1971a] echoes this by quoting Sekou Touré thus:

> The education that was given to us was designed to assimilate us, to depersonalize us, to Westernize us – to present our civilization, our culture, our own sociological and philosophical concepts, even our humanism as the appreciation of a savage and almost conscious primitivism – in order to create a number of complexes in us which would drive us to become more (English) French than the (English) French themselves.

And even after independence, most of those who possessed the language to an agreeable degree could not afford to lose it because they saw in it an enviable asset – good jobs, positions of political and economic power and above all, the core remnant of colonialism. Whitely beautifully states:

> There are leaders and democrats who still look upon the English way of life as a superior culture, and therefore English as the language of 'culture'. They seize every opportunity to speak English and flaunt their knowledge of English before peasants and workers in the fields and offices. Some of them will even proudly assert that they can only think in English . . . They do so because they subconsciously wish they were Englishmen.

The English language is a colonial heritage, and the leaders are the epitomes of the heritage. Colonialism was characterised by white supremacy (segregation), exploitation, oppression and vindictiveness. Although the leaders fought against these ills in their struggle for independence, they themselves had unconsciously incorporated them in their lifestyles and thus inherited a superiority complex which they could not mortgage. They could not as such liberalise the English language. They had to maintain it as a cult language, a capitalist language, a language of power by the few for the subjugation of the majority. This explains why PE, which is a nonethnic language and which is acquired freely by the majority, could not be adopted as the language of governance after independence. The English language is a protected language, a language of the status quo. Its value depends on its being closed, and this depends on its being expensive, difficult and time-consuming to learn.

Can PE survive?

The hostility against PE and the growing number of SMT children tend to suggest that with time, PE would decline. However, Lesley Milroy [1985] believes that:

Charles
Alobwede
d'Epie

> Many bidialectal and bilingual communities maintain, in a parallel way, low status dialects or languages in their repertoires which have the capacity to persist, often over centuries, in the teeth of powerful pressures from a legitimized norm. Social psychologists have concluded that it is the capacity of these low status varieties to symbolize solidarity and group identity, values important to their users, which accounts for their persistence.

PE has been a low status language under German, French and British administrations, and under each, in spite of the odds, it has shown the capacity to survive. Its survival rests on solid grounds. For one thing, it is the only language in Cameroon which expresses Cameroonian reality without provoking vertical or horizontal hostilities. Secondly, it is conveniently flexible and as such can be acquired at no cost. Finally, because of its horizontal spread, it is the language of consensus.

The controversy as to whether PE should be encouraged or discouraged rests on the language policy of the country. Cameroon has adopted English as her second official language. Some respondents think that, because PE vies for position and threatens the effective use of English, it (PE) should be discouraged. But is that discouragement ideal for the country? It is estimated that more than 70 per cent of our population speaks PE. To discourage PE is to alienate 70 per cent of the population from the basic collective identity.

This is where Cameroon language policy seems to have failed. The choice of French and English as official languages has relegated the HLs and PE to the background of international communication and divided the country into two linguistic loyalties. In choosing French and English, our leaders thought of avoiding the ethnic conflict which might result if they chose one HL in preference to another. They also thought that the two languages, as languages of worldwide communication, would be instrumental in the economic, political and administrative growth of the country. But is this true today, more than 30 years after independence and the use of French and English as official languages?

Cameroon's underdevelopment could be blamed on factors other than linguistics. But I stress the linguistic factor in agreeing with Fishman [1971a] that:

> A common indigenous language in the modern nation state is a powerful factor for unity. Cutting across tribal and ethnic lines, it promotes a feeling of single community. Additionally it makes possible the expression and development of social ideas, economic targets and cultural identity easily perceived by citizens. It is, in a word, a powerful factor for mobilization of people and resources for nationhood.

Cameroon elites and masses function at opposing realms of thought because they use codes of opposing status. This retardatory factor would have been eliminated if, upon independence, Cameroon had realised the divisive nature of English and had adopted and developed a neutral indigenous language (PE) to function alongside EdE. This would

**Charles
Alobwede
d'Epie**

have reduced the present stigma on PE and would have made it a participatory language for development. In East Africa, Tanzania is developing Swahili for such purposes. In the Philippines, Pilipino is functioning side by side with English. In Paraguay, a local language Guarani is being developed with the aim of using it to increase national awareness.

The division of a nation into high status language elites and low status language masses destroys national unity and cohesion; it leads to segregated quarters, schools, and so on. It enhances the exploitation of the masses by the minority and leads to the masses resisting policies formulated in the high status language. The masses identify the high status language and its objectives as belonging to exploiters, segretationists and oppressors. A language situation that recreates a colonial stereotype is what Orwell would call a decadent civilization – a civilization that leads to politico-economic and linguistic collapse.

Issues to consider

❏ In his controversial book *Language is Power*, John Honey (1997) argues that 'apparently egalitarian notions of Black English and other dialects can limit access to standard English – and hence power – for minority groups' (back cover). In your view, is this a valid argument for banning pidgin English in Cameroon? You might like to look back to the arguments and counter-arguments of Bisong and Phillipson in unit C1 regarding English in Africa.

❏ Exactly ten years after the publication of Alobwede d'Epie's article, Igboanusi (2008) presents similar findings in relation to Nigerian Pidgin (NP) English. Igboanusi identifies the same negative attitudes in Nigeria towards NP as those Alobwede d'Epie found in Cameroon towards Cameroon Pidgin English, and in particular, similarly strong views against its use in education. This, Igboanusi points out, is '[i]n spite of the fact that NP is probably the language with the highest population of users in Nigeria' (2008: 68). Why do you think these kinds of attitudes are so pervasive in these (and other) regions? What is it about Cameroon Pidgin English, NP, and the like, that people find so 'bad' (as Igboanusi puts it), even though they function very successfully in the lives of their speakers? If you have access to the journal *World Englishes*, you will find it useful to read Igboanusi's article in full and compare it with Alobwede d'Epie's.

❏ The following is an extract from the autobiographical *School Days* by Patrick Chamoiseau, in which he describes his school experiences in Martinique. Although the unfamiliar standard language he was forced to use at school in place of his native creole was French, the feelings he describes so graphically must have been very similar to those of children compelled to use standard English. How strong a 'case' does Chamoiseau make here for the use of creole in education?

But everything went well: no one had to speak, to write, to explain this-or-that. It was the Teacher who talked. And now the little boy realized something obvious: *the Teacher spoke French*. Mam Ninotte used snippets of French on occasion (a half-word here, a quarter-word there), bits of French that were automatic and unchanging. And the Papa, when he made a rum punch, ceremoniously unfurled a French that was less a language than an esoteric tool used for effect. As for the Big Kids, their natural mode of expression was creole, except with Mam Ninotte, other grownups, and most particularly the Papa. A certain respectful distance was maintained through the rituals of formality when speaking to them. And everything else for everyone else (pleasures, shouts, dreams, hatreds, the life in life . . .) was creole. This division of speech had never struck the little boy before. French (to which he didn't even attach a name) was some object fetched when needed from a kind of shelf, outside oneself, but which sounded natural in the mouth, close to creole. Close through articulation. The words, the sentence structure. But now, with the Teacher, speaking traveled far and wide along a single road. And this French road became strangely foreign. The articulation changed. The rhythm changed. The intonation changed. Words that were more or less familiar began to sound different. They seemed to come from a distant horizon and no longer had any affinity with creole. The Teacher's images, examples, references did not spring from their native country anymore. The Teacher spoke French like the people on the radio or the sailors of the French line. And he deliberately spoke nothing else. French seemed to be the very element of his knowledge. He savored this smooth syrup he secreted so ostentatiously. And his language did not reach out to the children, the way Mam Salinière's had, to envelop, caress, and persuade them. His words floated above them with the magnificence of a ruby-throated humming-bird hovering in the breeze. *Oh, the Teacher was French!*

❑ As you saw in the extract from Chamoiseau, the difference between the standard form of a language and the related creole (or pidgin) may seem as great as the difference between two completely independent languages. One recent development in English teaching, particularly in Europe, but also increasingly in East Asia, is **CLIL (Content and Language Integrated Learning)**. This is an approach to L2 learning in which school subjects such as science and geography are taught through the second language (see Graddol 2006: 86). Although in theory the approach can be applied to the learning of any L2, in practice the L2 is almost always English. What do you think the benefits for children of learning their school subjects through English might be? And what kinds of problems might arise when this approach is carried out in Expanding Circle contexts?

WHO OWNS ENGLISH TODAY?

D3

The ownership debate

In C3, you read the views of scholars such as Kachru, who argue that we need a paradigm shift in the teaching and testing of English, to reflect the fact that the majority of people who learn and use English today are not native speakers and do not even use it to communicate with them. In the paper that follows, still one of the most widely and frequently quoted papers in the field, Henry G. Widdowson argues in the strongest terms that native speakers of English no longer 'own' English or have the right to determine how it is, or should be, spoken around the world.

'The ownership of English'

Henry G. Widdowson (The Peter Strevens Memorial Lecture delivered at the 1993 IATEFL International Conference, Swansea, and reprinted from the *IATEFL Annual Conference Report: Plenaries 1993*: 5–8. A slightly different version (1994b) is more easily available).

[...]

I want to talk about how the English we teach is to be defined and how this is related to its position as an international language.

To start with, who determines the demarcation of the subject itself? We are teaching English and the general assumption is that our purpose is to develop in students a proficiency which approximates as closely as possible to that of native speakers. But who are these native speakers?

The English perhaps. And why not? A modest proposal. England is where the language originated and this is where the English live. The language and the people are bound together by both morphology and history. So they can legitimately lay claim to this linguistic territory. It belongs to them. And they are the custodians. If you want real or proper English, this is where it is to be found, preserved and listed like a property of the National Trust.

Of course, English of a kind is found elsewhere as well, still spreading, a luxuriant growth from imperial seed. Seeded among other people but not ceded to them. At least not completely. For the English still cling tenaciously to their property and try to protect it from abuse. Let us acknowledge (let us concede) that there are other kinds of English, offshoots and outgrowths, but they are not real or proper English, not the genuine article.

As an analogy, consider the French. They have, until just recently, successfully denied others the right to use the appellation 'Champagne' for any wine that does not come from the region of that name, where Dom Perignon first invented it. There may be all kinds of derivative versions elsewhere, excellent no doubt in their way, but they are not real or proper Champagne, even though loose talk may refer to them as such. Similarly, there is real English, *Anglais réal*, Royal English, Queen's English, or (for those unsympathetic to the monarchy) Oxford English. The vintage language.

I do not imagine that such a view would gain much support in present company. The response is more likely to be outrage. You cannot be serious. Well, not entirely, it is true. As I have expressed it, in somewhat extravagant terms, this position is one which very few people would associate themselves with. It is reactionary, arrogant, totally unacceptable. And the argument is patently absurd. Perhaps as I have expressed it. But then why is it absurd? The particular associations of England, Queen and country and Colonel Blimp which I invoked to demonstrate the argument also in some respects disguise it. If we now remove the position from these associations and strip the argument down to its essential tenets, is it so readily dismissed? Is it indeed so uncommon after

Henry G.
Widdowson

all? I want to suggest that the ideas and attitudes which I have presented in burlesque are still very much with us in a different and less obvious guise.

To return briefly to Champagne. One argument frequently advanced for being pro-tective of its good name has to do with quality assurance. The label is a guarantee of quality. If any Tom, Dick or Harry producing fizzy wine is free to use it, there can be no quality control. Recently an English firm won a court case enabling it to put Champagne on its bottles containing a non-alcoholic beverage made from elderflowers. The Cham-pagne lobby was outraged. Here, they said, was the thin end of the wedge. Before long, the label would be appearing on bottles all over the place containing concoctions of all kinds calling themselves Champagne, and so laying claim to its quality. The *appellation* would not be *controlée*. Standards were at stake.

They have a point. And the same point is frequently made about English. In this case, you cannot, of course, preserve exclusive use of the name and, indeed, it would work against your interests to do so (of which more later), but you can seek to preserve standards by implying that there is an exclusive quality in your own brand of English, aptly called 'standard English'. What is this quality, then? What are these standards?

The usual answer is quality of clear communication and standards of intelligibility. With standard English, it is argued, these are assured. If the language disperses into dif-ferent forms, a myriad of Englishes, then it ceases to serve as a means of international communication; in which case the point of learning it largely disappears. As the language spreads, there are bound to be changes out on the periphery; so much can be conceded. But these changes must be seen not only as peripheral but as radial also, and traceable back to the stable centre of the standard. If this centre does not hold, things fall apart, mere anarchy is loosed upon the world. Back to Babel.

In itself, this argument sounds plausible; and it is difficult to refute. But for all that, there is something about it which is suspect. Let us replay it again. Standard English promotes the cause of international communication so we must maintain the central stability of the standard as the common linguistic frame of reference.

To begin with, who are 'we'? Obviously the promoters of standard English must themselves have standard English at their disposal. But to maintain it is another matter. This presupposes authority. And this authority is claimed by those who possess the lan-guage by primogeniture and due of birth, as Shakespeare puts it. In other words, the native speakers. They do not have to be English, of course. That would be too restrictive a condition, and one it would be tactless to propose, but they have to be to the language born. Not all native speakers, you understand. In fact, come to think of it, not most native speakers, for the majority of those who are to the language born speak non-standard Eng-lish, and have themselves to be instructed in the standard at school. We cannot have any Tom, Dick or Harry claiming authority, for Tom, Dick and Harry are likely to be speakers of some dialect or other. So the authority to maintain the standard language is not conse-quent on a natural native speaker endowment. It is claimed by a minority of people who have the power to impose it. The custodians of standard English are self-elected members of a rather exclusive club. Now it is important to be clear that in saying this, I am not arguing against standard English. You can accept the argument for language maintenance, as indeed I do, without accepting the authority that claims the right to maintain it. It is, I think, very generally assumed that a particular subset of educated native speakers have the natural entitlement to custody of the language. That the preservation of its integrity is

Henry G.
Widdowson

in their hands: their right and their responsibility. It is this which I wish to question. Not in any spirit of radical rebellion against authority as such, but because I think such questioning raises a number of crucial issues about the learning and teaching of the language.

Consideration of who the custodians are leads logically on to a consideration of what it is exactly that is in their custody. What is standard English? The usual way of defining it is in reference to its grammar and lexis: it is a variety, a kind of superposed dialect which is socially sanctioned for institutional use, and therefore particularly well suited to written communication. In its spoken form it can be manifested by any accent. So it is generally conceded that standard English has no distinctive phonology. The same concession is not, however, extended to its graphology. On the contrary, it is deviant spelling which, in Britain at least, is most frequently singled out for condemnation. There is something of a contradiction here. If standard English is defined as a distinctive grammatical and lexical system which can be substantially realised in different ways, then what does spelling have to do with it? It is true that some spelling has a grammatical function (like apostrophe *s* which distinguishes the possessive form from the plural) but most of it does not. If you are going to ignore phonological variation, then, to be consistent, you should surely ignore graphological variation as well, and overlook it as a kind of written accent.

The reason it is not overlooked, I think, is that standard English, unlike other dialects, is essentially a written variety mainly designed for institutional purposes (education, administration, business and so on). Its spoken version is secondary, and typically used by those who control these institutions. This means that although it may not matter how it is spoken, it emphatically does matter how it is written. Furthermore, since writing, as a more durable medium, is used to express and establish institutional values, deviations from orthographic conventions undermine in some degree the institutions which they serve. They can be seen as evidence of social instability: a sign of things beginning to fall apart. So it is not surprising that those who have a vested interest in maintaining these institutions should be so vexed by bad spelling. It is not difficult to identify words through their unorthodox appearance. What seems to be more crucial is that good spelling represents conformity to convention and so serves to maintain institutional stability.

Similar points can be made about grammatical features. Since language has built-in redundancy, grammatical conformity is actually not particularly crucial for many kinds of communicative transaction. What we generally do in the interpretative process is actually to edit grammar out of the text, referring lexis directly to context, using lexical items as indexical clues to meaning. We edit grammar back in when we need it for fine tuning. If the reason for insisting on standard English is because it guarantees effective communication, then the emphasis should therefore logically be on lexis rather than grammar. But the champions of standard English do not see it in this way: on the contrary, they focus attention on grammatical abuse. Why should this be so? There are, I think, two reasons. Firstly, it is precisely because grammar is so often redundant in communicative transactions that it takes on another significance, namely that of expressing social identity. The mastery of a particular grammatical system, especially, perhaps, those features which are redundant, marks you as a member of the community which has developed that system for its own social purposes. Conversely, of course, those who are unable to master the system are excluded from the community. They do not belong. In short, grammar is shibboleth.

So when the custodians of standard English complain about the ungrammatical

Henry G.
Widdowson

language of the populace, they are in effect indicating that the perpetrators are out-siders, non-members of the community. The only way they can become members, and so benefit from the privileges of membership, is to learn standard English, and those privileges include, of course, access to the institutions which the community controls. Standard English is an entry condition and the custodians of it the gatekeepers. You can, of course, persist in your non-standard ways if you choose, but then do not be sur-prised to find yourself marginalised, perpetually kept out on the periphery. What you say will be less readily attended to, assigned less importance, if it is not expressed in the grammatically approved manner. And if you express yourself in writing which is both ungrammatical and badly spelled, you are not likely to be taken seriously. You are beyond the pale. Standard English, then, is not simply a means of communication but the sym-bolic possession of a particular community, expressive of its identity, its conventions and values. As such it needs to be carefully preserved, for to undermine standard English is to undermine what it stands for: the security of this community and its institutions. Thus it tends to be the communal rather than the communicative features of standard English that are most jealously protected: its grammar and spelling.

I do not wish to imply this communal function is to be deplored. Languages of every variety have this dual character: they provide the means for communication and at the same time express the sense of community, represent the stability of its conventions and values, in short, its culture. All communities possess and protect their languages. The question is, which community and which culture have a rightful claim to ownership of standard English? For standard English is no longer the preserve of a group of people living in an off-shore European island, even if some of them still seem to think that it is. It is an international language. As such, it serves a whole range of different communities and their institutional purposes, and these transcend traditional communal and cultural boundaries. I am referring to the business community, for example, and the community of researchers and scholars in science and technology and other disciplines. Standard English, especially in its written form, is their language. It provides for effective com-munication, but at the same time, it establishes the status and stability of the institu-tional conventions which define these international activities. These activities develop their own conventions of thought and procedure, customs and codes of practice; in short, they in effect create their own cultures, their own standards. And obviously for the maintenance of standards it is helpful, to say the least, to have a standard language at your disposal. But you do not need native speakers to tell you what it is. [...]

As I indicated earlier, the custodians of standard English express the fear that if there is diversity, things will fall apart and the language will divide up into mutually unintelligible varieties. But things in a sense have already fallen apart. The varieties of English used for international communication in science, finance, commerce and so on are mutually unintelligible. As far as lexis is concerned, their communicative viability depends on the development of separate standards, and this means that their communi-cation is largely closed off from the world outside.

The point, then, is that if English is to retain its vitality and its capability for con-tinual adjustment, it cannot be confined within a standard lexis. And this seems to be implicitly accepted as far as particular domains of use are concerned. Nobody, I think, says that the abstruse terms used by physicists or stock-brokers are non-standard Eng-lish. It is generally accepted that communities or secondary cultures which are defined

**Henry G.
Widdowson**

by shared professional concerns should be granted rights of ownership and allowed to fashion the language to their needs.

The same tolerance is not extended so readily to primary cultures and communities, where the language is used in the conduct of everyday social life. Lexical innovation here, equally motivated by communal requirement, is generally dismissed as dialect. Take, for example, the two words *depone* and *prepone*. The first is a technical legal term and therefore highly respectable. The second, *prepone*, is not. It is an Indian English word of very general currency, coined to contrast with 'to postpone'. To postpone an event means to put it back, to prepone an event is to bring it forward. The coinage exploits the morphology of English in an entirely regular way. It is apt. But it is also quaint. An odd Indian excrescence: obviously non-standard. And yet there is clearly nothing deviant in the derivational process itself and, indeed, we can see it at work in the formation of the related words *predate* and *postdate*. But these are sanctioned as entirely ordinary, proper, standard English words. What, then, is the difference? The difference lies in the origin of the word. Prepone is coined by a non-native speaking community, so it is not really a proper English word. It is not pukka. And of course the word *pukka* is itself only pukka because the British adopted it.

Where are we then? When we consider the question of standard English what we find, in effect, is double standards. The very idea of a standard implies stability and this can only be fixed in reference to the past. But language is of its nature unstable. It is essentially protean in nature, adapting its shape to suit changing circumstances. It would otherwise lose its vitality and its communicative and communal value. This is generally acknowledged in the case of specialist domains of use, but is not acknowledged in the case of everyday social uses of the language. So it is that a word like *depone* is approved and a word like *prepone* is not. But the basic principle of dynamic adaption is the same in both cases. And in both cases, the users of the language exploit its protean potential and fashion it to their needs, thereby demonstrating a high degree of linguistic capability. In both cases the innovation indicates that the language has been learned, not just as a set of fixed conventions to conform to, but as a resource for making meaning; and making meaning which you can call your own. This, surely, is a crucial condition. You are proficient in a language to the extent that you make it your possession, bend it to your will, assert yourself through it rather than simply submit to dictates of its form. It is a familiar experience to find oneself saying things in a foreign language because you can say them rather than because they express what you want to say. You feel you are going through the motions, and somebody else's motions at that. You are speaking the language but not speaking your mind. Real proficiency is when you are able to take possession of the language and turn it to your advantage. This is what mastery means. So in a way, proficiency only comes with non-conformity, when you can take the initiative and strike out on your own. Consider these remarks of the Nigerian writer, Chinua Achebe [1975]:

> I feel that the English language will be able to carry the weight of my African experience . . . But it will have to be a new English, still in Communion with its ancestral home but altered to suit its new African surroundings.

Achebe is a novelist and he is talking here about creative writing. But the point I have been making is that all uses of language are creative in the sense that they draw on linguistic

Henry G.
Widdowson

resources to express different perceptions of reality. English is called upon to carry the weight of all kinds of experience, much of it very remote indeed from its ancestral home.

The new English that Achebe refers to is locally generated, and although it must necessarily be related to, and so in communion with, its ancestral origins in the past, it owes no allegiance to any descendants of this ancestry in the present. And this point applies to all other new Englishes which have been created to carry the weight of different experience in different surrounding, whether they are related to specialist domains of use or to the contexts of everyday life. They are all examples of the entirely normal and necessary process of adaption, a process which obviously depends on non-conformity to existing conventions or standards. For these have been established else-where by other people as appropriate to quite different circumstances. The fact that these people can claim direct descent from the founding fathers has nothing to do with it. How English develops in the world is no business whatever of native speakers in England or anywhere else. They have no say in the matter, no right to intervene or pass judgement. They are irrelevant. The very fact that English is an international language means that no nation can have custody over it. To grant such custody of the language, particularly, one might add, to a nation disposed to dwell on the past, is necessarily to arrest its development and so undermine its international status. It is a matter of con-siderable pride and satisfaction for native speakers of English that their language is an international means of communication. But the point is that it is only international to the extent that it is not their language. It is not a possession which they lease out to others, while still retaining the freehold. Other people actually own it.

[. . .]

[A]s soon as you accept that English serves the communicative and communal needs of different communities, it follows logically that it must be diverse. An international language has to be an independent language. It does not follow logically, however, that the language will disperse into mutually unintelligible varieties. For it will naturally sta-bilise into a standard form to the extent required to meet the needs of the communities concerned. Thus it is clearly vital to the interests of the international community of, for example, scientists or business people, whatever their primary language, that they should preserve a common standard of English in order to keep up standards of com-municative effectiveness. English could not otherwise serve their purpose. It needs no native speaker to tell them that. Furthermore, this natural tendency towards standardi-zation will be reinforced by the extending of networks of interaction through develop-ments in telecommunications and information technology. For there is little point in opening up such amazing new transmission systems if what you transmit makes no sense at the other end. The availability of these new channels calls for the maintenance of a common code. And these are therefore likely to have greater influence on stabilising the language then the pronouncements of native speakers.

The essential point is that a standard English, like other varieties of language, devel-ops endo-normatively, by a continuing process of self-regulation, as appropriate to different conditions of use. It is not fixed, therefore, by native speakers. They have no special say in the matter, in spite of their claims to ownership of real English as associ-ated with their own particular cultural contexts of use.

[. . .]

Issues to consider

❑ Widdowson's paper argues uncompromisingly for precisely the kind of paradigm shift that Kachru calls for (see B3). To what extent do you agree or disagree with Widdowson's view that the standard English argument is suspect?

❑ Towards the end of his article, Widdowson claims that native English speakers do not have the right to determine the international development of English. While most authors who quote from the article tend to share his views, this particular point has received some negative comment. These are two such examples:

> Here is a quotation that has made a bewildering career [. . .]: 'How English develops in the world is no business whatever of native speakers in England, the United States, or anywhere else. They have no say in the matter, no right to intervene or pass judgement. They are irrelevant' (Widdowson 1994b: 385). Most readers will probably agree that this text is highly emotional, even hysterical. Whence comes this ascientific effect? Presumably from mixing matters linguistic with matters political-ideological (Sobkowiak 2005: 136).

> Widdowson . . . argues that 'how English develops in the world is no business whatever of native speakers [. . .] They have no say in the matter, no right to intervene or pass judgement'. No right, maybe, but I do think that some of us have an obligation, when asked, to ignore Widdowson's attempt to censor us. (Trudgill 2005: 86)

Do you agree with either or both? Why?/why not? Why do you think that some L2 English speakers (the first example) as well as some L1 English speakers (the second) have taken offence at Widdowson's point?

D4 FROM LANGUAGE TO LITERATURE

Although this section focuses on literature rather than language, many of the issues are the same. Underlying the extracts from Achebe and Ngũgĩ is the fundamental and unresolved question of whether the English language is able to (re)present the experience of speakers from other backgrounds, as well as the extent to which the language can or should be modified in the process. As you read through the two extracts, note the main points of disagreement between Achebe and Ngũgĩ on these issues.

'The African writer and the English language'

Chinua Achebe (reprinted from *Morning yet on Creation Day*, New York: Anchor, 1975)

Chinua
Achebe

I have indicated somewhat off-handedly that the national literature of Nigeria and of many other countries of Africa is, or will be, written in English. This may sound like a controversial statement, but it isn't. All I have done has been to look at the reality of present-day Africa. This 'reality' may change as a result of deliberate, e.g. political, action. If it does an entirely new situation will arise, and there will be plenty of time to examine it. At present it may be more profitable to look at the scene as it is.

What are the factors which have conspired to place English in the position of national language in many parts of Africa? Quite simply the reason is that these nations were created in the first place by the intervention of the British which, I hasten to add, is not saying that the peoples comprising these nations were invented by the British.
[…]

Of course there are areas of Africa where colonialism divided up a single ethnic group among two or even three powers. But on the whole it did bring together many peoples that had hitherto gone their several ways. And it gave them a language with which to talk to one another. If it failed to give them a song, it at least gave them a tongue, for sighing. There are not many countries in Africa today where you could abolish the language of the erstwhile colonial powers and still retain the facility for mutual communication. Therefore those African writers who have chosen to write in English or French are not unpatriotic smart alecs with an eye on the main chance – outside their own countries. They are by-products of the same process that made the new nation states of Africa.

You can take this argument a stage further to include other countries of Africa. The only reason why we can even talk about African unity is that when we get together we can have a manageable number of languages to talk in – English, French, Arabic.

The other day I had a visit from Joseph Kariuki of Kenya. Although I had read some of his poems and he had read my novels we had not met before. But it didn't seem to matter. In fact I had met him through his poems, especially through his love poem, 'Come Away My Love' in which he captures in so few words the trial and tensions of an African in love with a white girl in Britain.

> Come away my love, from streets
> Where unkind eyes divide
> And shop windows reflect our difference.

By contrast, when in 1960 I was travelling in East Africa and went to the home of the late Shabaan Robert, the Swahili poet of Tanganyika, things had been different. We spent some time talking about writing, but there was no real contact. I knew from all accounts that I was talking to an important writer, but of the nature of his work I had no idea. He gave me two books of his poems which I treasure but cannot read – until I have learnt Swahili.

And there are scores of languages I would want to learn if it were possible. Where am I to find the time to learn the half-a-dozen or so Nigerian languages each of which can sustain a literature? I am afraid it cannot be done. These languages will just have to develop as tributaries to feed the one central language enjoying nation-wide currency. Today, for good or ill, that language is English. Tomorrow it may be something else, although I very much doubt it.

Those of us who have inherited the English language may not be in a position to appreciate the value of the inheritance. Or we may go on resenting it because it came as part of a package deal which included many other items of doubtful value and the positive atrocity of racial arrogance and prejudice which may yet set the world on fire. But let us not in rejecting the evil throw out the good with it.

[...]

I think I have said enough to give an indication of my thinking on the importance of the world language which history has forced down our throat. Now let us look at some of the most serious handicaps. And let me say straight away that one of the most serious handicaps is *not* the one people talk about most often, namely, that it is impossible for anyone ever to use a second language as effectively as his first. This assertion is compounded of half-truth and half bogus mystique. Of course, it is true that the vast majority of people are happier with their first language than with any other. But then the majority of people are not writers. We do have enough examples of writers who have performed the feat of writing effectively in a second language. And I am not thinking of the obvious names like Conrad. It would be more germane to our subject to choose African examples.

The first name that comes to my mind is Olaudah Equiano, better known as Gustavus Vassa, the African. Equiano was an Ibo, I believe from the village of Iseke in the Orlu division of Eastern Nigeria. He was sold as a slave at a very early age and transported to America. Later he bought his freedom and lived in England. In 1789 he published his life story, a beautifully written document which, among other things, set down for the Europe of his time something of the life and habit of his people in Africa in an attempt to counteract the lies and slander invented by some Europeans to justify the slave trade.

[...]

It is when we come to what is commonly called creative literature that most doubt seems to arise. Obi Wali [...] has this to say:

> ... Until these writers and their Western midwives accept the fact that any true African literature must be written in African languages, they would be merely pursuing a dead end, which can only lead to sterility, uncreativity and frustration.

But far from leading to sterility the work of many new African writers is full of the most exciting possibilities.

[...]

[T]ake the poem 'Night Rain' in which J. P. Clark captures so well the fear and wonder felt by a child as rain clamours on the thatch-roof at night and his mother walking about in the dark, moves her simple belongings

> Out of the run of water
> That like ants filing out of the wood

Will scatter and gain possession
Of the floor . . .

I think that the picture of water spreading on the floor 'like ants filing out of the wood' is beautiful. Of course if you have never made fire with faggots you may miss it. But Clark's inspiration derives from the same source which gave birth to the saying that a man who brings home antridden faggots must be ready for the visit of lizards.

I do not see any signs of sterility anywhere here. What I do see is a new voice coming out of Africa, speaking of African experience in a world-wide language. So my answer to the question: *Can an African ever learn English well enough to be able to use it effectively in creative writing?* is certainly yes. If on the other hand you ask: *Can he ever learn to use it like a native speaker? I* should say, I hope not. It is neither necessary nor desirable for him to be able to do so. The price a world language must be prepared to pay is submission to many different kinds of use. The African writer should aim to use English in a way that brings out his message best without altering the language to the extent that its value as a medium of international exchange will be lost. He should aim at fashioning out an English which is at once universal and able to carry his peculiar experience. [. . .]

Allow me to quote a small example from *Arrow of God* which may give some idea of how I approach the use of English. The Chief Priest in the story is telling one of his sons why it is necessary to send him to church:

I want one of my sons to join these people and be my eyes there. If there is nothing in it you will come back. But if there is something there you will bring home my share. The world is like a Mask, dancing. If you want to see it well you do not stand in one place. My spirit tells me that those who do not befriend the white man today will be saying *had we known* tomorrow.

Now supposing I had put it another way, like this for instance:

I am sending you as my representative among these people – just to be on the safe side in case the new religion develops. One has to move with the times or else one is left behind. I have a hunch that those who fail to come to terms with the white man may well regret their lack of foresight.

The material is the same. But the form of the one is *in character* and the other is not. It is largely a matter of instinct, but judgment comes into it too.
[. . .]

One final point remains for me to make. The real question is not whether Africans could write in English but whether they *ought to*. Is it right that a man should abandon his mother-tongue for someone else's? It looks like a dreadful betrayal and produces a guilty feeling.

But for me there is no other choice. I have been given this language and I intend to use it. I hope, though, that there will always be men, like the late Chief Fagunwa, who will choose to write in their native tongue and ensure that our ethnic literature will flourish side-by-side with the national ones. For those of us who opt for English there is much work ahead and much excitement.

Chinua Achebe

Writing in the London *Observer* recently, James Baldwin said:

> My quarrel with English language has been that the language reflected none of my experience. But now I began to see the matter another way . . . Perhaps the language was not my own because I had never attempted to use it, had only learned to imitate it. If this were so, then it might be made to bear the burden of my experience if I could find the stamina to challenge it, and me, to such a test.

I recognise, of course, that Baldwin's problem is not exactly mine, but I feel that the English language will be able to carry the weight of my African experience. But it will have to be a new English, still in full communion with its ancestral home but altered to suit its new African surroundings.

The language of African literature

Ngũgĩ wa Thiong'o

Ngũgĩ wa Thiong'o (reprinted from *Decolonising the Mind: The Politics of Language in African Literature*, London: James Currey, 1986)

It was after the declaration of a state of emergency over Kenya in 1952 that all the schools run by patriotic nationalists were taken over by the colonial regime and were placed under District Education Boards chaired by Englishmen. English then became the language of my formal education. In Kenya, English became more than a language: it was *the* language, and all the others had to bow before it in deference.

Thus one of the most humiliating experiences was to be caught speaking Gĩkũyũ in the vicinity of the school. The culprit was given corporal punishment – three to five stokes of the cane on bare buttocks – or was made to carry a metal plate around the neck with inscriptions such as 'I am stupid' or 'I am a donkey'. Sometimes the culprits were fined money they could hardly afford. And how did the teachers catch the culprits? A button was initially given to one pupil who was supposed to hand it over to whoever was caught speaking his mother tongue. Whoever had the button at the end of the day would sing who had given it to him and the ensuing process would bring out all the culprits of the day. Thus children were turned into witch-hunters and in the process were being taught the lucrative value of being traitor to one's immediate community.

The attitude to English was the exact opposite: any achievement in spoken or written English was highly rewarded; prizes, prestige, applause; the ticket to higher realms. English became the measure of intelligence and ability in the arts, the sciences, and all the other branches of learning. English became the main determinant of a child's progress up the ladder of formal education.

As you may know, the colonial system of education in addition to its apartheid racial demarcation had the structure of a pyramid: a broad primary base, a narrowing secondary middle, and an even narrower university apex. Selections from primary into secondary were through an examination, in my time called Kenya African Preliminary Examination, in which one had to pass six subjects ranging from Maths to Nature Study and Kiswahili. All the papers were written in English. Nobody could pass the exam who failed the English language paper no matter how brilliantly he had done in the other

Ngũgĩ wa
Thiong'o

subjects. I remember one boy in my class of 1954 who had distinctions in all subjects except English, which he had failed. He was made to fail the entire exam. He went on to become a turn boy in a bus company. I who had only passes but a credit in English got a place at the Alliance High School, one of the most elitist institutions for Africans in colonial Kenya. The requirements for a place at the University, Makerere University College, were broadly the same: nobody could go on to wear the undergraduate red gown, no matter how brilliantly they had performed in all the other subjects unless they had a credit – not even a simple pass! – in English. Thus the most coveted place in the pyramid and in the system was only available to the holder of an English language credit card. English was the official vehicle and the magic formula to colonial elitedom.

Literary education was now determined by the dominant language while also reinforcing that dominance. Orature (oral literature) in Kenyan languages stopped. In primary school I now read simplified Dickens and Stevenson alongside Rider Haggard. Jim Hawkins, Oliver Twist, Tom Brown – not Hare, Leopard and Lion – were now my daily companions in the world of imagination. In secondary school, Scott and G. B. Shaw vied with more Rider Haggard, John Buchan, Alan Paton, Captain W. E. Johns. At Makerere I read English: from Chaucer to T. S. Eliot with a touch of Graham Greene.

Thus language and literature were taking us further and further from ourselves to other selves, from our world to other worlds.

What was the colonial system doing to us Kenyan children? What were the consequences of, on the one hand, this systematic suppression of our languages and the literature they carried, and on the other the elevation of English and the literature it carried? To answer those questions, let me first examine the relationship of language to human experience, human culture and the human perception of reality.

Language, any language, has a dual character: it is both a means of communication and a carrier of culture. Take English. It is spoken in Britain and in Sweden and Denmark. But for Swedish and Danish people English is only a means of communication with non-Scandinavians. It is not a carrier of their culture. For the British, and particularly the English, it is additionally, and inseparably from its use as a tool of communication, a carrier of their culture and history. Or take Swahili in East and Central Africa. It is widely used as a means of communication across many nationalities. But it is not the carrier of a culture and history of many of these nationalities. However in parts of Kenya and Tanzania, and particularly in Zanzibar, Swahili is inseparably both a means of communication and a carrier of the culture of those people to whom it is a mother-tongue. [. . .]

But there is more to it: communication between human beings is also the basis and process of evolving culture. In doing similar kinds of things and actions over and over again under similar circumstances, similar even in their mutability, certain patterns, moves, rhythms, habits, attitudes, experiences and knowledge emerge. Those experiences are handed over to the next generation and become the inherited basis for their further actions on nature and on themselves. There is a gradual accumulation of values which in time become almost self-evident truths governing their conception of what is right and wrong, good and bad, beautiful and ugly, courageous and cowardly, generous and mean in their internal and external relations. Over a time this becomes a way of life distinguishable from other ways of life. They develop a distinctive culture and history. Culture embodies those moral, ethical and aesthetic values, the set of spiritual

Ngũgĩ wa
Thiong'o

eyeglasses, through which they come to view themselves and their place in the universe. Values are the basis of a people's identity, their sense of particularity as members of the human race. All this is carried by language. Language as culture is the collective memory bank of a people's experience in history. Culture is almost indistinguishable from the language that makes possible its genesis, growth, banking, articulation and indeed its transmission from one generation to the next.

Language as culture [. . .] has three important aspects. Culture is a product of the history which it in turn reflects. Culture in other words is a product and a reflection of human beings communicating with one another in the very struggle to create wealth and to control it. But culture does not merely reflect that history, or rather it does so by actually forming images or pictures of the world of nature and nurture. Thus the second aspect of language as culture is as an image-forming agent in the mind of the child. Our whole conception of ourselves as a people, individually and collectively, is based on those pictures and images which may or may not correctly correspond to the actual reality of the struggles with nature and nurture which produced them in the first place. But our capacity to confront the world creatively is dependent on how those images correspond or not to that reality, how they distort or clarify the reality of our struggles. Language as culture is thus mediating between me and my own self; between my own self and other selves; between me and nature. Language is mediating in my very being. And this brings us to the third aspect of language as culture. Culture transmits or imparts those images of the world and reality through the spoken and written language, that is through a spe-cific language. [. . .] Written literature and orature are the main means by which a par-ticular language transmits the images of the world contained in the culture it carries.

Language as communication and as culture are then products of each other. Com-munication creates culture: culture is a means of communication. Language carries cul-ture, and culture carries, particularly through orature and literature, the entire body of values by which we come to perceive ourselves and our place in the world. How people perceive themselves affects how they look at their culture, at their politics and at the social production of wealth, at their entire relationship to nature and to other beings. Language is thus inseparable from ourselves as a community of human beings with a specific form and character, a specific history, a specific relationship to the world.

So what was the colonialist imposition of a foreign language doing to us children?

The real aim of colonialism was to control the people's wealth [. . .]. But its most im-portant area of domination was the mental universe of the colonised: the control, through culture, of how people perceived themselves and their relationship to the world. Eco-nomic and political control can never be complete or effective without mental control. To control a people's culture is to control their tools of self-definition in relations to others.

For colonialism this involved two aspects of the same process: the destruction or the deliberate undervaluing of a people's culture, their art, dances, religions, history, geography, education, orature and literature, and the conscious elevation of the language of the coloniser. The domination of a people's language by the languages of the colonising nations was crucial to the domination of the mental universe of the colonised.

Take language as communication. [. . .] Since the new language as a means of com-munication was a product of and was reflecting the 'real language of life' elsewhere, it could never as spoken or written properly reflect or imitate the real life of that commu-nity. This may in part explain why technology always appears to us as slightly external, *their* product and not *ours*. The word 'missile' used to hold an alien far-away sound until I recently learnt its equivalent in Gĩkũyũ, *ngurukuhi*, and it made me apprehend it differently. Learning, for a colonial child, became a cerebral activity and not an emotionally felt experience.

But since the new, imposed languages could never completely break the native languages as spoken, their most effective area of domination was [. . .] the written. The language of an African child's formal education was foreign. The language of the books he read was foreign. Thought, in him, took the visible form of a foreign language. So the written language of a child's upbringing in the school (even his spoken language within the school compound) became divorced from his spoken language at home. There was often not the slightest relationship between the child's written world, which was also the language of his schooling, and the world of his immediate environment in the family and the community. [. . .] This resulted in the disassociation of the sensibility of that child from his natural and social environment, what we might call colonial alienation. The alienation became reinforced in the teaching of history, geography, music, where bourgeois Europe was always the centre of the universe.

This disassociation, divorce, or alienation from the immediate environment becomes clearer when you look at colonial language as a carrier of culture.

[. . .]

Since culture does not just reflect the world in images but actually, through those very images, conditions a child to see that world in a certain way, the colonial child was made to see the world and where he stands in it as seen and defined by or reflected in the culture of the language of imposition.

And since those images are mostly passed on through orature and literature it meant the child would now only see the world as seen in the literature of his language of adoption. From the point of view of alienation, that is of seeing oneself from outside oneself as if one was another self, it does not matter that the imported literature carried the great humanist tradition of the best in Shakespeare, Balzac, Tolstoy, Gorky, Brecht, Sholokhov, Dickens. The location of this great mirror of imagination was necessarily Europe and its history and culture and the rest of the universe was seen from that centre.

But obviously it was worse when the colonial child was exposed to images of his world as mirrored in the written languages of his coloniser. Where his own native languages were associated in his impressionable mind with low status, humiliation, corporal punishment, slow-footed intelligence and ability or downright stupidity, non-intelligibility and barbarism, this was reinforced by the world he met in the works of such geniuses of racism as a Rider Haggard or a Nicholas Monsarrat; not to mention the pronouncement of some of the giants of western intellectual and political establishment, such as Hume ('. . . the negro is naturally inferior to the whites . . .'), Thomas Jefferson ('. . . the blacks . . . are inferior to the whites on the endowments of both body and mind . . .'), or Hegel with his Africa comparable to a land of childhood still enveloped in the dark mantle of the night as far as the development of self-conscious history was concerned. Hegel's statement that there was nothing harmonious with humanity to be found in the African character is representative of the racist images of Africans and Africa such a colonial child was bound to encounter in the literature of the colonial languages. The results could be disastrous.

[. . .]

Ngũgĩ wa Thiong'o

In history books and popular commentaries on Africa, too much has been made of the supposed differences in the policies of the various colonial powers, the British indirect rule (or the pragmatism of the British in their lack of a cultural programme!) and the French and Portuguese conscious programme of cultural assimilation. These are a matter of detail and emphasis. The final effect was the same: [. . .] Chinua Achebe's gratitude in 1964 to English – 'those of us who have inherited the English language may not be in a position to appreciate the value of the inheritance'. The assumptions behind the practice of those of us who have abandoned our mother-tongues are not different either. [. . .] It is the final triumph of a system of domination when the dominated start singing its virtues.

Issues to consider

❏ In his book *Decolonising the Mind* Ngũgĩ (1986: xiv) declares: 'This book, *Decolonising the Mind*, is my farewell to English as a vehicle for any of my writings. From now on it is Gĩkũyũ and Kiswahili all the way. However, I hope that through the age-old medium of translation I shall be able to continue dialogue with all'. Achebe, on the other hand, argues eloquently in favour of writing in English, but one adapted to its 'New English' users. With which of these two perspectives do you find yourself in greater sympathy?

❏ Ngũgĩ has indeed written his later works in his mother-tongue Gĩkũyũ for his local readers, and then translated them into English for a wider readership. In a review of Ngũgĩ's 2006 book *Wizard of the Crow*, Phillipson (2007) applauds his decision, arguing that '[i]nvesting in other languages, which Ngũgĩ is doing in a pioneering way, represents the creation of linguistic and cultural capital that can challenge English linguistic hegemony'. Do you agree with Phillipson that it is important to challenge the 'hegemony' of English by actions such as writing literature in the mother tongue? Why?/why not?

❏ Achebe argues above that '[t]he price a world language must be prepared to pay is submission to many different kinds of use'. How far do you agree in terms of both literary and non-literary use? It might help you, as regards non-literary use, to refer back to the earlier sections of strand 4, especially B4.

D5   IS LANGUAGE (STILL) POWER?

The book *Language is Power* (Honey 1997) promotes the author's belief that 'schoolchildren should be given maximum access to standard English' (p. 5), and attacks what he sees as the obstacle to such access: 'the consensus that has existed among linguists . . . for at least three decades now, around the hypothesis that I will call "linguistic equality", the notion that all languages, and all dialects of any language, are equally good'. This 'liberal orthodoxy', Honey believes, far from protecting underprivileged children, has 'inflicted lasting educational damage' on them (back cover) and is in need of remediation in both Britain and the US.

In 1998 a book taking a rather different view was published: *Language Myths* edited by the linguist Laurie Bauer and the sociolinguist Peter Trudgill. This book sets out to do precisely the opposite of Honey's. That is, its twenty-one articles each take a particular belief about 'correct' English, and demonstrate its mythical nature. The article reproduced below focuses on English grammar, discussing it in precisely the 'liberal' manner so despised by Honey. It is followed by two articles which appeared in May 2001 in the Singaporean newspaper, *The Straits Times*, one by the Speak Good English movement supporter (see C4) Alfred Lee lamenting the deterioration in the use of English by its native speakers in Britain, the other a response two days later from the non-prescriptivist Dennis Bloodworth.

'Bad grammar is slovenly'

Lesley Milroy (reprinted from Laurie Bauer and Peter Trudgill (eds) *Language Myths*, London: Penguin, 1998: 94–101)

Lesley Milroy

Like most language myths this one begs a number of questions, such as the following:

- ❑ What is meant by 'bad grammar'?
- ❑ What is meant by 'grammar'?

Can particular sentences of the English language reasonably be described as 'slovenly' – or 'lacking in care and precision', according to one dictionary definition? The quest for answers exposes the myth to critical scrutiny.

Newspaper features, letter columns and the mailboxes of the BBC are good places to find complaints about bad grammar. A rich harvest may be gathered if language use becomes the subject of public debate or if current educational policies are focusing on English teaching and testing. In Britain recently many judgemental remarks have been aired about 'Estuary English', the name given to a variety of the language which is spreading both socially and geographically.

Examples of specific constructions often described as bad grammar can be placed in at least three categories. The first, exemplified in sentences (1)–(3) along with the (presumed) correct form in italics, regularly occur in the speech and writing of educated people.

1   Who am I speaking to? / *To whom am I speaking?*
2   Martha's two children are completely different to each other / *Martha's two children are completely different from each other.*
3   I want to quickly visit the library / *I want to visit the library quickly.*

Two well-known 'errors' appear in (1), namely the preposition in the sentence final position and the nominative form of the relative pronoun 'who' rather than the oblique form 'whom' which is prescribed after a preposition. In (2) the expression 'different to' is used rather than the prescribed 'different from'; and in (3) there is a 'split infinitive'. In fact,

Lesley Milroy

the 'correct' versions were prescribed as such relatively recently in the history of the language, as part of the flurry of scholarly activity associated with the codification of the English language in the eighteenth century. Since the goal of codification is to define a particular form as standard, this process entailed intolerance of the range of choices which speakers and writers had hitherto taken for granted. In earlier centuries all these 'errors' appeared in highly sophisticated writing; in 1603, for example, Thomas Decker wrote 'How much different art thou to this cursed spirit here?' Different rationalizations were introduced to support these new prescriptions. The model of Latin was invoked to argue that a preposition should not end a sentence, that the inflected form of who should not appear anywhere other than in the subject of the sentence, and that an infinitive should not be split. The reason advanced by one writer of a popular manual of correctness for preferring 'different from' is that 'different to' is illogical, since no one would say 'similar from'. But it is not difficult to construct an equally logical argument in support of 'different to', since it falls into a set of words with comparative meanings such as similar, equal, superior, which require to. Not only are prescriptive arguments difficult to sustain, but if taken seriously they are likely to create problems. For example, 'Who am I speaking to?' is normal in most contexts, while 'To whom am I speaking?' will generally be interpreted as marking social distance. Thus the real difference between these forms is stylistic; both are good English sentences in appropriate contexts. Sometimes an attempt to follow the prescribed rules produces odd results.

4   A good author needs to develop a clear sense of who she is writing for.
5   A good author needs to develop a clear sense of for whom she is writing.

The prescription which outlaws (4) and yields (5), does not work because it is not based on a principled analysis of the structure of English but is a response to cultural and political pressures. By the eighteenth century Britain needed a standardised language to meet the needs of geographically scattered colonial government servants and to facilitate mass education. It did not too much matter which of a set of variants emerged as standard, as long as only one was specified as such. The prescribed standard was codified in grammars (such as Robert Lowth's) and dictionaries (the most famous being Dr Johnson's). No systematic grammar of English existed at that time, but Latin had a particular prestige as the lingua franca of scholars throughout Europe; hence the appeal not only to logic but to the model of Latin to justify particular prescriptions. But as we shall see shortly, English rules are very different from Latin rules, though equally complex; like all Germanic languages, English quite naturally places prepositions in sentence final position.

By 'bad grammar' then is sometimes meant expressions which are not in line with even unrealistic prescriptions. But what is grammar? Our myth refers to a *prescriptive* grammar, which is not a systematic description of a language, but a sort of linguistic etiquette, essentially an arbitrary set of *dos* and *don'ts*. [. . .]

Prescriptive rules are never as complex as properly formulated descriptive rules, and are easily dealt with by descriptive grammars. For example, *different from/to* would simply be specified as options; the split infinitive would not be an issue since the infinitive form of the verb is *visit*, not *to visit*; 'Who am I speaking to?' would be viewed as a normal sentence following the rules of English.

Sentences like (11) and (12) are also subject to popular criticism:

11 So I said to our Trish and our Sandra, 'Yous wash the dishes.'
12 Was you watching the game when the rain started?

Lesley
Milroy

Unlike (1)–(6), which are regularly used by educated speakers and writers, both of these are characteristic of low-status speakers. They were recorded respectively in Belfast and London, although the grammatical patterns which they illustrate are found elsewhere. It is the low social status of these speakers, indexed by details of their language use, which seems in this case to form the basis of negative evaluation. In such a way is social class prejudice disguised as neutral intellectual commentary, and for this reason one linguist has described linguistic prescriptivism as the last open door to discrimination. But note that (11) makes a systematic distinction between 'you' (singular) and 'yous' (plural) simi-lar to many languages of the world but lacking in standard English. Thus (11) cannot be argued to be in any sense linguistically impoverished (another common rationalization in defence of prescribed variants). Languages and dialects simply vary in the meaning distinctions they encode, regardless of their social status.

Note that (12) is a perfectly formulated question. Earlier in the history of English *was* and *were* in such sentences were acceptable alternatives (recall that the process of standardization has narrowed the range of socially and stylistically acceptable linguistic choices). But if we ask whether such sentences are 'slovenly' ('lacking in care and pre-cision') we must surely concede that the care and precision needed to implement the question-formation rule is considerable, placing in perspective the triviality of requiring *were* with a plural subject.

Let us look finally at two sentences which seem to be subject to criticism for yet a different reason:

13 Me and Andy went out to the park.
14 it's very awkward/it's difficult mind you/with a class of thirty odd/occasionally with the second form/you'll get you know/well we'll we'll have erm a debate/

Neither (13) nor (14) are clearly marked as belonging to a particular region, but between them they display a number of characteristics of informal spoken English. Uttered by an adolescent boy, (13) is criticised on the grounds that the wrong pronoun case (*me* instead of *I*) is used inside a conjoined phrase. Speakers are so conscious of this Latin-based prescription that even linguistically self-conscious and quite prescriptively minded individuals sometimes hypercorrect and use *I* where *me* is prescribed (a par-ticularly large number of complaints about these patterns of pronoun use are received by the BBC). Thus Margaret Thatcher once announced, 'It is not for you and I to con-demn the Malawi economy,' and Bill Clinton pleaded, 'Give Al Gore and I a chance.' But a systematic analysis of English grammar reveals underlying rules which permit variation between *me* and *I* only within conjoined phrases. Thus, adolescent boys do not habitually say 'Me went out to the park,' Clinton would not plead 'Give I a chance,' and not even Margaret Thatcher would have said 'It is not for I to condemn the Malawi economy.' With respect to *prescriptive* rules, there is often such a disparity between what speakers believe is correct and what they actually do; but *descriptive* rules are neither subject to violation nor are they part of our conscious knowledge of language.

Although conversation is often thought to be unstructured, ungrammatical and

Lesley Milroy

slovenly (presumably when judged against the norms of writing or formal speech), its complex organizational principles are quite different from those of planned spoken or written discourse; it is not simply spoken prose. Transcribed from a coffee-break conversation between two teachers, (14) is typical of informal conversation in its chunks (marked by slashes), which do not correspond to sentences of written English. Also in evidence are fillers such as *erm*, hesitations (marked by full stops), repairs, repetitions, and discourse tokens such as *you know*, *mind you*. Most of these features are attributable to conversation's interactive, online mode of production, and the two discourse tokens function as 'participation markers', signalling to the interlocutor that interactional involvement or response is expected. Thus, it hardly seems appropriate to describe even the apparently unstructured utterance (14) as 'slovenly'.

So what are we to say in conclusion about our current 'myth'? 'Bad grammar' is a cover term to describe a number of different kinds of English expressions. Some are widely used by educated speakers and writers but are outlawed by traditional prescriptions which are difficult to sustain; some appear to attract covert social prejudice by virtue of their association with low-status groups; and some follow the very characteristic but still rule-governed patterns of informal speech. All are perfectly grammatical, providing evidence of a complex body of rules which constitute mental grammars, the unconscious knowledge which speakers have of their own language. In comparison, the prescriptions which are recommended as 'good grammar' are revealed as at best marginal and frequently as unrealistic and trivial.

'English to get English lessons'

Alfred Lee

Alfred Lee (reprinted from *The Straits Times*, Tuesday, 15 May 2001)

A society has been set up to teach the English language to adults in England. Retired newspaper sub-editor John Richards was so appalled at public misuse of apostrophes that he formed the Apostrophe Protection Society.

After news of his society was revealed, hundreds of people, including teachers, writers, academics and others rushed to support his campaign and to join his society. They have now decided to expand the aims of the organisation – and to highlight common errors in English made by English people.

'English people are supposed to write excellent English – but many can't,' said Mr Richards, 75. 'My local fruiterer writes on posters that he sells bunch's of banana's. The public library has a sign saying that it has CD's. The largest supermarket in town promises 1000's of products at reduced prices. I was so irritated by the mistakes in the use of apostrophes that I had to do something.'

Headmaster Anthony Macrory said the group had 'a tremendous fight on our hands, with the Internet and e-mails responsible for "weblish" and mobile phone text messages undoing all that is taught in English classes'.

In 'weblish', e-mails are often sent in lower case or all in capital letters, because Internet users are too lazy to use the capital letter key. Punctuation is often left out. It is as though apostrophes, full stops and initial capital letters for proper nouns never

Alfred
Lee

existed, he said, adding that in the world of text messages, abbreviations and acronyms fly through cyberspace.

'Good English has nothing to do with messages that read RUF2T – Are you free to talk?; CUL8R – See you later; IJC2SaILuvU – I just called to say I love you,' he said.

A recent survey placed the literacy of adults in England among the lowest of any developed country. When Britain's education authority tried to fill some administrative posts, only six of 33 candidates with A-level qualifications passed a test in literacy. One 19-year-old applicant, asked to write a short essay on how he would organise a campaign against the use of narcotics, started by saying: 'I wud reed all the leaflets and complied a questionair concerning how the bodies system was effected by drugs.'

As Mr Tony Maher of the Plain English Campaign put it: 'Sadly, there is a huge army of grown-up English people who are illiterate. They cannot spell properly and their grammar and punctuation are atrocious.'

Professor Roger Holliday, an English expert, said he believed that things have been going downhill in Britain ever since the Rolling Stones sang, 'I Can't Get No Satisfaction'.

Checklist of common mistakes:

Split infinitives: 'Its five-year mission is to boldly go where no man has gone before.' Should be: 'to go boldly'.

You, I and me: 'Between you and I, Nicole Kidman and Tom Cruise were always going to separate.' Should be: 'between you and me'.

To lay and lie: 'I always lay down to sleep after a big meal.' Should be: 'always lie'.

Who or whom: 'Who do you think you are kidding, Mr Hitler?' Should be: 'whom do you think'.

Herewith: 'Enclosed herewith with this letter, please find another one.' 'With' should be deleted.

Prepositions: 'That was the Prime Minister I gave my vote *to*.' The sentence should *not* end with a preposition.

'Go on, dare to boldly split the infinitive'

Dennis Bloodworth (reprinted from *The Straits Times*, Thursday, 17 May 2001)

Dennis
Bloodworth

I was fascinated by the box ('Checklist of common mistakes') which accompanied the report, 'English to get English lessons' (*The Straits Times*, 15 May). *The Straits Times* listed splitting infinitives as one common mistake that people make. But what do the pundits say about this?

In his *Penguin Dictionary of Troublesome Words*, Bill Bryson writes that 'one (misconception) is the belief that the split infinitive is a grammatical error. It is not. Another is that the split infinitive is widely condemned. That too is untrue'.

He cites, as an example of the folly of religiously avoiding a split infinitive, this sentence

Dennis Bloodworth

from *The Times* (of London): 'The education system had failed adequately to meet the needs of industry and commerce.' Failed adequately? Well, thank goodness for that – or, no, wait a minute . . .

Sir Ernest Gowers writes about the split infinitive: 'Broadminded grammarians have described it as . . . a bad rule, and many people (including so good a writer as Bernard Shaw) have regarded it as a mere fetish'.

Eric Partridge quotes H. W. Fowler, who said that, though not desirable in itself, the split infinitive was preferable to ambiguity and 'patent artificiality', citing as an example, 'in not combining to forbid flatly hostilities'. Forbid flatly hostilities? What on earth does it mean?

Fowler himself points out that to avoid that patent artificiality, Byron wrote 'to slowly trace the forest's shady scene' and Thomas Hardy, 'she wants to honestly and legally marry that man'. He quotes sentences from Bernard Levin, Anita Brookner, John Updike, Julian Barnes, Iris Murdoch and others to show that when literary sense and rhythm and grace, clarity and style demanded it, they were ready to split with the best, and to hell with academic nitpickers.

The Times commented in fun in 1992: 'The most diligent search can find no modern grammarian to pedantically, to dogmatically, to invariably condemn a split infinitive'.

The Straits Times box correctly attacks 'Between you and I', but then it denounces 'I always lay down to sleep after a big meal'. It should be 'always lie', you say, but you are not 'always' right. If you are talking about the past, 'lay' *is* correct.

Next comes 'who or whom'. Your checklist quotes 'Who do you think you are kidding, Mr Hitler?', saying it should be 'whom do you think . . .' Spot on. Except that (if I remember rightly), this was the first line of a music-hall ditty sung during the Second World War in Cockney, and might well have begun (phonetically) not with 'who' or 'whom' at all, but 'Oo do you fink . . ., Mr 'itler?' And anyway that was about 60 years ago.

Do you really consider it a valid example of bad English today that you should pass on to Singaporeans in your newspaper? Are you suggesting that instead of 'Who do you think you're talking to?', they should learn to say 'To whom do you think you are talking?' And what about these examples from Fowler that flout the rigid rules you echo: 'Who wouldst thou strike?' (The Bible) and 'To who, my Lord?' (Shakespeare).

Gowers quotes Addison ('Who would I see there?') and Winston Churchill ('Moves made to displace their leader by someone whom they imagined would be a more vigorous President'). Partridge simply wants to abandon 'whom' altogether.

Finally, we come to prepositions: A sentence should not end with a preposition, says your box. Really? Bryson writes: 'Anyone who believes that it is wrong to end a sentence with a preposition . . . is about a century out of date . . . Today, happily, it is universally condemned as a ridiculous affectation'.

Gowers: 'Do not hesitate to end a sentence with a preposition if your ear tells you it is where the preposition goes best . . . no good writer ever heeded the rule, except Dryden'.

Fowler: 'One of the most persistent myths about prepositions is that they . . . should not be placed at the end of a clause or sentence'. Shakespeare obviously would have agreed with him; take 'Who servest though (*sic*) under?' or 'Who do you speak to?'

Pundits have asked how else would you write 'This bed hasn't been slept in' or 'What is the world coming to?'. Winston Churchill reputedly gave his opinion on the matter by saying 'This is the sort of English up with which I will not put'.

So what have you scored? According to my calculations, two out of six – all right, two and a half. I certainly wouldn't advise you to take the hot seat in 'Who Wants to Be a Millionaire?'

Dennis
Bloodworth

But, more seriously, your London correspondent Alfred Lee has excelled by finding yet another story that puts the British in a bad light, this one about their ignorance of their own language. The ignorance is real enough, unhappily. But, surely, that is all the more reason for not misleading poor Singaporeans with bogus dogma when they are already struggling with the wiles of English, the writing of which is an art, not a geo-metrical theorem in a secondary-school exam. I feel that Mr Lee should at least make sure that his sources know what they are talking about. Or do you really believe that sentence ought to read 'know about what they are talking'? Bunkum!

Issues to consider

❑ How far do you agree with Milroy and Bloodworth, and how far do you think that Honey's and Lee's positions (which are shared by many members of the British general public and right-wing press) are valid? In particular, do you believe that standard English use *still* provides people with power, and vice versa, or do you think that ten years on, things are changing, e.g. among younger users of English?

❑ Compare what is said about the language of texting in Lee's article with the views on texting presented in C5. Does this either reinforce or weaken your response to the previous question?

❑ Mugglestone (2003: 42) argues that '[p]rescriptive ideology . . . in spite of its pro-fessed egalitarianism, instead merely reinforces notions of the cultural hegemony of one social group above others'. She describes as 'fictions of "empowerment"' the attempts of eighteenth-century elocutionists such as Thomas Sheridan and John Walker to encourage the disadvantaged to 'emulate their "betters"' on the grounds that use of the standard would be a social leveller. Do you agree with Mugglestone that the 'language is power' argument actually works against rather than for the disadvantaged in society, and that equality can only result from acknowledging all language varieties as equal (the descriptive position)? Do you think either the prescriptive or descriptive position is achievable in practice?

❑ Milroy mentions speech/writing differences. In your view, do her arguments hold good for both, or are they more appropriate to one or other channel? (You might like to refer back to the section on speech and writing in C5.)

❑ Prepare a questionnaire that will enable you to compare the attitudes of older and younger English speakers in your own country towards specific 'incorrect' usages (use either your own examples or those provided above by Milroy, Blood-worth and Lee), and to the present-day grammatical competence in general of native speakers of English. After you have administered your questionnaire to a sufficient number of respondents (I suggest a minimum of six for each of the two groups), look for patterns relating to the age of the respondents. Do you think you would obtain different responses if you asked these questions in an L1 English-speaking country if yours is an L2 English-speaking one, or vice versa? Why might this be?

POSITIONING ENGLISH AS A LINGUA FRANCA

English as a Lingua Franca (ELF) was introduced in C6, where we examined a number of its potential features and looked briefly at some of the more negative attitudes towards them. In the reading in this unit, the author explores ELF in more detail, discussing its implications for notions such as 'speech community', 'language variety' and 'appropriate English', and considering the causes of negative attitudes towards ELF.

'English as a lingua franca and communities of practice'

**Barbara
Seidlhofer**

Barbara Seidlhofer (reprinted from *Anglistentag 2006 Halle Proceedings*, ed. S. Volk-Birke and J. Lippert 2007, Trier: Wissenschaftlicher Verlag: 307–18)

[. . .]
The most salient development of 'English' over recent years has obviously been its global spread and its concomitant variation and change. This global spread has taken place with unprecedented rapidity because air travel and electronic technology have effectively diminished the constraints of space. Whereas change was previously regulated by factors of physical proximity, these constraints have to a large extent now been eliminated.
[. . .]
   With the rise in numbers of speakers worldwide, norms have been diversifying and changing at an unprecedented pace, and to an unprecedented extent. This process has been most obvious in the assertion and recognition of essentially postcolonial uses of English as institutionalised, indigenised varieties, but it is increasingly being discussed with reference to contexts where English has traditionally been a foreign language with strictly native English models, such as continental Europe, China and Latin America.
[. . .]

Contradictory conceptions
In what follows, I would like to address what to me seem to be crucial underlying conceptual questions pertaining to why English as a lingua franca [. . .] has turned into a hotly disputed issue.
   [. . .] I propose to home in on what I see as the two most important contradictions in the intensifying and often controversial discussion of ELF. [. . .] one of these contradictions relates to descriptive and applied linguistics, and the other to language teaching.
   Here is the first contradiction – consider the following facts:
   Fact 1: Linguists are keen to describe language as it is 'really used' – witness the current preference for large-scale corpus studies of attested language and the focus on data obtained through observation rather than elicitation or intuition. This observation captures interactions as they happen, whether a researcher is there to record them or not. English linguistics is at the forefront of this development, and the claim thus is that descriptions have now become available of 'Real English'.
   Fact 2: The most widespread use of English, i.e. that which from a global perspective

Barbara
Seidlhofer

actually constitutes the prevailing reality of English, with the largest number of speakers, is English as a lingua franca, in interactions in which more often than not no native speaker participates. Seen globally, this is the English that is a reality for most speakers, and in this sense ELF is the most 'Real English'.

So we come to the first contradiction:

From Facts 1 and 2 it would seem reasonable to conclude that considerable descriptive effort should be going into understanding the real state of affairs of how speakers make use of English as a lingua franca. However, the only Englishes that have been deemed worthy of major descriptive research efforts so far are those spoken by what actually constitutes the minority of English speakers, namely those who speak it as their first language (i.e. the people in what Braj Kachru calls the Inner Circle) and, more recently, those that use it as an additional / official language, usually in postcolonial settings (what Kachru calls the Outer Circle). Hardly any descriptions are available of how ELF works – ELF is not regarded as 'Real English'. And few anglicists seem to think that this is a deficit.

Now two more facts, relating to teaching:

Fact 3: In the era of communicative language teaching and its contemporary variants such as task-based language teaching, English language teaching experts have been keen to emphasise that the language presented for learning should not be an idealised 'textbook English', but that it should be 'authentic', that is, the kind of language that is 'really used' for communication, by real people in real settings for real purposes. Again, the slogan 'Real English' is employed here to designate this desirable goal.

Fact 4: The reality of most speakers all over the world when they use English for a vast array of real purposes in real settings is that they are using it not as their native language, nor even to speak to somebody whose native language it is, but as a convenient means of communication with interlocutors with whom they do not share a first language. So the 'most real English' spoken by the largest number of speakers is English as a lingua franca, and most of today's learners of English will be tomorrow's users of ELF.

So the second contradiction is:

From Facts 3 and 4 one would expect one priority of current theorising in English language teaching to be a serious and substantial consideration of how learners can be helped to use ELF to achieve their actual communicative purposes, most likely with other non-native speakers of English. However, this concern is practically non-existent in current language teaching orthodoxy. And a good thing too, many anglicists would say.

The need for reconceptualisation

In what follows, I propose to try and shed some light on the reasons why these contradictions may have arisen and why they are proving so persistent. The thrust of my argument will be that new conditions require new conceptual frameworks, and unprecedented conditions may require unprecedented conceptual reframing. While this may seem difficult at present, my prediction is that in ten or twenty years these new concepts will be taken for granted and people will wonder what the fuss was all about. This requirement for re-appraisal is not, of course, universally recognised. There is a parallel here with another area of English studies. When I was discussing ELF and reactions to it with one of my literary colleagues, she remarked that early researchers in postcolonial literature encountered similar resistance, and that this is difficult to imagine nowadays, when there is probably no *Anglistik* department anywhere that does not conduct

Barbara
Seidlhofer

research into, and offer courses on, postcolonial literature. And the same observation could be made about the recognition of postcolonial, indigenised varieties of English, which was a hotly contested, controversial issue a couple of decades ago. As recently as in 1996, Kachru commented on reactions to his view that indigenised varieties of English should be recognised as varieties in their own right rather than stigmatised as interlanguages, and he found it necessary to say the following:

> There are essentially two types of response. One is to view this overwhelming linguistic phenomenon as an age-old process of language dynamics accentuated by the complex culturally and linguistically pluralistic contexts of language acquisition, language function, language contact, and language creativity. This response demands questioning the earlier paradigms, asking new probing questions, and looking for fresh theoretical and methodological answers. The second response, from a number of active scholars, is to marginalize any questions – theoretical, methodological, and ideological – which challenge the earlier paradigms or seek answers appropriate to new global functions of English.
>
> (Kachru 1996: 242)

Some ten years on there are not many linguists who would dispute that Indian English has its own recognised identity. Postcolonial literature, featuring as it does various Englishes around the world, has long been granted the academic seal of approval.

But when it comes to the largest group of speakers of English, namely those who use it as a lingua franca, the majority opinion still seems to be that the way they use the language does not constitute a worthwhile object of investigation in its own right. The prevailing view is that these speakers are actually simply unsuccessful learners who are using an interlanguage that is a language form belonging to an interim stage of learning that they would need to move away from in their striving for English as native speakers use it, even though it remains unclear just which English this is, and which native speakers use it. From the perspective as to what deserves attention in linguistic research, the prevailing view is that ELF is not a serious candidate, despite its undeniable presence and pervasiveness all around us.

Here is an example provided by Peter Trudgill, arguably the most eminent living British sociolinguist. In his book *Sociolinguistic Variation and Change*, Trudgill, like many other commentators, acknowledges the sheer scale on which English is being used and the way it is spreading in the world:

> There are many languages which have played important roles as institutionalised lingua francas: Latin was the lingua franca of the Roman Empire, and continued to play an important role in European learning until quite recently. But the extent to which English is employed like this is without parallel. Never before has a language been used as a lingua franca by so many people in so many parts of the world. English is also remarkable in having more non-native than native speakers ...
>
> (Trudgill 2002: 150ff)

Now you have just read this passage, what do you expect to come next? Being a sociolinguist, Trudgill might go on to say that the fact that the situation of English in today's

Barbara
Seidlhofer

world is without parallel should make for an exciting time for sociolinguists, since it is to be expected that some of the theoretical and descriptive linguistic research it gives rise to is likely to be without parallel, too. Given the increase in language variation and eventually also the acceleration of language change to be expected as a consequence of the global spread of English, he will probably say that this is the stuff that sociolinguists' dreams are made of. This is how he continues:

> There are . . . anglophone people who regard this expansion of English as a danger to the language. One reason is an irrational fear that one just cannot trust foreigners with one's language: who knows what they will get up to with it if native speakers are not at all times totally vigilant? After all, some foreigners seem to think that English is their language: some French and German speakers have invented English words which do not exist in English, such as lifting, or wellness, or handy, or pullun- der. This, however, is not a danger to English.
>
> (Trudgill 2002: 150f)

I agree: this is not a danger to English, but a fascinating development, a research arena opening up that will allow us to study close-up how the entirely natural language devel- opment of ELF exemplifies the ways in which a language can spread and vary, and ulti- mately change, in reaction to circumstances and conditions of use – and not just at the most obvious, lexical, level of course. The accelerated spread of English and the resulting tension between stability and variation would seem to be precisely the kind of phenom- enon that should interest sociolinguists, on whom the richness of functions and forms of English in the world is bound to exert particular fascination. So is this the gist of what Trudgill says next? Well, here is what does come next:

> . . . This, however, is not a danger to English. It is on the contrary quite interesting and amusing, and does not make any difference to anything important. It is a [sic] even a kind of compliment, perhaps. The true repository of the English language is its native speakers, and there are so many of them that they can afford to let non- natives do what they like with it so long as what they do is confined to a few words here and there.
>
> (Trudgill 2002: 151)

As one of those 'non-natives' I feel an urgent need to comment on this passage.

First of all, it seems odd (not to say patronising) for an eminent sociolinguist to call any naturally occurring, regularly attested forms of language use 'interesting and amus- ing' if they were not intended to be. Secondly, it is a simple fact that in the unparalleled situation English finds itself in, native speakers have ceased to be the only 'true reposi- tory' of the language: if – following precisely Trudgill's own logic – it is the number of speakers that is important, then ELF speakers might say that numerically, it is they that now are 'the true repository of the English language', and that there are so many of them that they can afford to let natives do what they like with it so long as what they do is confined to their own native-speaker communities.

We might also take issue with some lexical choices in the above passage: what exactly does it mean to say that something 'does not make any difference to anything

**Barbara
Seidlhofer**

important'? What would be 'something important'? And who is to be the arbiter of importance? And note that native speakers are called native speakers, not natives. But then aren't the 'non-natives' speakers too? Most importantly, there is the apodictic statement that 'the true repository of the English language is its native speakers' – this is asserted like an axiom, a dogma that by definition does not require any substantiation or justification. But academic enquiry is essentially incompatible with dogmatic assertions, so an explanation is called for. But it is not given.

What Peter Trudgill says here, and the way he says it, seem to me to be symptomatic of an attitude of denial which is paradoxically contradictory to Trudgill's own views on language variation. What I am arguing is that by denying the existence of ELF as a linguistic reality and therefore as something that deserves to be recognised and described as a natural language development, socio- and other linguists are acting against their very own academic principles. What they really need to explain is why ELF should be an exception, why this type of spread, variation and change should *not* be a legitimate object of study.

This is where we come back to the contradictions I sketched at the outset, and with Trudgill's quotation we have looked at an example of the kind of objections that are most often raised against ELF. As with his 'true repository' remark, objections usually centre around the argument that ELF speakers do not constitute a proper, stable speech community, and that therefore ELF cannot be like a variety used by people who live in proximity of each other and have regular contact. The implication of this objection is that if the investigation is unlikely to yield a complete system, a set of clear oppositions in structuralist terms, then it is not worth undertaking. Apart from the fact that this perspective ignores the inherent fuzziness and arbitrariness of boundaries between any varieties, it also, and this seems crucial to me, operates with concepts which may have been adequate to the world up to the 20th century but are in need of rethinking now. The most important ones in this context are the concepts of *community* and *variety* [...].

Rethinking 'community' and 'variety'

These concepts have to do with the relationship between language and society, and they derive from certain states of affairs, and have indeed arisen from an account of particular situations. If the situations they account for undergo radical change, then the concepts too will have to be reconsidered, and equally radically.

The traditional view of varieties – and this is simplifying somewhat – has been that a distinct variety in its own right can be acknowledged as such when it is used extensively and consistently by a community of speakers with their own sociocultural identity, primarily in regular face-to-face contact (cf. Schneider 2003). This of course has, over the last couple of decades, been the argument for recognising indigenised varieties of English, typically in postcolonial contexts. So it is identification with a particular community that makes a variety a variety.

But just what is a community? This surely is the crucial question here on which everything depends. [...]

In sociolinguistic terms, the idea of a speech community, according to Fishman (1971[b]: 232) 'probably translated from the German *Sprachgemeinschaft*', builds on this traditional sense of 'community' in its simplest definition as the '[t]otal set of speakers of the same (native) language' (Bussmann 1996, s.v. *speech community*).

Barbara
Seidlhofer

But the situation regarding communities has changed radically in recent times, particularly over the last decade or so. While previously it might have been reasonable to think of varieties as dialects which have to do with *primary socialisation*, up-bringing and with most interactions happening within a *primary community*, in the postmodern world the metaphor of 'international, or global, community' has turned into an everyday reality in a different literal sense. Countless interaction networks are independent of physical proximity and are instantiated through interaction over vast distances, often without the participants ever meeting 'in the flesh'. This means that *virtual communities* have achieved considerable significance in the sum of global interactions, giving rise to a very different meaning of 'community'. In contrast with local speech communities, such global communities tend to be referred to as discourse communities with a common communicative purpose or, more recently, as communities of practice, i.e. in Eckert and McConnell-Ginet's definition, 'aggregate[s] of people who come together around mutual engagement in an endeavour' (1992: 464). For Wenger (1998), the community of practice is defined by a process of social learning where three basic criteria hold:

1   mutual engagement in shared practices,
2   taking part in some jointly negotiated enterprise, and
3   making use of members' shared repertoire.

This repertoire consists of linguistic and other resources which are the agreed result of internal negotiations. Even from such a short characterisation it should be obvious that describing the language – or rather, the processes of languaging – in such communities poses quite different questions from those involved in the description of dialects as reified entities – a far cry from speech communities defined 'by the same (native) language'. Indeed, what may well characterise communities of practice on a global scale is that they do *not* have the same native language.

So with the current proliferation of possibilities created by electronic means and effortless global mobility, changes in *communications* have accelerated and forced changes in the nature of *communication*: the *media* now available have changed the *modes* of use. And in all this, English is in a pivotal position: already established as a widespread language, it is particularly well placed to play a crucial role in these changed conditions, where communities can no longer be defined mainly in terms of face-to-face contact, and certainly not by a common native language. It is now commonplace, and indeed necessary, for people who want 'to get on in the world', to use a means of communication that takes them beyond traditional community boundaries: wider networking needs a lingua franca.

What is important here of course is that English as a lingua franca is a language of *secondary socialisation*, a means of wider communication to conduct transactions outside one's primary social space and speech community. So instead of varieties in the sense of 'dialects' as used in different kinds of primary 'community', in the case of ELF we are looking at varieties in terms of 'registers' as used in different kinds of 'communication'. The distinction introduced by Halliday (Halliday 1978; Halliday et al. 1964) between dialect as a variety with reference to *user* and register as a variety with reference to *use* captures this difference very neatly while according both kinds of variety equal importance. It is likely that at the time when this distinction was proposed, the notion of

**Barbara
Seidlhofer**

'dialect' was considered primary, and dialectology as the study of varieties in particular locations has, after all, always been a staple area of enquiry in sociolinguistics.

But dialect maps with their isoglosses that demarcate local usages need now to be complemented with accounts that capture the processes of ongoing global change in English. What we are witnessing now in worldwide communication mostly via ELF, is an exponential increase in 'dislocated' interactions driven by needs and wants in specific domains of use, thus foregrounding and upgrading the significance of 'registers' as experientially equally salient. Any professionals worth their salt are expected to feel at home in international networks. All areas of knowledge and expertise worth taking note of, and certainly anything that makes serious money, ignores national boundaries and is global by its very nature; research projects without an international dimension stand no chance of being funded. Many young people communicate happily in chatrooms populated by interactants from all over the world and say that the communities they are part of there are as real to them as their classroom ones. [. . .]

The main argument I am attempting to outline here is, then, that with radical technology-driven changes in society, inevitably our sense of what constitutes a *legitimate community* and a *legitimate linguistic variety* has to change, too. Along-side local speech communities sharing a dialect we are witnessing the increased emergence of global discourse communities, or communities of practice sharing their particular registers, with English being the most widely used code. This development has a momentum of its own, and is happening at a pace that gives us little time to adjust our conceptual categories.

And this is what I was getting at when sketching, at the beginning of this paper, the two contradictions as I see them in the contemporary description and teaching of English: they reflect a time-lag, a lack of fit between the role of English in the contemporary world and current practices and priorities in the description and teaching of English. These can only be resolved by looking afresh at familiar ideas and labels. The operative word to use here, I would suggest, is 'appropriate'.

Appropriate English

What effectively I have been talking about is what *appropriate* language use in *particular communities* is. Appropriateness is of course one of the four factors of Communicative Competence discussed by Hymes in his familiar programmatic model. [. . .] Interestingly, and of particular relevance to the argument I am pursuing here, appropriateness is generally interpreted as relating to primary social communities of native-speaker users and not to communities of practice which cut across the native–non-native distinction. But logically, of course, the criteria for appropriateness also need to take into account the broader needs and purposes of lingua franca English use. And indeed here one has to accept that it is likely to be appropriate in many, if not most contexts in which English is currently used, *not* to fully conform to native speaker conventions. This is because these native speaker conventions derive from quite different, local communities of users and are replete with in-group markers of shared sociocultural identity, conditions that just do not obtain in the same way in ELF situations. [. . .]

The interpretation of appropriateness as pertaining only to primary speech communities relates, of course, to the Real English issue which I mentioned earlier. What is appropriate effectively becomes what is normally produced in contexts of native speaker use. Thus appropriateness is a feature of norms of behaviour. A norm is a descriptive category:

Barbara
Seidlhofer

it is an account of what actually, customarily or normally, occurs. When this is prescribed as something that needs to be conformed to it becomes a standard [. . .]. It is entirely desirable and reasonable to describe the norms of native speaker use as is now extensively done in corpus linguistics, but it is entirely undesirable and unreasonable to suppose that those norms should automatically serve as the default standards for pedagogic purposes. Of course there need to be standards in language pedagogy, and this must involve pre-scribing some model of use that calls for conformity, otherwise both teachers and learners would be in limbo and no teaching or learning would be possible, let alone measurement of learning outcomes. But the question arises as to what criteria such a model needs to meet. Traditionally, it has been assumed that to have any standards for effective use or learning of English there needs to be an absolute adherence to standard English as ratified by native speakers. What has been persistently misunderstood is that there is no denial of the importance of standards in considering the possibility – and at this stage it is only a possibility until more descriptive work is done – of using insights into how ELF commu-nication works for formulating appropriate and relevant goals for learning. Standards there must be, but in the changed world of English that I have been discussing the question is, what is a valid and realistic – and therefore appropriate – way of defining them? [. . .]

Until we have more description of ELF as it actually occurs, we are in no position to make any pedagogic suggestions. But even the interim results from ELF research so far indicate the need at least to think again about the assumptions generally made about norms and standards. At the very least, teachers, especially if they claim to be 'reflective practitioners', surely need to be able to reflect on ideas that have been taken as received wisdom, but which are grounded in past states of affairs which no longer obtain. I am not arguing for the promotion of any specific new approach or paradigm. Far from it, I am arguing the need for a critical reappraisal of received ideas and an open-minded reconsideration of what is pedagogically relevant. [. . .]

Conclusion

Established ideas, as I have already indicated, will always prime people to interpret things in a certain way. This, of course, applies to this paper as well. It is my experi-ence that since people have, and indeed need to have, certain established ideas about standard English and English as a lingua franca, many are naturally resistant to my argu-ment and may be prone to misinterpret what I am saying. So in conclusion, let me there-fore summarise the points I have been trying to make, and clarify my position. I am not advocating throwing out the old categories and replacing them by new ones. Nor do I think, however, that existing concepts should be bent in order to accommodate drastic new developments. As always, changed circumstances call for a rethinking of established ideas. I am therefore certain that it is not helpful to transfer familiar ideas to as yet unfamiliar contexts, where we are bound to find them wanting; or worse, to accuse new concepts of not making sense while actually, caught in a conceptual straightjacket based on previous circumstances, it is us that fail to make sense of them. Thus there is little to be gained by closing our eyes to the contemporary reality of English as a lingua franca, whatever name we choose to give it, just because we cannot neatly slot it into categories of 'variety' and do not wish to call its users a 'community'. [. . .]

Issues to consider

❏ Seidlhofer argues that we need to rethink how we interpret the notion of 'language variety', because the traditional interpretation (a dialect used by a clearly definable group of speakers) does not account for global communities and the ways they use English. Do you think it will be possible for people to conceive of legitimate English in ways that do not conform to the norms of particular L1 groups of English speakers? Why/why not? And either way, what kinds of obstacles do you predict?

❏ Another concept that needs rethinking in terms of ELF, according to Seidlhofer, is that of 'speech community'. One important aspect of any language community is often said to be the shared identity of its speakers. To what extent do you think ELF speakers might have or might develop some sort of shared identity, whether global or local (e.g. European, south-east Asian, Japanese, German, or the like)? Do you agree with House (1999, 2001, 2003) that ELF is purely a 'language of communication' and that ELF speakers use their L1 as a 'language of identification'? Or do you agree with Cogo (Cogo and Dewey 2006), Erling and Bartlett (2006), and others who argue that ELF speakers wish to project their identities in their English?

❏ Seidlhofer critiques Trudgill's (2002) perspective on ELF in some detail in her paper. However, much more recently, Trudgill has adjusted his view:

. . . it may be that there are developing in some parts of the world varieties that we can call *ELF* – English as a lingua franca – in the sense that, say, the way Europeans speak English to each other may be taking on a relatively stable common form, different from [ENL], which could be described and taught to learners if they so wish.

(Trudgill and Hannah 2008: 7–8)

Does this suggest to you that some of the more negative attitudes towards ELF may soften over time in the light of increasing empirical evidence and/or first-hand experience of ELF communication?

❏ If you have access to the internet, take a look at the VOICE website (at www. univie.ac.at/voice), where the entire VOICE corpus was put online in 2009. Does the material on this website make you want to rethink your answers to any of the previous questions? If so, how?

ATTITUDES TO LOCAL NORMS IN THE EXPANDING CIRCLE   **D7**

Two views about local norms in the Expanding Circle

In unit C6, I made the point that ELF does not only consist of features shared by all its speakers: ELF speakers also use features that relate specifically to their *own* L1 variety of English. In the two readings in this unit, scholars from two very different parts of the Expanding Circle, China and Germany, consider the implications of the spread of English in relation to norms for English users from their own region. In the first reading, Hu argues in support of the legitimacy of her own English variety, China English. Whereas most of the debate about English in the Expanding Circle has focused on its spoken forms, Ammon, in his discussion of German English in the second reading, extends the debate to written forms. As you read through the two extracts, observe how, despite their different linguistic backgrounds, the two authors share a number of similar concerns and views.

'Why China English should stand alongside British, American, and the other "world Englishes"'

Hu Xiao Qiong (reprinted from *English Today*, vol. 20, no. 2, 2004: 26–33)

Hu Xiao Qiong

[...]

English as a global language
English has for some time been learned worldwide, and is now spoken in every country of the globe. Some 380 million people speak it as their first language and perhaps two-thirds as many again as their second. A billion are learning it, about a third of the world's population are in some sense exposed to it, and by 2050, it is predicted, half the world will be more or less proficient in it. It is the language of globalization: of international business, politics and diplomacy. It is the language of computers and the Internet. Truly, the tongue spoken in the 14th century only by the 'low people' of England has come a long way.

In Asia, the number of English users has reached *c.* 350 million, a figure that is equal to the combined population of the United States, Britain and Canada. It is estimated that the proportion of English users in non-English-speaking countries and English-speaking countries is something like 2–4: 1 (Kachru 1997). Such estimates indicate that English, as a lingua franca, is playing an increasingly important role in every corner of the world and in many sectors of society. Phillipson (1992) employs the term 'linguistic imperialism' to describe this phenomenon. However, former colonies have no wish to be recolonized; on the contrary, the reverse is happening. As he quotes one Filipino poet as saying, speaking in effect for all Asian users of the language: 'English is now our language. We too have colonized it.' It is clear from this that English is now no longer the exclusive property of its native speakers.[...]

Hu Xiao
Qiong

China English versus Chinese English/Chinglish

In China, one major variety, now widely known as 'China English', is attracting growing attention from linguists, researchers and educators there (cf. Jia Delin 1990; Jia Guanjie and Xiang Mingfa 1997; Jiang Yajun 1995; Li Wenzhong 1993; Wang Rongpei 1991). However, before we can proceed further, we need to be clear what we mean by not only 'China English' but also the older terms 'Chinese English' and 'Chinglish' in relation to China English. When attempting to distinguish them, it will be useful to start from Rudzka's comment on categories and language (1985: 242–43):

> Categories are not uniform entities with clear boundaries and strictly defined sets of properties . . . Cognitive grammarians view language as a network of open-ended categories. There are no strict boundaries.

In a similar vein, we can say that there is no clear boundary between Chinglish and Chinese English on the one side and China English on the other, it is not possible to place them neatly into two categories. Instead, they are situated on a continuum and progressively merge.

At the 'bottom' end of the continuum we have a kind of pidgin, Chinglish, in its most marked form: words are ungrammatically strung together, with often inappropriate lexis and probably only a partially comprehensible pronunciation. The link between this form of language and standard English is tenuous. The internal flight system within China is rich with examples of Chinglish: messages in English rapidly given by the air hostess over the intercom are almost totally incomprehensible to any speaker of English, the main problem being pronunciation. Comparably, on the backs of seats, one reads the message 'Use the bottom cushion for flotation', which is perfect grammatically, but one is lost for a meaning, especially as one looks in vain for a cushion. At the airport, the sign 'Departure Arrive' is lexically sound but quite ungrammatical, and one can see attractive cabin bags for sale, advertised as 'Refiand: Buy rave refland bags', where a real effort is required to interpret *refined* in both instances and many people must wonder about the intended meaning of *rave*.

At the other end of the continuum we have China English: a language which is as good a communicative tool as standard English. The pronunciation is close enough not to pose much of a problem; there may be some syntactic and grammatical differences attributable to the influence of Chinese; and the lexis may occasionally differ, reflecting cultural differences – as pointed out by Ge Chuanghui (1980), who first introduced the term *China English*. An example: the word *face* is strongly stressed in Chinese culture; it means honour, dignity, pride, or even identity. So expressions like *give face, save face, no face, lose face* are very often used. Take, for example, the following:

1   I lost a lot of face by being unable to answer this question.
2   This saved me a great deal of face.
3   They started quarrelling. I didn't know where to hide my face.
4   How can you do that to me? I really got no face now.
5   You must go to his son's wedding dinner. You must give him face (from [Honna] Nobuyuki 2001).

Although the expression *to lose face* has worked its way into standard British English, meaning to look ridiculous or lose the respect of others, in the course of cultural transition it has lost much of its original meaning, and the other expressions are not commonly used – although they might well be understood if heard or read. We cannot, however, say that for this reason they should be condemned as 'incorrect English' or 'bad English' just because people in the Inner Circle do not use (or know) them.

Hu Xiao
Qiong

The criterion for situating an utterance at a point on the continuum, in respect of grammar, syntax, lexis and pronunciation, must be the degree of proximity to, or distance from, a standard variety. Li Wenzhong (1993) has suggested that China English be defined as a variety of English whose vocabulary, sentences and discourse have Chinese characteristics. It is based on standard English, and has been adapted to express characteristics of Chinese culture in terms of phonetic translation, borrowing and meaning reproduction.

Why use China English as a standard?

There are at least three reasons.

1 As indicated above, China English is quite different from Chinglish, since it retains a 'common core' that renders it as intelligible to speakers of other varieties of English as Hiberno-English or Australian English. However, other varieties of English are unable to transmit many of the cultural references that Chinese speakers of the language will want to communicate. Both in old China and new China, there are many things that are unique, for which English equivalents cannot be found. We can give the following examples:

> *baihua*: modern-style Chinese writing and speaking
> *the four modernizations*: the modernization of industry, agriculture, science and technology
> *develop-the-west*: the name or slogan of a policy of investing money and talent to develop the western regions of the country
> *trans-century talent*: talented people in the new century; ethical and cultural progress conserving the spirit of Chinese civilization
> *pay New Year calls*: what people do when they give greetings to each other at the Spring Festival

The study of China English could both further enrich general English vocabulary and introduce to other countries unique features of the culture so that China will be better understood.

2 British English tends to be the variety of English that is taught in many European second- and third-level educational institutions, for the simple reason that it is more useful (and closer) to them than American English. Similarly, other countries in Asia may find that China English is more useful to them, politically, economically and culturally, than other varieties, as it reflects more accurately their needs, both culturally and in business. Not long ago, the British Government was severely criticized by the German ambassador to London when it announced a reduction in the foreign-language component of the national curriculum (*BBC News*, February 2002). The government's attitude was that

Hu Xiao Qiong

English was so widely spoken that the money could be used for other resources. The German ambassador, however, made the point that one needs to know the culture of one's business partners, and at least make an attempt to show an interest in the language, even if the actual business itself is conducted in English – if, that is, one wants to be successful in business.

3 The huge population of China, the country's recent entry into the World Trade Organization, and the ensuing international cultural and business contacts may all mean that China will be using English more and more, providing a basis from which its own variety of the language may very well dominate, due – if nothing else – to the sheer numbers of Chinese speakers and foreigners' new contacts with China.
[…]
     This leads us to the question of why a native-speaker standard should be imposed upon learners of English, when most of its speakers are in fact learning English as a second or foreign language. Is there any good reason to justify the native-speaker monopoly of the 'standard' variety of English?
     It is up to the people who speak English as a second or foreign language to determine its future development: that is, the people in the Outer Circle and the Expanding Circle, in particular the Indians and the Chinese, whose countries are by far the most heavily populated. It can therefore be seen why the study of World Englishes assumes great importance.
[…]

Implications for teaching
The study of China English and World Englishes has provided some insights into English teaching and learning in China.

     First, it is clear that China English should be further and more fully studied and that the English taught and learned should not be only British or American English. There are other members of the Inner Circle who have thrown off the yoke of colonialism in the past century and are proud of their standard variety of English, e.g. the Australians and the Irish. Today, people using English do not communicate solely with native speakers. More often than not, they communicate with non-English speakers; their English therefore does not need to reflect Anglo-Saxon culture. English is no longer a colonial language; it is a tool with which Asian people, among others, communicate with the world […]. [Honna] Nobuyuki (2001) writes: 'We learn English not only because we use it to communicate with British or American people. What is more important, we use English to communicate with Chinese, Koreans, Thais, Indonesians …'
     English has become an international language in the sense that it is a language for communication between people from different cultures. It is therefore natural that Japanese to speak English with a Japanese accent, and Chinese with a Chinese accent. It follows that the English of different cultures should be highly encouraged as it reflects the user's identity and culture. Nowadays many people in the Outer Circle are proud to speak English with their native accent. Tommy Koh (Kirkpatrick 2000) writes: 'When I speak English I want the world to know I'm a Singaporean.'
     China has joined the WTO and won the right to host the Olympics for 2008, so

Hu Xiao
Qiong

learning English is becoming an important part of people's daily lives. Even elderly ladies in Beijing are beginning to learn it enthusiastically! It is predicted that English will be many people's second language and it is likely that China English will become the variety of English spoken by the largest number of people in the world. In that case, British or American English should not be the focus of language teaching in the classroom. Instead, we must systematise China English in terms of phonetics, grammar, vocabulary, culture, etc., and learners need to be more exposed to a China English through which Chinese culture can be better and more thoroughly understood.

Second, we should integrate China English into textbooks and other teaching materials. As English is sweeping the world as a lingua franca, nativization is inevitable. Currently, the situation in China is that almost all English textbooks and readings, from kindergarten to university, either originate in the Inner Circle countries or represent their culture. Why cannot we give courses in Chinese literature and Chinese politics, for example, in an English that reflects our culture? Many Chinese students know a great deal about the West, but very little about their own country. This is largely the fault of the teaching materials used. Sadly, there are many young people who seem to be acquiring a higher regard for Western culture than for their own.

At present, teachers, researchers and other specialists in English language learning in China are considering the streamlining of English teaching and learning, from kindergarten to university (cf. [Dai] Weidong 2002 [. . .]). It would be good to make China English the standard. The native speaker models could be incorporated as external models, but not as a must, since they are unrealistic (cf. Kirkpatrick 2000) and, as we have argued, virtually unattainable objectives.

Thirdly, let students be widely exposed to World Englishes and take communicative responsibility for what they themselves say. Studies have shown that where communication is not a problem, it is a non-standard pronunciation rather than syntax, grammar or even lexis that produces a negative reaction. The following dialogue from the film *Falling Down* perfectly illustrates this, where the customer, after a momentary lack of comprehension, adopts a highly aggressive stance:

Asian (shopkeeper): Eighdy fie sen.
D-Fens (customer): What?
Asian: Eighdy fie sen.
D-Fens: I can't understand you . . . I'm not paying eighty-five cents for a stinking soda. I'll give you a quarter. You give me seventy 'fie' cents back for the phone. What is a fie? There's a 'v' in the word. Fie-vuh. Don't they have 'v's' in China?
Asian: Not Chinese. I am Korean.
D-Fens: Whatever. What difference does that make? You come over here and take my money and you don't even have the grace to learn to speak my language.

(Lippi-Green 1997: 100–2)

Hu Xiao
Qiong

Those who have not gone through the arduous process of learning another language are often oblivious of the difficulties in not only producing certain sounds in the target language but even of hearing them (Winitz 1977). It is a well-established fact that beyond the age of puberty, it is virtually impossible to acquire a standard pronunciation in the target language (cf. Lenneberg 1967 [. . .]; Lippi-Green 1997). Tolerance and flexibility, the key words for attaining world peace, must necessarily be reflected in language. Exposure of language learners to different varieties of English, particularly through movies, sound recordings and television, can considerably reduce the problem. It should not be forgotten that native speakers of English encounter similar difficulties with other varieties of English. When American films were first shown in English in Britain, many viewers believed that they were listening to a foreign language! In the Chinese context, we further recommend that English teachers from countries from the Outer Circle and the Expanding Circle, like India, Singapore, Korea, Russia, Saudi Arabia, etc., be employed to teach English in our country.

Conclusion

The focus of English language teaching and learning in China needs to change, the materials need to be changed, attitudes need to change, and it is to be hoped that in the course of time China English will become an honored member of the Inner Circle. If the members of the Inner Circle adjust to the variety of English of the other members and accept it, then there is no reason why they cannot do so with other varieties of the language; once this has taken place, it will no longer be necessary (as is the case with the author of this article who, incidentally, has never set foot in an [Inner Circle] English-speaking country) to have her China English adapted to one of the two standard varieties by a member of the Inner Circle, in order to ensure its acceptance at an international level. We need one circle, not three, in the interests of cultural transmission, understanding and world peace. There must be give and take on all sides.

'Towards more fairness in international English: linguistic rights of non-native speakers?'

Ulrich
Ammon

Ulrich Ammon (reprinted from Robert Phillipson (ed.) *Rights to Language: Equity, Power, and Education*, Mahwah, NJ: Lawrence Erlbaum, 2000: 112–16)

[. . .]

In spite of the majority of non-native speakers of the non-inner-circle countries, many of whom use the language actively and regularly in institutional frameworks, the native speakers of the inner-circle countries retain the hold to the yardstick of linguistic correctness. The inner-circle countries' population is usually equalised, at least roughly, with the native speakers of the language. That their command of the language be superior to any others' is by and large taken for granted. Even researchers who are aware of the numerical proportions of speaker groups or who deal with globalization of the language finally stick to this assumption. Crystal (1997: 130–9) or Graddol (1997: 10–11), for instance, go a long way in presenting and justifying the 'New Englishes' of the outer or even the expanding-circle countries and underlining their values, but

Graddol is probably right in pointing out that they, in spite of forming 'distinct varieties', often follow an 'underlying model of correctness' of either Britain or the USA (p. 11). Graddol also, like Crystal, finally retains traditional correctness judgments – contrary to what he seems to profess in some sections of his book. This is at least how I read some of his remarks. I see nothing wrong with his ranking *fluency* in spoken English from 'native-like' to 'extremely poor' (p. 11). But he also states, when reporting on the production of a book written in English, that '[t]he development and writing of the book require advanced "native-speaker" skills' (p. 42). Advanced non-native speaker skills wouldn't do, one must conclude. Native-speaker norms remain the final basis of correctness judgments.

Correctness judgment along these lines seems to be particularly rigorous with respect to written scientific or scholarly texts. British or US English language standards relate to different aspects of texts: orthography, vocabulary, grammar, pragmatic and discourse features as well as text structure in the narrower sense. Clyne (1987) has shown that English and German academic texts are structured differently in various respects (linearity/digression (Exkurs), symmetry, advance organisers, and hedging) and that English texts written by Germans tend to retain typical Germain structures which, as a rule, are evaluated negatively by English readers or reviewers (cf. also the literature on comparisons of English and other languages with respect to text structure in Clyne 1987). The British reviewer of a handbook of German editors found 'some of the English written by non-native speakers so bad (. . .) as to be almost incomprehensible' (cf. Ammon 1989: 267). Similarly, a US reviewer of another book of a German editor, in fact myself, complained about 'near unintelligibility', because 'the grammatical mistakes are so severe'. He also did not appreciate that a 'decidedly German substratum peeks through in many of the papers written in English' (Di Pietro 1990: 301, cf. for other examples Coulmas 1987: 106ff).

In contrast to such criticism of British or US reviewers, I am doubtful whether the texts under scrutiny were really unintelligible, or even especially hard to understand. Generally, I dare to assume that unintelligibility is not the main reason why texts in non-native English are often rejected or judged negatively by native speakers. One indication is that the native speakers who 'corrected' or 'polished' my own English language texts have never had serious difficulty understanding them correctly except in a few instances. Similar experiences were confirmed by about a dozen German colleagues whom I queried. One should also be aware of the fact that texts produced by native speakers can contain unclarities too, especially ambiguities, and as a consequence be unintelligible at some points.

The question of intelligibility of non-native-speaker texts can of course not be answered without comprehensive empirical research. There is evidence with respect to spoken language – and similar results would probably be found with respect to written language – that non-native English is indeed harder to understand for native speakers than is native English (Nelson 1982). It has, however, also been confirmed that 'speakers with shared cultural and linguistic norms obtain higher degrees of intelligibility in their language interactions' (Nelson 1982: 60). Non-native speakers of English understand non-native speakers of the same linguistic background better than non-native speakers of another linguistic background. In addition, non-native speakers of English or any linguistic background probably understand native speakers of British or American standard

Ulrich Ammon

English better than they do non-native speakers of another linguistic background other than their own. Nevertheless, there are reasons to assume that native speakers' negative evaluations of non-native-speaker texts are not only, or often not primarily, based on problems with intelligibility. Do they arise from what has been called 'linguicism'? Are they a special type of linguistic prejudice?

Linguicism?

Linguicism has been characterised as using the languages of different groups as defining criteria and as the basis for hierarchization (Skutnabb-Kangas and Phillipson 1994: 104, 1996a). there are various aspects of such hierarchization, and the delimitation of linguicism is not always easy. A clear case of linguicism, which seems widespread in the scientific community, are quality judgments of texts according to the language in which they are written. Vandenbroucke (1989: 1461) assumes with respect to medical dissertations in the Netherlands: 'By the language a thesis is written in you immediately judge its quality,' meaning that a thesis in English is valued more highly – as to its content! – than a thesis in Dutch. Matched-guise technique with written texts in Scandinavia confirmed the possibility of such judgment. Two different texts, each in two language versions: the national Scandinavian language and English, were presented to referees: 'the majority of different aspects of scientific content was assessed to be better in English than in the national language version for both manuscripts' (Nylenna, Riis and Karlsson: 1994: 151).

It could also be argued that it is linguicism if native speakers of a prestige language are ranked higher socially (in some way) than non-native speakers. Is it, however, still linguicism if texts in line with native-speaker standards are valued more highly than those with 'deviations' from these standards? Calling this linguicism seems to be justified if the native-speaker standards do not guarantee more communicative efficiency. They in fact may not, at least in the future, with the growing number of non-native speakers. Reasonably safe judgment would of course require comprehensive empirical research. Yet even dealing theoretically with this question in a convincing manner is, to my view, beyond the scope of this short paper, which will therefore be limited to some general suggestions.

Any alternative to native-speaker standards would have to specify in which way they should be extended or changed. Doing away with standards altogether would certainly be no viable option, since it would endanger successful communication. Would it be possible to encorporate special features of non-native English – of Indian, Chinese, Japanese, French, Spanish, German or other Englishes – as elements of International English (or World English)? Which elements could that be? Would these elements have to be explicitly defined in some manual (codex) of International English, so that they could be studied by anyone interested? Or would it suffice to appeal to all the participants in international communication to be as tolerant as possible with respect to any linguistic peculiarity, as long as the text remains intelligible? This appeal would of course also imply very serious attempts at comprehension. Perhaps, new international standards, different from native-speaker standards, would gradually develop on the basis of such a new culture of communication and could finally be codified. There is a bulk of publications dealing with related questions which should be scrutinised for ideas and evidence, like for instance the literature on modified (mostly simplified) English for international communication or on EFL teaching objectives (closeness to native-speaker competence). Harmut Haberland proposed some of these ideas in a much earlier article, in which he suggested to develop a 'new, independent norm of academic English . . . which would be different from US or British English to the degree that speakers of those dialects would have to learn it, if they want to write it or speak it properly . . .' and which 'would serve the purposes of its community of speakers better than any existing standard of English would, since it would be far less culture-bound and ethnocentric than all the other Englishes we can choose between today' (Haberland 1989: 936–7).

Language rights?

Those difficult questions will finally have to be answered if any postulate of 'the non-native speakers' right to linguistic peculiarities' (Ammon 1998: 278–82) is to be taken seriously, i.e. put into practice. Obviously, not all linguistic peculiarities are acceptable if communication is to function. It might be for these difficulties, why Skutnabb-Kangas and Phillipson (1994) mention no such 'linguistic human right.' It even seems hard to place any non-native speakers' right to linguistic peculiarities into their system. Rather, any such a right straddles across their 'necessary' and their 'enrichment-oriented rights' (ibid.: 102), depending on the function of English as a non-native language, but doesn't really fit into either. The deeper reason might be that their system of linguistic rights is itself based on the ideal of native-speaker standards or norms.

It seems to me, however, that systematic provision for such a right should seriously be considered in face of the disadvantages of the non-native speakers of English and actually non-native speakers of any prestige language with rigorous standards. Murray and Dingwall (1997: 56) concede that the dominance of English as a language of science 'may give native speakers of English an unfair advantage in the competition to publish results'. When they point out, however, that native speakers of English too need extensive training before they are capable of writing scientific articles, they seem to forget that the Swiss scientists, whose fate they examine, get the equivalent training. It is even a central objective of university courses in Switzerland, particularly seminars. Swiss scientists are therefore, as a rule, very well capable of writing scientific texts – but according to their own and not anglosaxon norms. Disadvantaging such users of English could be called 'discrimination' with respect to the non-native speakers' right to linguistic peculiarities, if we had it, and be criticised accordingly. It would of course be necesssary to show functioning alternatives to the present situation.

There have been demands of learners' rights which seem to be related to our suggestions. Thus, Gomes de Matos (1998: 15) postulated for EFL learners '[t]he right (as non-native speakers) to deviate [from native-speaker standards! U.A.] in noncrucial areas that do not affect intelligibility or communication (. . .)' His ideals remain, however, the native-speaker competence or the standards of the inner-circle countries. In contrast, I would like to challenge the inner-circle countries' exclusive control of the standards of International English. It seems to me that there is no real justification for this kind of control in a world with a growing majority of speakers of the language outside the inner-circle countries. In the case of a planned standard, or set of standards, one could think of a transnational institution, perhaps similar to that for Esperanto, to be put in charge. However, an unplanned, spontaneous development of standards through interaction might be more practical. Changes along the suggested lines probably presuppose long-lasting persistence and growing self-confidence on the side of the non-native speakers with respect to their own use of English.

Ulrich
Ammon

The non-native speakers' right to linguistic peculiarities remains at the moment a rather helpless postulate. It needs more elaboration as well as integration into an extended system of linguistic human rights. It also needs support through political action. It should become part of the agenda of linguistic and other scholarly or scientific associations, or their conferences, and be presented to political parties or institutions, for instance of the European Union. – For a start, the non-native speakers of English could as a minimum try to raise awareness of their problems (cf. Ammon 1990) and demand more linguistic tolerance from the language's native speakers. They should use their growing number as their argument, among others. In fact of these numbers, rigorous enforcement of native-speaker standards amounts to the suppression of a disadvantaged majority by a privileged minority.

Issues to consider

❏ Despite coming from very different parts of the world, these two authors share some similar views. How do you explain these similarities? On the other hand, do you find any major differences in their perspectives? Again, how do you explain these?

❏ In the light of Ammon's request for tolerance for non-native English users and to be allowed 'linguistic peculiarities' (i.e. his L1 German influence on his English), how different from standard British or American English do you find his and Hu's writing? Make a note of any features that you think or know are examples of China English and/or German English. If you are unable to identify (m)any, do you think this is because writing, especially academic, is much slower to change than speech, or because the authors have had their articles edited by Inner Circle speakers (the point that Hu makes in her conclusion)? If the latter, to what extent do you think this practice is acceptable for articles that are published in journals and books for an international readership?

❏ In another article on the same theme, Ammon (2006: 25) questions 'the justification, and even the functional necessity, of native-like language norms for scientific [i.e. academic] texts', and argues that '[e]stablishing, instead, new language norms, close to but systematically different from native-speaker English' would make better sense. He proposes calling these new norms 'Globalish' in order to raise awareness of the fundamental difference from ENL of this 'lingua franca, whose norms are no longer under the control of native speakers of English', and which has 'a pluricentric structure' (2006: 1). How similar to ELF does Ammon's 'Globalish' seem to you? Finally, how far does it fit with Hu's conclusion that '[w]e need one circle, not three'? And how much does it have in common with Canagarajah's proposed reframing of the circle model (see A3), which also takes a pluricentric approach?

❏ If you are able to, consult the ELFA website (English as a Lingua Franca in Academic Settings) at www.uta.fi/laitokset/kielet/engf/research/elfa. To what extent does the material on this website strengthen your support for Ammon's stated and Hu's implicit position on the legitimacy of non-Inner Circle norms for academic English?

❑ In C7, I quoted Deterding et al. (2006: 195) who argue that in light of the current and potential massive growth in the number of Chinese speakers of English, China English 'may start to have a major impact on the way the [English] language evolves'. Do you think it is possible that in future years, China English will not only become a legitimate variety for its Chinese users, but will also start to influence other English varieties in the way that British and American English have done up to now?

LOOKING AHEAD . . .

D8

Graddol's 1997 book *The Future of English?* was, at the time of its publication, the most detailed and up-to-date examination available of the likely future of English. In the following extract from the final chapter of Graddol's 1997 book, he considers what sort of English is likely to be spoken in the future, which languages may come to rival English at the global level, and the influences that may affect the roles and types of English spoken in years to come. Next is an article by Crystal that was published in 2008 (Crystal 2008a) in the journal *English Today* alongside an extract from an article 'How many millions use English?' that Crystal had published in the same journal in 1985. In his 2008 article, he comments on what he had said 23 years earlier, and revises his predictions for the future of English.

English in the future

David Graddol (reprinted from *The Future of English?* London: British Council, 1997: 56–9 and 62–3)

David Graddol

Will a single world standard for English develop?

One question which arises in any discussion of global English is whether a single world standard English will develop, forming a supranational variety which must be learned by global citizens of the 21st century. Like most questions raised in this book, this demands a more complicated answer than those who ask probably desire.

There are, for example, at least two dimensions to the question: the first is whether English will fragment into many mutually unintelligible local forms; the second is whether the current 'national' standards of English (particularly US and British) will continue to compete as models of correctness for world usage, or whether some new world standard will arise which supersedes national models for the purposes of international communication and teaching.

The widespread use of English as a language of wider communication will continue to exert pressure towards global uniformity as well as give rise to anxieties about 'declining' standards, language change and the loss of geolinguistic diversity. But as English shifts from foreign-language to second-language status for an increasing number of people, we can also expect to see English develop a larger number of local varieties.

David
Graddol

These contradictory tensions arise because English has two main functions in the world: it provides a vehicular language for international communication and it forms the basis for constructing cultural identities. The former function requires mutual intelligibility and common standards. The latter encourages the development of local forms and hybrid varieties. As English plays an ever more important role in the first of these functions, it simultaneously finds itself acting as a language of identity for larger numbers of people around the world. There is no need to fear, however, that trends towards fragmentation will necessarily threaten the role of English as a lingua franca. There have, since the first records of the language, been major differences between varieties of English.

The mechanisms which have helped maintain standard usage in the past may not, however, continue to serve this function in the future. Two major technologies have helped develop national, standard-language forms. The first was printing, the invention of which provided a 'fixity' in communication by means of printed books. According to scholars such as Anderson (1983), such fixity was a necessary requirement for the 'imagined communities' of modern nation states. But with increasing use of electronic communication much of the social and cultural effect of the stability of print has already been lost, along with central 'gatekeeping' agents such as editors and publishers who maintain consistent, standardised forms of language.

The second technology has been provided by broadcasting, which in many ways became more important than print in the socially mobile communities of the 20th century. But trends in global media suggest that broadcasting will not necessarily play an important role in establishing and maintaining a global standard. Indeed, the patterns of fragmentation and localisation, which are significant trends in satellite broadcasting, mean that television is no longer able to serve such a function. How can there be such a thing as 'network English' in a world in which centralised networks have all but disappeared?

Meanwhile, new forms of computer-mediated communication are closing the gap between spoken and written English which has been constructed laboriously over centuries. And cultural trends encourage the use of informal and more conversational language, a greater tolerance of diversity and individual style, and a lessening deference to authority. These trends, taken together, suggest that a weakening of the institutions and practices which maintained national standard languages is taking place: that the native-speaking countries are experiencing a 'destandardisation' of English.

The ELT industry, however, may play an important role in maintaining an international standard, as Strevens (1992) suggested.

[. . .]

Since the ELT publishers from native-speaking countries are likely to follow markets – most of the large publishers already provide materials in several standards – it will be non-native speakers who decide whether a US model, a British one, or one based on a second-language variety will be taught, learned and used. At the very least, English textbooks in countries where English is spoken as a second language are likely to pay much more attention to local varieties of English and to localise their product by incorporating materials in local varieties of English.

The most likely scenario thus seems to be a continued 'polycentrism' for English – that is, a number of standards which compete. It will be worth monitoring the global

ELT market for signs of shifting popularity between textbooks published in different standards.

[...]

Will the British 'brand' of English play an important role in the world in the 21st century?

The conventional wisdom is that US English is the most influential variety worldwide. Recent American studies of the cultural consequences of globalisation suggest:

> The global culture speaks English – or, better, American. In McWorld's terms, the queen's English is little more today than a high-falutin' dialect used by advertisers who want to reach affected upscale American consumers. American English has become the world's primary transnational language in culture and the arts as well as science, technology, commerce, transportation, and banking . . . The war against the hard hegemony of American colonialism, political sovereignty, and economic empire is fought in a way which advances the soft hegemony of American pop culture and the English language.
>
> (Barber 1996: 84)

> By 2000, English was the unchallenged world lingua franca . . . This language monopoly bestowed upon the United States an incalculable but subtle power: the power to transform ideas, and therefore lives, and therefore societies, and therefore the world.
>
> (Celente 1997: 298)

It will be clear from the discussion elsewhere in this book that these commentaries already have a slightly old-fashioned feel to them. The hegemony of English may not be so entrenched as writers such as Barber and Celente fear. But Barber may also be dismissing the position of British English too readily. Much of the negative reaction to English in the world is directed towards the US; most territories in which English is spoken as a second language still have an (ambiguous) orientation to British English . . . British publishers have a major share of the global ELT market and there are signs that even US companies are using the British variety to gain greater acceptance in some world markets. Microsoft, for example, produces two English versions of intellectual property on CD-ROM, such as the *Encarta Encyclopedia*: a domestic (US English) edition and a 'World English edition' based on British English.

The future of British English in the world will depend in part on continued, careful management of its 'brand image'. Some useful groundwork has already been undertaken. The support of 'British Studies' courses in overseas universities, for example, has helped shift the focus from cultural heritage to a more balanced understanding of Britain's place in the modern world. There is also a growing appreciation of the importance of British audio-visual products in projecting an image of Britain as a leader of style and popular culture.

**David
Graddol**

Which languages may rival English as a world lingua franca in the 21st century?

There is no reason to believe that any other language will appear within the next 50 years to replace English as the global lingua franca. The position of English has arisen from a particular history which no other language can, in the changed world of the 21st century, repeat.

We have argued, however, that no single language will occupy the monopolistic position in the 21st century which English has – almost – achieved by the end of the 20th century. It is more likely that a small number of world languages will form an 'oligopoly', each with particular spheres of influence and regional bases.

As trade, people movement and communication between neighbouring countries in Asia and South America become more important than flows between such regions and Europe and North America, so we can expect languages which serve regional communication to rise in popularity. But it is actually very difficult to foresee more precisely what will occur.

For example, we have noted that economic activity, telecommunications traffic and air travel between Asian countries will greatly increase. But there are at least three possible linguistic scenarios which may develop from this. One is that English will remain the preferred language of international communication within Asia, since the investment in English may be regarded as too great to throw away, or the social elites who have benefited from English in the past may be reluctant to let their privileged position become threatened. Or it may simply be the most common shared language. A second scenario is that Mandarin becomes regionally more important, beginning as a lingua franca within Greater China (for communication between the regions of Hong Kong, Beijing, Shanghai and Taiwan) and building on increased business communication between the overseas Chinese in South-East Asia.

The third scenario is that no single language will emerge as a dominant lingua franca in Asia and a greater number of regional languages will be learned as foreign languages. If intraregional trade is greatest between adjacent countries, then there is likely to be an increased demand for neighbouring languages. In this case, the pattern of demand for foreign languages will look different in each country.

The position of Russian in Central and North Asia is subject to similar problems of prediction. But it does seem clear that the global fortunes of Spanish are rising quite rapidly. Indeed, the trading areas of the south (Mercosur, Safta) are expected to merge with Nafta in the first decade of the new millennium. This, taken together with the expected increase in the Hispanic population in the US, may ensure that the Americas emerge as a bilingual English–Spanish zone.

[...]

What gives a language global influence and makes it a 'world language'?

No one has satisfactorily answered the question of what makes a language a 'world' language. It is clear from earlier discussion in this book that sheer numbers of native speakers do not in themselves explain the privileged position of some language.

David Crystal suggests that 'a language becomes an international language for one chief reason: the political power of its people – especially their military power' (Crystal

**David
Graddol**

1997: p. 7). Historically that may have been true: in the future, it will be less clearly military power which provides the international backing for languages, because of changes
in the nature of national power, in the way that cultural values are projected and in the
way markets are opened for the circulation of goods and services.

What we need is some sense of what makes a language attractive to learners, so that
we can identify languages which newly meet such criteria in the future. This would also
allow us to chart and ideally anticipate, the decline of erstwhile popular languages.

In this book we have focused on economic and demographic factors. Some combination of these might usefully form a starting point for an understanding of what makes
a language acquire importance. The engco model provides an illustration of the kind of
approach that can be taken. The model calculates an index of 'global influence' taking
into account various economic factors which have been discussed earlier, including
Gross Language Product and openness to world trade (Traded Gross Language Product). The model also includes demographic factors, such as the numbers of young speakers and rates of urbanisation. Finally, it takes into account the human development index
(HDI) for different countries. This is a composite figure produced by the UN, which
combines measures of quality of life with those for literacy and educational provision. In
this way, HDI provides an indicator of the proportion of native speakers who are literate
and capable of generating intellectual resources in the language.

The engco model of global influence thus generates a new kind of league table
among languages, which weights languages not only by the number and wealth of their
speakers, but also by the likelihood that these speakers will enter social networks which
extend beyond their locality: they are the people with the wherewithal and ambition
to 'go about' in the world, influence it and to have others work to influence them. The
calculations for the mid 1990s for the 'basket' of languages we have surveyed in this book
are as shown in Table D8.1.

Table D8.1 Engco model of the global influence of English. (Note: an index score of
100 represents the position of English in 1995.)

1	English	100
2	German	42
3	French	33
4	Japanese	32
5	Spanish	31
6	Chinese	22
7	Arabic	8
8	Portuguese	5
9	Malay	4
10	Russian	3
11	Hindi/Urdu	0.4
12	Bengali	0.09

No strong claims are made for the validity of this index, but it does seem to capture
something of the relative relations between world languages which other indices, based

David
Graddol

crudely on economic factors or numbers of native speakers, do not convey. It shows that English is, on some criteria at least, a long way ahead of all other languages including Chinese.

The advantage of the engco index is the way it can be used to generate projections. As the model is refined and the full demographic and economic projections for the countries concerned are taken into account, league tables will be published for the decades up to 2050. Preliminary results indicate that on this basis Spanish is one of the languages which will rise most quickly. The nearest rivals to English – German, French and Japanese – will grow much more slowly. The relative positions of the 'top six' are likely to change during the coming decades, but it is unlikely that any other language will overtake English.

The changing status of language will create a new language hierarchy for the world. Figure [D1.1] shows how this might look in the middle of the 21st century, taking into account economic and demographic developments as well as potential language shift. In comparison with the present-day hierarchy there are more languages in the top layer. Chinese, Hindi/Urdu, Spanish and Arabic may join English. French and other OECD languages (German, Japanese) are likely to decline in status. But the biggest difference between the present-day language hierarchies and those of the future will result from the loss of several thousand of the world's languages. Hence there may be a group of languages at the apex, but there will be less linguistic variety at the base. The shift from linguistic monopoly to oligopoly brings pluralism in one sense, but huge loss of diversity in another. This will be offset only in part by an increasing number of new hybrid language varieties, many arising from contact with English.

[...]

[Figure D1.1] The world language hierarchy in 2050?

Can anything be done to influence the future of English?

Can anything be done by institutions and decision-makers to influence the future of
English?

David
Graddol

    This is a difficult question to answer. There is an argument that global processes are
too complex, too overwhelming in their momentum and too obscure in their outcomes
to permit the activities of a few people and institutions, even with coherent policies, to
make any difference. David Crystal suggests that the English language may have passed
beyond the scope of any form of social control:

> It may well be the case . . . that the English language has already grown to be inde-
> pendent of any form of social control. There may be a critical number or critical
> distribution of speakers (analogous to the notion of critical mass in nuclear phys-
> ics) beyond which it proves impossible for any single group or alliance to stop its
> growth, or even influence its future. If there were to be a major social change in
> Britain which affected the use of English there, would this have any real effect on the
> world trend? It is unlikely.
>
>   (Crystal 1997: 139)

Even if the English language cannot, in any comprehensive sense, be managed, there is
an argument that complex systems have an unpredictability in their behaviour which
needs to be taken into account by strategic management. The institutions and organisations which will best survive the potentially traumatic period of global reconstruction
which has only just begun, and even thrive during it, will be those which have the best
understanding of the changing position of English in local markets, which can adapt the
products and services they offer most quickly and effectively and which know how to
establish appropriate alliances and partnerships.

    But the function of strategic management can extend beyond ensuring either sur-
vival or the effective exploitation of changing conditions in the marketplace. In complex
systems, small forces, strategically placed, can lead to large global effects. There is no
way, at present, of knowing what nudges placed where will have what consequences. But
careful strategic planning, far-sighted management, thoughtful preparation and focused
action now could indeed help secure a position for British English language services in
the 21st century.

[. . .]

    The indications are that English will enjoy a special position in the multilingual
society of the 21st century: it will be the only language to appear in the language mix
in every part of the world. This, however, does not call for an unproblematic celebration
by native speakers of English. Yesterday it was the world's poor who were multilingual;
tomorrow it will also be the global elite. So we must not be hypnotised by the fact that
this elite will speak English: the more significant fact may be that, unlike the majority of
present-day native English speakers, they will also speak at least one other language –
probably more fluently and with greater cultural loyalty.

'Two thousand million?'

David
Crystal

David Crystal, 'Two thousand million?', updates on the statistics of English (reprinted from
English Today, vol. 24, no. 1, 2008: 3–6)

Reading this article again, almost a quarter of a century on, the most noticeable change,
it seems to me, has been in the amount and colour of the author's hair! That aside, I
am struck by my final comment: 'I shall stay with this figure for a while' – a billion. It
appears I stayed with it for a decade. In the first edition of my *English as a Global Language* (1997: 61) I raised my estimate, suggesting a middle-of-the-road figure of 1,350
million. In the second edition (2003a: 69), a 'cautious temperament', I said, would suggest 1,500 million. And these days, having read the more sophisticated assessments by
David Graddol and others, I am prepared to revise upwards again in the direction of
2 billion. In short, we have moved in 25 years from a fifth to a quarter to a third of the
world's population being speakers of English.

India – and South Asia generally – was a preoccupation of the 1985 article, and
that would not change if the article were being written today. On my last visit to India,
in 2005, I bored every linguistic professional I met by asking for their estimate of
the number of English speakers in their country today. Kachru's figure of 3 per cent,
referred to in the 1985 article, was evidently history. Although answers varied greatly,
depending on the levels of English assumed, most people thought that around a third of
the population were these days capable of carrying on a domestic conversation in English. An *India Today* survey in 1997 had reached the same conclusion (Kachru 2001: 411).
Given that India's population is now well over a billion, this meant a total of around 350
million people – more than the combined English-speaking populations of the leading
first-language countries.

China also receives a special mention in the 1985 article. If India is the significant
factor in relation to second-language speakers (in the sense of countries where English
has some sort of special status), then China is surely the corresponding factor in relation
to foreign-language speakers (in the sense of countries where the language has no official status). Estimates coming out of China in the late 1990s suggested that the number
of speakers there was around 220 million; but the motivation provided by the Olym-
pics has caused that figure to double. As with India, the estimates cited vary depending
on the level of English the estimators have in mind. But commentators I have talked to
assert that China will have nearly half its population capable of at least a basic level of
conversational competence in English by the end of 2008. I would not be at all surprised
if this came to pass.

Taken together, the estimates for second- and foreign-language competence reinforce the point that has been made with increasing emphasis over the past ten years
– that the centre of gravity of the English language has moved from the native speaker
to the non-native speaker. For every one native speaker, there are now three or four
non-native speakers, a ratio that will increase as time goes by (Graddol, 1999). And as
the non-native group is the primary force fostering the emergence of 'new Englishes',
there are going to be implications for the future character of the language.

Can I be specific? It is always dangerous making predictions about languages. Who
would have dared suggest, a thousand years ago, that Latin would today be of such little

David
Crystal

consequence? And the same tentativeness must apply to predictions about the future formal character of English. But let me make a couple of guesses. For example, given the difficulty that many foreign learners have in pronouncing interdental fricatives (as in *thin, this*) I would not be surprised to see them disappear completely within the next fifty years (they are already gone in some accents, such as Cockney and Irish). And in grammar, I can see several uncountable nouns developing a countable use – usages such as *informations*, for example, which are widespread in second/foreign language situations. Some people might think these 'un-English', but in fact *informations* was in [native] English once: *an information* and *informations* can be traced back to Middle English, and are found in Chaucer, Shakespeare, Swift, and many other authors. It may only be a matter of time before they are back.

Issues to consider

❑   What points of similarity and difference do you notice between Graddol's 1997 and Crystal's 2008a accounts? How far can any differences be explained by the time difference?

❑   To what extent do you believe that the situation Graddol described in 1997 has changed since then? Have any of his predictions been proved or disproved, or the indications become any clearer?

❑   One thing that Graddol himself believes has changed since 1997 is the situation concerning challengers to English:

> People have wondered for some years whether English had so much got its feet under the global office desk that even the rise of China – and Mandarin – could ever shift it from its position of dominance. The answer is that there is already a challenger, one which has quietly appeared on the scene whilst many native speakers of English were looking the other way, celebrating the rising hegemony of their language. The new language which is rapidly ousting the language of Shakespeare as the world's lingua franca is English itself – English in its new global form . . . this is not English as we have known it, and have taught it in the past as a foreign language. It is a new phenomenon, and if it represents any kind of triumph it is probably not a cause of celebration by native speakers.
>
> (Graddol 2006: 11)

What is your reaction to Graddol's claim? And what do you think he means by 'English in its *new global form*'?

❑   In the reading from Graddol (1997) above, he hints that the spread of English could become a problem for native English speakers once the 'global elite' is multilingual. How far do you agree with him? He takes this issue up again in his later book (2006: 114–15), arguing that there is a 'native speaker problem' involving the following:

– native speakers bring with them 'cultural baggage in which learners wanting to use English primarily as an international language are not interested';

- 'native speaker accents may seem too remote from the people that learners expect to communicate with';
- 'as teachers, native speakers may not possess some of the skills required by bilingual speakers, such as those of translation and interpreting';
- 'as the English-speaking world becomes less formal, and more democratic, the myth of a standard language becomes more difficult to maintain';
- in addition, Phillipson (2003a: 167) argues that '[i]n many international fora, competent speakers of English as a second language are more comprehensible than native speakers, because they can be better at adjusting their language for people from different cultural and linguistic backgrounds'.

❏ What is your response to the above points? If you are a native English speaker, compare your response with that of a non-native English speaker, and vice versa. How far do you (dis)agree?

❏ How plausible do you find Crystal's predictions about the future character of English? Do you agree with him that 'th' might disappear completely, and that usages such as 'informations' will become widespread?

❏ In unit A6, one of the reasons listed as to why people still learn English was entertainment, and within that, music, and particularly hip hop. In what ways do you think the hybrid forms of hip hop, with their fusion of African American English, 'standard' English, and local (e.g. Japanese or Korean) English might influence the kinds of English that spread around the world?

❏ Taking a radically different approach from that of most World Englishes scholars is Pennycook (2007: 20), who argues that the 'World Englishes framework has consistently avoided the broader political implications of the global spread of English' and 'places nationalism at its core'. He considers (2007: 5–6) that the term 'global Englishes' is preferable to 'world Englishes' because 'English is closely tied to processes of globalization'. We need, he says, 'to move beyond arguments about homogeneity or heterogeneity, or imperialism and nation states, and instead focus on translocal and transcultural flows'. According to this perspective, 'English is a translocal language . . . that moves across, while becoming embedded in, the materiality of localities and social relations'. At the same time, Pennycook argues, 'locating English within a complex view of globalization' does not mean 'we are necessarily witnessing increasing levels of global similarity'. How do you see the link between English and globalisation? Read Pennycook 2007 (chapter 2) to learn more about his interpretation.

❏ At the end of this second edition, I still leave you with more questions than answers. You can probably do little more than make educated guesses in relation to some of these issues and (those of you young enough to do so) wait and see what happens. But in the meantime, how do *you* see the future of English?

FURTHER READING

The following groupings relate to the respective strand of the book, for example, the first grouping, 'English and colonialism/postcolonialism', relates to units A1, B1, C1 and D1. The only exception is Estuary English, which has been moved from the fourth to the fifth grouping to join the other references to Inner Circle Englishes.

English and colonialism/postcolonialism

For more detail on the historical background, see Crystal (2003a); for sociopolitical interpretations, see Bailey (1991), Holborow (1999), Pennycook (1994, 1998), Phillipson (1992), and Watts and Trudgill (2002) among many others.

Kachru et al. (eds) (2006) is a useful reference work on current linguistic, social, cultural and political issues relating to a wide range of Englishes.

Good sources of material on a range of colonial and postcolonial issues are the collections in Ashcroft et al. (eds) (1995), Burke et al. (eds) (2000) and Fishman (ed.) (1999).

On issues concerning English in Africa, see also Rubagumya (2004), and the special issue of *World Englishes*, 21/1 (2002), 'English in South Africa'.

For more on English Only, see Baugh (2000), Dicker (2000) and May (2008).

Pidgins and creoles

Of the many books on this subject, I recommend Singh (2001) and Todd (1990) as introductory texts, and Mühlhäusler (1997) and Sebba (1997) for more detail.

Mufwene (2001) provides a detailed account of the evolution of creole languages.

A good source of information on the Ebonics debate is the symposium in *World Englishes* journal vol. 19, no. 1 (2000).

On London Jamaican, see Hewitt (1986) and Sebba (1993, 2007), and on the phenomenon of language crossing, see Rampton (1995/2005).

The current ownership of English

The classic reading on this topic, and still highly relevant, is Widdowson (1994b).

On the implications for teaching materials and methods, see Canagarajah (1999, (ed.) 2005), Holliday (1994, 2005), Kirkpatrick (2007a), and the papers in Gnutzmann (ed.) (1999), Gnutzmann and Intemann (eds) (2005) and Hughes (ed.) (2006).

On the implications for English testing, see Lowenberg (2000, 2002), and for a detailed critique of language testing, McNamara and Roever (2006).

For recent research into the teaching of World Englishes and ELF, see Jenkins (2006b).

Good sources on the native/non-native teacher debate are the papers in Braine (ed.) (1999), Luk and Lim (2006), Kirkpatrick (2007a) and Seidlhofer (1999).

On language policy and planning, see Ferguson (2006), and on rights in language teaching/learning, see Brumfit (2001).

Outer Circle varieties of English

Detailed sources for Outer Circle varieties include Cheshire (ed.) (1991) and Mesthrie and Bhatt (2008), while Kachru et al. (2006) cover a vast amount of ground but in less detail.

To learn more about Asian Englishes, see Kachru (2005) and Y. Kachru and Nelson (2006); on Singapore English and Singlish, see Deterding (2007), Rubdy (2001) and Wee (2005); and on English language teaching in East Asia, see Ho and Wong (eds) (2003).

On postcolonial literatures, see Carter and McRae (2001), Talib (2002) and Thumboo (1992).

Standardisation and Inner Circle varieties of English

On standard language ideology, see Bauer and Trudgill (eds) (1998), Bex and Watts (eds) (1999), Crowley (2003) and Milroy and Milroy (1999).

To find out more about the processes involved in standardisation, see the classic work, Haugen (1966).

For a detailed discussion of Estuary English, see Przedlacka (2001, 2002), as well as the Estuary English website at UCL: www.phon.ucl.ac.uk/home/estuary

You will find more information on the development of writing, differences between (Inner Circle) speech and writing, and e-discourse in Baron (2000), on texting in Crystal (2008b), and on language and the internet in Crystal (2006).

For a detailed description of Inner Circle varieties of English, see Melchers and Shaw (2003); for further detail on American English, see Wolfram and Schilling-Estes (2006); and for more on British English, see the papers in Britain (ed.) (2007).

English as a Lingua Franca

The most useful overview of research in this field is Seidlhofer (2004), though this will soon be complemented and expanded by Seidlhofer (forthcoming).

On ELF corpora, see Mauranen (2003), Seidlhofer (2001) and the ELFA and VOICE websites (details in C6).

On ELF linguistic levels and the use of ELF in different contexts of use, see Deterding and Kirkpatrick (2006), Jenkins (2000), Seidlhofer et al. (2006), and the special issue of *Nordic Journal of English Studies*, 5/2 (2006), which focuses particularly on ELF in academic settings.

For a range of views on ELF, see Rubdy and Saraceni (eds) (2006), and on attitudes towards ELF, see Jenkins (2007).

Asian and European Englishes

For more on second language aquisition (SLA) and the interlanguage/fossilisation controversy, see Firth and Wagner (1997, 2007).

On Indian English, see Parasher (2001); on Hong Kong English, see Bolton (ed.) (2002), and on China English, see Bolton (2003), Deterding (2006), and *World Englishes* 21/1, a special issue on English in China.

On English in Europe, see Phillipson (2003a) and the papers in Cenoz and Jessner (eds) (2000), and Gubbins and Holt (eds) (2002).

World Englishes in the future

See the final chapter of McArthur (2002) for a range of perspectives on likely future developments in World Englishes. For the most recent wide-ranging discussion of the possibilities, see Graddol (2006).

On English and globalisation, see the articles in Block and Cameron (eds) (2002), Pennycook (2007) and *Journal of Sociolinguistics*, vol. 7, no. 4 (2003), a special issue on 'Sociolinguistics and globalisation'; on ELF and globalisation see Dewey (2007b); on hip hop, English and globalisation see Pennycook (2007) and *World Englishes*, vol. 25, no. 2, a special issue on 'World Englishes in pop culture'.

To keep informed of contemporary developments in World Englishes, it is a good idea to consult the various journals in the field. Two that I recommend in particular are *World Englishes* (published by Blackwell), which provides lengthy detailed studies on a wide range of Englishes and related issues, and *English Today* (published by Cambridge University Press), which contains shorter but equally relevant discussions of the latest developments in the field.

REFERENCES

Achebe, C. (1975) 'The African writer and the English language', in *Morning yet on Creation Day*, New York: Anchor.

Aitchison, J. (1991) *Language Change: Progress or Decay?*, 2nd edition, Cambridge: Cambridge University Press.

Aitchison, J. (1996) *The Seeds of Speech*, Cambridge: Cambridge University Press.

Alobwede d'Epie, C. (1998) 'Banning pidgin English in Cameroon', *English Today*, 14/1: 54–60.

Alsagoff, L. and Ho, C. L. (1998) 'The grammar of Singapore English' in J. Foley et al. (eds) (1998).

Ammon, U. (1989) 'Die Schwerigkeiten der deutschen Sprachgemeinschaft aufgrund der Dominanz der englischen Sprache', *Zeitschrift für Sprachwissenschaft*, 8/2: 257–72.

Ammon, U. (1990) 'German or English?: the problems of language choice experienced by German-speaking scientists' in P. Nelde (ed.) *Language Conflict and Minorities*, Bonn: Dümmler.

Ammon, U. (1998) *Ist Deutsch noch internationale Wissenschaftssprache? Englisch auch für die Lehre an den deutschprachigen Hochschulen*, Berlin and New York: de Gruyter.

Ammon, U. (2000) 'Towards more fairness in international English: linguistic rights of non-native speakers' in R. Phillipson (ed.) (2000) *Rights to Language. Equity, Power, and Education*, Mahwah, NJ: Lawrence Erlbaum.

Ammon, U. (2006) 'Language planning for international scientific communication: an overview of questions and possible solutions', *Current Issues in Language Planning*, 7/1: 1–30.

Anderson, B. (1983) *Imagined Communities*, London: Verso.

Andreasson, A.-M. (1994) 'Norm as a pedagogical paradigm', *World Englishes*, 13/3: 395–409.

Ashcroft, B., Griffiths, G. and Tiffin, H. (eds) (1995) *The Post-colonial Studies Reader*, London: Routledge.

Baik, M. and Shim, R. (2002) 'Teaching World Englishes via the internet', *World Englishes*, 21/3: 423–30.

Bailey, R. (1991) *Images of English*, Cambridge: Cambridge University Press.

Bamgboṣe, A. (1998) 'Torn between the norms: innovations in World Englishes', *World Englishes*, 17/1: 1–14.

Barber, B. (1996) *Jihad vs McWorld*, New York: Ballantine Books.

Baron, N. (2000) *Alphabet to Email*, London: Routledge.

Bauer, L. and Trudgill, P. (eds) (1998) *Language Myths*, London: Penguin.

Baugh, J. (2000) 'Educational malpractice and the miseducation of language minority students' in J. K. Hall and W. Eggington (eds) (2000).

Bautista, M. (1998) 'Tagalog–English code-switching and the lexicon of Philippine English', *Asian Englishes*, 1/1: 51–67.

Bautista, M. and Gonzalez, A. (2006) 'Southeast Asian Englishes' in B. B. Kachru, Y. Kachru and C. Nelson (eds) (2006).

Berns, M. (1995) 'English in the European Union', *English Today* 11/3: 3–11

Bex, T. and Watts, R. (eds) (1999) *Standard English: The Widening Debate*, London: Routledge.

Bickerton, D. (1981) *Roots of Language*, Ann Arbor: Karoma.

Bickerton, D. (1984) 'The language bioprogram hypothesis', *The Behavioral and Brain Sciences*, 7: 173–88.

Bisong, J. (1995) 'Language choice and cultural imperialism: a Nigerian perspective', *ELT Journal*, 49/2: 122–32.

Block, D. and Cameron, C. (eds) (2002) *Globalization and Language Teaching*, London: Routledge.

Bloodworth, Dennis (2001) 'Go on, dare to boldly split the infinitive', *The Straits Times*, Thursday, 17 May.

Bolton, K. (2000) 'The sociolinguistics of Hong Kong and the space for Hong Kong English', *World Englishes*, 19/3: 265–85.

Bolton, K. (ed.) (2002) *Hong Kong English: Autonomy and Creativity*, Hong Kong: Hong Kong University Press.

Bolton, K. (2003) *Chinese Englishes: A Sociolinguistic History*, Cambridge: Cambridge University Press.

Bonfiglio, T. (2002) *Race and the Rise of Standard American*, Berlin: Mouton de Gruyter.

Bourhis, R. and Marshall, D. (1999) 'The United States and Canada' in J. Fishman (ed.) (1999).

Braine, G. (ed.) (1999) *Non-Native Educators in English Language Teaching*, Mahwah, New Jersey: Lawrence Erlbaum Associates.

Britain, D. (ed.) (2007) *Language in the British Isles*, 2nd edition, Cambridge: Cambridge University Press.

Brown, A. (1999) *Singapore English in a Nutshell: An Alphabetic Description of Its Features*, Singapore: Federal.

Brown, K. and Peterson, J. (1997) 'Exploring conceptual frameworks: framing a world Englishes paradigm' in L. Smith and M. Forman (eds) (1997).

Brumfit, C. (1995) 'The role of English in a changing Europe: where do we go from here?', Best of ELTECS, the British Council.

Brumfit, C. (2001) *Individual Freedom in Language Teaching*, Oxford: Oxford University Press.

Brumfit, C. (2002) 'Has everything changed?' *EL Gazette*, no. 265, February 2002: 11.

Bruthiaux, P. (2003) 'Squaring the circles: issues in modeling English worldwide', *International Journal of Applied Linguistics*, 13/2: 159–78.

Brutt-Griffler, J. (2002) *World English: A Study of Its Development*, Clevedon, UK: Multilingual Matters.

Brutt-Griffler, J. and Samimy, K. (2001). 'Transcending the nativeness paradigm', *World Englishes*, 20/1: 99–106.

Bryson, B. (1990) *Mother Tongue: The English Language*, London: Hamish Hamilton.

Burke, L., Crowley, T. and Girvin, A. (eds) (2000) *The Routledge Language and Cultural Theory Reader*, London: Routledge.

Burnett, L. (1962) *The Treasure of Our Tongue*, London: Secker and Warburg.

Bussmann, H. (1996) *Routledge Dictionary of Language and Linguistics*, London: Routledge.

Butler, S. (1997) 'World Englishes in the Asian context: why a dictionary is important' in L. Smith and M. Forman (eds) (1997).

Cameron, D. (1995) *Verbal Hygiene*, London: Routledge.

Canagarajah, A. S. (1999) *Resisting Linguistic Imperialism in English Teaching*, Oxford: Oxford University Press.

Canagarajah, A. S. (ed.) (2005) *Reclaiming the Local in Language Policy and Practice*, Mahwah, NJ: Lawrence Erlbaum.

Carter, R. (1999) 'Standard grammars, spoken grammars: some educational implications' in T. Bex and R. Watts (eds) (1999).

Carter, R. and McCarthy, M. (1995) 'Grammar and the spoken language', *Applied Linguistics*, 16/2: 141–58.

Carter R. and McRae, J. (2001) *The Routledge History of Literature in English*, London: Routledge.

Celente, G. (1997) *Trends 2000: How to Prepare for and Profit from the Changes of the 21st Century*, New York: Warner Books.

Cenoz, J. and Jessner, U. (eds) (2000) *English in Europe: The Acquisition of a Third Language*, Clevedon, UK: Multilingual Matters.

Chamoiseau, P. (1998) *School Days*, translated by Linda Coverdale, London: Granta Books.

Cheshire, J. (ed.) (1991) *English around the World*, Cambridge: Cambridge University Press.

Cheshire, J. (2002) 'Who we are and where we're going' in P. Gubbins and M. Holt (eds) (2002).

Claiborne, R. (1983) *The Life and Times of the English Language: The History of Our Marvellous Tongue*, London: Bloomsbury.

Clyne, M. (1987) 'Cultural differences in the organization of academic texts', *Journal of Pragmatics*, 11: 211–47.

Cogo, A. (2007) 'Intercultural communication in English as a lingua franca: a case study', doctoral thesis submitted at King's College London.

Cogo, A. and Dewey, M. (2006) 'Efficiency in ELF communication: from pragmatic motives to lexico-grammatical innovation' in A. Mauranen and M. Metsä Ketelä (eds) (2006): 59–93.

Coleman, J. (2006) 'English-medium teaching in European higher education', *Language Teaching*, 39: 1–14.

Collins, B. and Mees, I. (2007) *Phonology and Phonetics*, 2nd edition, London: Routledge.

Cook, G. and Seidlhofer, B. (eds) (1995) *Principle and Practice in Applied Linguistics: Studies in Honour of H. G. Widdowson*, Oxford: Oxford University Press.

Coppieters, R. (1987) 'Competence differences between native and near-native speakers', *Language*, 63: 544–73.

Coulmas, G. (1987) 'Why speak English?' in K. Knapp, E. Werner and A. Knapp-Potthoff (eds) *Analyzing Intercultural Communication*, Berlin: Mouton de Gruyter.

Crowley, T. (1989) *The Politics of Discourse: The Standard Language Question in British Cultural Debates*, London: Macmillan.

Crowley, T. (2003) *Standard English and the Politics of Language*, 2nd edition, Hound-mills, Basingstoke: Palgrave Macmillan.

Crystal, D. (1985) 'How many millions use English?', *English Today*, 1.

Crystal, D. (1997) *English as a Global Language*, Cambridge: Cambridge University Press.

Crystal, D. (1999) 'The future of Englishes', *English Today*, 15/2: 10–20.

Crystal, D. (2000) *Language Death*, Cambridge: Cambridge University Press.

Crystal, D. (2002) 'Broadcasting the nonstandard message' in R. Watts and P. Trudgill (eds) (2002).

Crystal, D. (2003a) *English as a Global Language*, 2nd edition, Cambridge: Cambridge University Press.

Crystal, D. (2003b) *The Cambridge Encyclopedia of the English Language*, 2nd edition, Cambridge: Cambridge University Press.

Crystal, D. (2006) *Language and the Internet*, 2nd edition, Cambridge: Cambridge University Press.

Crystal, D. (2008a) 'Two thousand million?', *English Today*, 24/1: 3–6.

Crystal, D. (2008b) *txtg the gr8 db8*, Oxford: Oxford University Press.

Dai, W. (2002) 'Constructing a streamline institution of English teaching and learning with Chinese characteristics', *Foreign Language Teaching and Research Journal*, vol. 5.

de Klerk, V. (1999) 'Black South African English: where to from here?', *World Eng-lishes*, 18/2: 311–24.

de Quincey, T. (1862) *Recollections of the Lakes and the Lake Poets*, Edinburgh: Adam and Charles Black.

D'Souza, J. (1999) 'Afterword', *World Englishes*, 18/2: 271–4.

D'Souza, J. (2001) 'Contextualizing range and depth in Indian English', *World Eng-lishes*, 20/2: 145–59.

Deterding, D. (2006) 'The pronunciation of English by speakers from China', *English World-Wide*, 27/2: 175–98.

Deterding, D. (2007) *Singapore English*, Edinburgh: Edinburgh University Press.

Deterding, D. and Kirkpatrick, A. (2006) 'Emerging South-East Asian Englishes and intelligibility', *World Englishes*, 25/3–4: 391–409.

Deterding, D., Wong, J. and Kirkpatrick, A. (2006) 'The pronunciation of Hong Kong English', *English World-Wide*, 29/2: 148–75.

Dewey, M. (2007a) 'English as a lingua franca: an empirical study of innovation in lexis and grammar', doctoral thesis submitted at King's College London.

Dewey, M. (2007b) 'English as a lingua franca and globalization: an interconnected perspective', *International Journal of Applied Linguistics*, 17/3: 332–54.

Dicker, S. (2000) 'Official English and bilingual education: the controversy over lan-guage pluralism in US society' in J. K. Hall and W. Eggington (eds) (2000).

Di Pietro, R. (1990) Review of Ulrich Ammon (ed.) 'Status and function of languages and language varieties', *Language Problems and Language Planning*, 14: 288–91.

Dorian, N. (1998) 'Western language ideologies and small-language prospects' in L. Grenoble and L. Whaley (eds) (1998) *Endangered Languages*, Cambridge: Cambridge University Press.

Dörnyei, Z., Csizér, K. and Németh, N. (2006) *Motivation, Language Attitudes and Globalisation: A Hungarian Perspective*, Clevedon, UK: Multilingual Matters.

Dziubalska-Kołaczyk, K. and Przedlacka, J. (eds) (2005) *English Pronunciation Models: A Changing Scene*, Bern: Peter Lang.

Ebunlola Adamo, G. (2005) 'Globalization, terrorism, and the English language in Nigeria', *English Today*, 21/4: 21–6.

Eckert, P. and McConnell-Ginet, S. (1992) 'Think practically and look logically: language and gender as community-based practice', *Annual Review of Anthropology*, 21: 461–90.

Elmes, S. (2001) *The Routes of English 4*, London: BBC.

Erling, B. and Bartlett, T. (2006) 'Making English their own: the use of ELF among students of English at the FUB' in A. Mauranen and M. Metsä Ketelä (eds) (2006): 9–40.

Evans, S. (2000) 'Hong Kong's new English language policy in education', *World Englishes*, 19/2: 185–204.

Fairclough, N. (1989) *Language and Power*, London: Longman.

Ferguson, G. (2006) *Language Planning and Education*, Edinburgh: Edinburgh University Press.

Filppula, M. (1991) 'Urban and rural varieties of Hiberno-English', in J. Cheshire (ed.) (1991).

Firth, A. (1996) 'The discursive accomplishment of normality: on "lingua franca" English and conversational analysis', *Journal of Pragmatics*, 26: 237–59.

Firth, A. and Wagner, J. (1997) 'On discourse, communication and (some) fundamental concepts in SLA research', *Modern Language Journal*, 81: 285–300.

Firth, A. and Wagner, J. (2007) 'Second/foreign language learning as a social accomplishment: elaborations on a reconceptualized SLA', *Modern Language Journal*, 91: 798–817.

Fishman, J. (1971a) 'National languages and languages of wider communication in developing nations' in W. H. Whiteley (ed.) (1971) *Language Use and Social Change*, Oxford: Oxford University Press.

Fishman, J. (1971b) 'The sociology of language: an interdisciplinary social science approach to language in society' in J. Fishman (ed.) (1971) *Advances in the Sociology of Language*, The Hague: Mouton.

Fishman, J. (ed.) (1999) *Handbook of Language and Ethnic Identity*, Oxford: Oxford University Press.

Fishman J. (2001) 'Why is it so hard to save a threatened language?' in J. Fishman (ed.) 2001. *Can Threatened Languages Be Saved?* Clevedon, UK: Multilingual Matters.

Foley, J., Kandiah, T., Fraser Gupta, A., Alsagoff L., Lick, H., Wee, L., Talib, I. and Bokhorst-Heng, W. (eds) (1998) *English in New Cultural Contexts: Reflections from Singapore*, Singapore: Singapore Institute of Management and Oxford University Press.

Gardner, R. (1985) *Social Psychology and Second Language Learning: The Role of Attitudes and Motivation*, London: Edward Arnold.

Gargesh, R. (2006) 'South Asian Englishes' in B. B. Kachru, Y. Kachru and C. Nelson (eds) (2006).

Ge, C. (1980) 'About translation from Chinese to English', *Translation Journal*, vol. 2.

George, J. (1867) *The Mission of Great Britain to the World, or Some of the Lessons Which She Is Now Teaching*, Toronto: Dudley and Burns.

Gill, S. K. (2002) *International Communication: English Language Challenges for Malaysia*, Serdang: Universiti Putra Malaysia Press.

Gnutzmann, C. (ed.) (1999) *Teaching and Learnng English as a Global Language*, Tübingen: Stauffenberg Verlag.

Gnutzmann, C. and Intemann, F. (eds) (2005) *The Globalisation of English and the English Language Classroom*, Tübingen: Gunter Narr.

Gomes de Matos, F. (1998) 'Learners' pronunciation rights', *Braz-TESOL Newsletter*, September: 14–15.

Gordon, E. and Sudbury, A. (2002) 'The history of southern hemisphere Englishes' in R. Watts and P. Trudgill (eds) (2002).

Görlach, M. (1988) 'The development of standard Englishes' in M. Görlach (1990), *Studies in the History of the English Language*, Heidelberg: Carl Winter.

Görlach, M. (2002) *Still More Englishes*, Amsterdam: John Benjamins.

Graddol D. (1997) *The Future of English?* London: British Council. Available at: www. britishcouncil.org/learning-research

Graddol D. (1999) 'The decline of the native speaker', *AILA Review*, 13, The English Company (UK) Ltd.

Graddol, D. (2006) *English Next: Why Global English May Mean the End of 'English as a Foreign Language'*, London: British Council, available at: www.britishcouncil. org/learning-research

Graham, L. (2000) 'Talkin' Jamaican', unpublished master's dissertation, King's College London.

Gramley, S. (2001) *The Vocabulary of World English*, London: Arnold.

Grenoble, L. and Whaley, L. (eds) (1998) *Endangered Languages*, Cambridge: Cambridge University Press.

Gubbins, P. and Holt, M. (eds) (2002) *Beyond Boundaries: Language and Identity in Contemporary Europe*, Clevedon, UK: Multilingual Matters.

Gupta, A. (1994) *The Step-Tongue: Children's English in Singapore*, Clevedon, UK: Multilingual Matters.

Gupta, A. (1999) 'Standard Englishes, contact varieties and Singapore Englishes' in C. Gnutzmann (ed.) (1999).

Haarmann, H. (1997) 'On European identity, fanciful cosmopolitanism and problems of modern nationalism', *Sociolinguistica*, 11: 142–52.

Haberland, H. (1989) 'Whose English, nobody's business', *Journal of Pragmatics*, 13: 927–38.

Hall, J. K. and Eggington, W. (eds) (2000) *The Sociopolitics of English Language Teaching*, Clevedon, UK: Multilingual Matters.

Halliday, M. (1978) *Language as a Social Semiotic*, London: Edward Arnold.

Halliday, M., McIntosh, A. and Strevens, P. (1964) *The Linguistic Sciences and Language Teaching*, London: Longman.

Haugen, E. (1966) 'Dialect, language and nation', *American Anthropologist*, 68: 922–35 in J. Pride and J. Holmes (eds) (1972) *Sociolinguistics: Selected Readings*, Harmondsworth, UK: Penguin Books.

Hewitt, R. (1986) *White Talk Black Talk*, Cambridge: Cambridge University Press.

Hinton, L. (1999) 'Trading tongues: loss of heritage languages in the United States', *English Today*, 15/4: 21–30.

Ho, W. K. and Wong, R. (2003) *English Language Teaching in East Asia Today*, Singapore: Times Academic Press.

Holborow, M. (1999) *The Politics of English*, London: Sage Publications.

Holliday, A. (1994) *Appropriate Methodology and Social Context*, Cambridge: Cambridge University Press.

Holliday, A. (2004) '"Non-natives" and "natives"', *IATEFL 2004: Liverpool Conference Selections*, Canterbury: IATEFL.

Holliday, A. (2005) *The Struggle to Teach English as an International Language*, Oxford: Oxford University Press.

Holm, J. (2000) *An Introduction to Pidgins and Creoles*, Cambridge: Cambridge University Press.

Honey, J. (1997) *Language is Power*, London: Faber & Faber.

Honna, N. (2001) 'English as an international language and Japan's English language teaching' in *Foreign Language Teaching Research Journal*, 5.

House, J. (1999) 'Misunderstanding in intercultural communication' in C. Gnutzmann (ed.) (1999).

House, J. (2001) 'A "stateless" language that Europe should embrace', *Guardian Weekly, Learning English Supplement*, April 2001: 1–3.

House, J. (2003) 'English as a lingua franca: a threat to multilingualism?', *Journal of Sociolinguistics*, 7/4: 556–78.

Hu, X. Q. (2004) 'Why China English should stand alongside British, American, and the other "world Englishes"', *English Today*, 20/2: 26–33.

Hu, X. Q. (2005) 'China English, at home and in the world', *English Today*, 21/3: 27–38.

Hudson, R. (1996) *Sociolinguistics*, 2nd edition, Cambridge: Cambridge University Press.

Hughes, R. (ed.) (2006) *Spoken English, TESOL and Applied Linguistics*, Houndmills, Basingstoke: Palgrave Macmillan.

Hughes, A. and Trudgill, P. (1979) *English Accents and Dialects*, London: Arnold.

Hughes, A. and Trudgill, P. (1996) *English Accents and Dialects*, 2nd edition, London: Arnold.

Hung, T. (2000) 'Towards a phonology of Hong Kong English', *World Englishes*, 19/3: 337–56.

Igboanusi, H. (2008) 'Empowering Nigerian Pidgin: a challenge for status planning?', *World Englishes*, 27/1: 68–82.

James, A. (2000) 'English as a European lingua franca: current realities and existing dichotomies' in J. Cenoz and U. Jessner (eds) (2000).

Jenkins, J. (1996) 'Native speaker, non-native speaker and English as a foreign language: time for a change?', *IATEFL Newsletter*, 131: 10–11.

Jenkins, J. (2000) *The Phonology of English as an International Language*, Oxford: Oxford University Press.

Jenkins, J. (2006a) 'The spread of English as an international language: a testing time for testers', *ELT Journal*, 60/1: 42–50.

Jenkins, J. (2006b) 'Current perspectives on teaching World Englishes and English as a lingua franca', *TESOL Quarterly*, 40/1: 157–81.

Jenkins, J. (2006c) 'Points of view and blind spots: ELF and SLA', *International Journal of Applied Linguistics*, 16/2: 137–62.

Jenkins, J. (2007) *English as a Lingua Franca: Attitude and Identity*, Oxford: Oxford University Press.

Jenkins, S. (1995) 'The triumph of English', *The Times*, 25 February.

Jespersen, O. (1938/1982) *Growth and Structure of the English Language*, Oxford: Basil Blackwell.

Jia, D. (1990) 'A model of thinking and linear order: linguistic features of Chinese English', *Foreign Language Journal*, vol. 5.

Jia, G. and Xiang, M. (1997) 'Debating on China English', *Foreign Language and Foreign Language Teaching and Learning*, vol. 5.

Jiang, Y. (1995) 'Chinglish and China English', *English Today*, 41: 51–3.

Jones, G. M. (1997) 'Immersion programs in Brunei' in *Bilingual Education*, vol. 5 of J. Cummins and D. Corson (eds) *Encyclopedia of Language and Education*, Dordrecht: Kluwer Academic Publishers.

Joseph, J. (2004) *Language and Identity*, Houndmills, Basingstoke: Palgrave Macmillan.

Kachru, B. B. (1982/1992) 'Models for non-native Englishes' in B. B. Kachru (ed.) (1992).

Kachru, B. B. (1985) 'Standards, codification and sociolinguistic realism: the English language in the outer circle' in R. Quirk and H. G. Widdowson (eds) (1985) *English in the World: Teaching and Learning the Language and Literatures*, Cambridge: Cambridge University Press.

Kachru, B. B. (1988) 'The sacred cows of English', *English Today*, 16: 3–8.

Kachru, B. B. (1991) 'Liberation linguistics and the Quirk concern', *English Today*, 25: 3–13.

Kachru, B. B. (1992) 'Teaching world Englishes' in B. B. Kachru (ed.) (1992).

Kachru, B. B. (ed.) (1992) *The Other Tongue: English across Cultures*, 2nd edition, Urbana, IL: University of Illinois Press.

Kachru, B. B. (1996) 'The paradigms of marginality', *World Englishes*, 15/3: 241–55.

Kachru, B. B. (1997) 'World Englishes 2000: resources for research and teaching' in L. Smith and M. Forman (eds) (1997).

Kachru, B. B. (2001) 'World Englishes and culture wars' in T. C. Kiong, A. Pakir, B. K. Choon and R. B. Goh (eds) *Ariels: Departures and Returns*, Singapore: Oxford University Press.

Kachru, B. B. (2005) *Asian Englishes: Beyond the Canon*, Hong Kong: University of Hong Kong Press.

Kachru, B. B. (2006) 'World Englishes and culture wars' in B. B. Kachru, Y. Kachru and C. Nelson (eds) (2006).

Kachru, Y. (1993) 'Interlanguage and language acquisition research', review of L. Selinker: *Rediscovering Interlanguage*, *World Englishes*, 12/1: 265–8.

Kachru, Y. (1994) 'Monolingual bias in SLA research', *TESOL Quarterly*, 28/4: 795–800.

Kachru, Y. (2005) 'Teaching and learning of World Englishes' in E. Hinkel (ed.) *Handbook of Research in Second Language Learning and Teaching*, Mahwah, NJ: Lawrence Erlbaum.

Kachru, Y. and Nelson, C. (2006) *World Englishes in Asian Contexts*, Hong Kong: University of Hong Kong Press.

Kachru, Y. and Smith, L. (2008) *Cultures, Contexts, and World Englishes*, New York: Routledge.

Kachru, B. B., Kachru, Y. and Nelson, C. (eds) (2006) *The Handbook of World Englishes*, Oxford: Blackwell.

Kandiah, T. (1991) 'South Asia' in J. Cheshire (ed.) (1991).

Kandiah, T. (1998) 'The emergence of new Englishes' in J. Foley et al. (eds) (1998).

Kaur, J. (2008) 'The co-construction of understanding in English as a lingua franca', doctoral thesis submitted at the University of Lancaster.

Kerswill, P. (2007) 'Standard and non-standard English' in D. Britain (ed.) (2007).

Kfua, B. (1996) 'Time is up for pidgin English' in *The Herald* (Cameroon bi-weekly), 359, 20–22 September.

Kiernan, V. (1969) *The Lords of Human Kind: European Attitudes towards the Outside World in the Imperial Age*, London: Weidenfeld & Nicolson.

Kirkpatrick, A. (2007a) *World Englishes: Implications for International Communication and English Language Teaching*, Cambridge: Cambridge University Press.

Kirkpatrick, A. (2007b) 'Setting attainable and appropriate English language targets in multilingual settings: a case for Hong Kong', *International Journal of Applied Linguistics*, 17/3: 376–91.

Kirkpatrick, A. and Xu, Z. (2002) 'Chinese pragmatic norms and "China English"', *World Englishes*, 21/2: 269–80.

Klimpfinger, T. (2007) '"Mind you, sometimes you have to mix" – The role of code-switching in English as a lingua franca', *Vienna English Working Papers*, 16/2: 36-61.

Koenig, E., Chia, E. and Povey, J. (eds) (1983) *A Sociolinguistic Profile of Urban Centres in Cameroon*, Los Angeles: Crossroads Press, University of California.

Lee, A. (2001) 'English to get English lessons', *The Straits Times*, 15 May.

Leech, G., Deuchar, M. and Hoogenraad, R. (1982) *English Grammar for Today*, Houndmills, Basingstoke: Macmillan.

Leith, D. (1996) 'English: colonial to postcolonial' in D. Graddol, D. Leith and J. Swann (eds) *English History, Diversity and Change*, London: Routledge.

Lenneberg, E. (1967) *Biological Foundations of Language*, New York: Wiley.

Leung, C., Harris, R. and Rampton, B. (1997) 'The idealised native speaker: reified ethnicities, and classroom realities', *TESOL Quarterly* 31/3: 543–60.

Li, D. (2002) 'Hong Kong parents' preference for English-medium education: passive victims of imperialism or active agents of pragmatism?' in A. Kirkpatrick (ed.) *Englishes in Asia: Communication, Identity, Power and Education*, Melbourne: Language Australia.

Li, W. (1993) 'China English and Chinese English', *Foreign Language Teaching and Research Journal*, vol. 4.

Lightbown, P. and Spada, N. (2006) *How Languages Are Learned*, 3rd edition, Oxford: Oxford University Press.

Lindquist, H., Klintborg, S., Levin, M. and Estling, M. (eds) (1998) *The Major Varieties of English: Papers from MAVEN 97*, Växjö: Acta Wexionensia.

Lippi-Green, R. (1997) *English with an Accent*, London: Routledge.

Lowenberg, P. (2000) 'Non-native varieties and the sociopolitics of English proficiency assessment' in J. K. Hall and W. Eggington (eds) (2000).

Lowenberg, P. (2002) 'Assessing English proficiency in the Expanding Circle', *World Englishes*, 21/3: 431–5.

Luk, J. and Lin, A. (2006) 'Uncovering the sociopolitical situatedness of accents in the world Englishes paradigm' in R. Hughes (ed.) 2006.

McArthur, A. (1987) 'The English languages?', *English Today*, 11: 9–13.

McArthur, A. (1998) *The English Languages*, Cambridge: Cambridge University Press.

McArthur, A. (2002) *The Oxford Guide to World English*, Oxford: Oxford University Press.

McArthur, A. (2003) 'World English, Euro English, Nordic English?', *English Today*, 19/1: 54–8.

McCarty, T. and Zepeda, O. (1999) 'Amerindians' in J. Fishman (ed.) (1999).

McCrum, R., MacNeil, R. and Cran, W. (1992) *The Story of English*, 2nd edition, London: Faber & Faber.

McKay, S. (2002) *Teaching English as an International Language*, Oxford: Oxford University Press.

McNamara, N. and Roever, C. (2006) *Language Testing: The Social Dimension*, Oxford: Blackwell.

Maidment, J. (1994) 'Estuary English: hybrid or hype?', paper presented at the 4th New Zealand conference on Language and Society, Lincoln University, Christchurch, New Zealand, August 1994, available at http://www.phon.uck.ac.uk/home/estuary/maidment.htm

Mar-Molinero, C. (2006) 'The European linguistic legacy in a global era: linguistic imperialism, Spanish, and the *Instituto Cervantes*' in C. Mar-Molinero and P. Stevenson (eds) *Language Ideologies, Policies and Practices*, Houndmills, Basingstoke: Palgrave Macmillan.

Mar-Molinero, C. (2008) 'Subverting Cervantes: language authority in global Spanish', *International Multilingual Research Journal*, 2: 27–47.

Mar-Molinero, C. and Stewart, M. (eds) (2006) *Globalization and Language in the Spanish-Speaking World*, Houndmills, Basingstoke: Palgrave Macmillan.

Matsuda, A. (2000) 'The use of English among Japanese returnees', *English Today*, 16/4: 49–55.

Mauranen, A. (2003) 'The corpus of English as a lingua franca in academic settings', *TESOL Quarterly*, 37/3: 513–27.

Mauranen, A. and Metsä Ketelä, M. (eds) (2006) 'English as a lingua franca', special issue of *Nordic Journal of English Studies*, 5/2.

May, S. (2008/2001) *Language and Minority Rights*, London: Routledge.

Mbassi-Manga, F. (1973) 'English in Cameroon: a study of historical contacts, patterns of usage and current trends', unpublished PhD thesis, University of Leeds.

Medgyes, P. (1994) *The Non-native Teacher*, London: Macmillan.

Meierkord, C. (1996) *Englisch als Medium der interkulturellen Kommunikation. Untersuchungen zum non-native/non-native speaker Diskurs*, Frankfurt am Main: Peter Lang.

Melchers, G. and Shaw, P. (2003) *World Englishes*, London: Arnold.

Mesthrie, R. (2002) 'Building a new English dialect' in R. Watts and P. Trudgill (eds) (2002).

Mesthrie, R. (2008) 'English circling the globe', *English Today*, 24/1: 28–32.

Mesthrie, R. and Bhatt, R. (2008) *World Englishes: The Study of New Linguistic Varieties*, Cambridge: Cambridge University Press.

Metcalf, T. (1995) *Ideologies of the Raj*, Cambridge: Cambridge University Press (Indian edition: New Delhi: Foundation Books).

Milroy, J. (2001) 'Language ideologies and the consequences of standardisation', *Journal of Sociolinguistics*, 5/4: 530–55.

Milroy, J. and Milroy, L. (1999) *Authority in Language: Investigating Standard English*, London: Routledge.

Milroy, L. (1985) 'Social network and language maintenance' in A. K. Pugh, V. J. Lee and J. Swann (eds) *Language and Language Use*, London and Milton Keynes: Heinemann Educational Books and The Open University Press.

Milroy, L. (1998) 'Bad grammar is slovenly' in L. Bauer and P. Trudgill (eds) (1998).

Milroy L. (1999) 'Standard English and language ideology in Britain and the United States' in T. Bex and R. Watts (eds) (1999).

Mitchell, R. (1993) 'Diversity or uniformity?: multilingualism and the English teacher in the 1990s', *IATEFL Annual Conference Report: Plenaries 1993*: 9–16.

Modiano, M. (1999a) 'International English in the global village', *English Today*, 15/2: 22–34.

Modiano, M. (1999b) 'Standard English(es) and educational practices for the world's lingua franca', *English Today*, 15/4: 3–13.

Moreno-Fernández, F. and Otero, J. (2008) 'The status and future of Spanish among the main international languages: quantitative dimensions', *International Multilingual Research Journal*, 2: 67–83.

Mufwene, S. (1997) 'The legitimate and illegitimate offspring of English' in L. Smith and M. Forman (eds) (1997).

Mufwene, S. (2001) *The Ecology of Language Evolution*, Cambridge: Cambridge University Press.

Mugglestone, L. (2003) *'Talking Proper': The Rise of Accent as Social Symbol*, Oxford: Oxford University Press.

Mühlhäusler, P. (1997) *Pidgin and Creole Linguistics*, London: University of Westminster Press.

Murray, H. and Dingwall, S. (1997) 'English for scientific communication at Swiss universities: God helps those who help themselves', *Babylonia*, 4: 54–9.

Nayar, P. B. (1998) 'Variants and varieties of English: dialectology or linguistic politics?' in H. Lindquist et al. (1998).

Nelson, C. (1982) 'Intelligibility and non-native varieties of English' in B. B. Kachru (ed.) (1982) *The Other Tongue: English across Cultures*, Urbana, IL: University of Illinois Press.

Nettle, D. and Romaine, S. (2000) *Vanishing Voices*, Oxford: Oxford University Press.

Ngũgĩ wa Thiong'o (1986) *Decolonising the Mind: The Politics of Language in African Literature*, London: James Currey.

Nylenna M., Riis, P. and Karlsson, Y. (1994) 'Multiple blinded reviews of the same two manuscripts: effects of reference characteristics and publication language', *The Journal of the American Medical Association*, 272/2: 149–51.

Obeng, S. and Adegbija, E. (1999) 'Sub-Saharan Africa' in J. Fishman (ed.) (1999).

Odlin, T. (1992) 'Transferability and linguistic substrates', *Second Language Research*, 8: 171–202.

Omoniyi, T. (1999) 'Afro-Asian rural border areas' in J. Fishman (ed.) (1999).

Pakir, A. (1991) 'The range and depth of English-knowing bilinguals', *World Englishes*, 10/2: 167–79.

Pakir, A. (1995) 'Expanding triangles of English expression in Singapore' in Teng S. C. and Ho M. L. (eds) *The English Language in Singapore: Implications for Teaching*, Singapore: SAAL.

Pakir, A. (1997) 'Standards and codification for World Englishes' in L. Smith and M. Forman (eds) (1997).

Pakir, A. (2002) 'The matter of English, the matter with English: maintaining language standards in teaching of English in the 21st century', in Low E. L. and Teng S. C. (eds) *The Teaching and Use of Standard English*, Singapore: SAAL.

Pandey, A. (2000) 'Symposium on the Ebonics debate and African-American language', *World Englishes*, 19/1: 1–4.

Parakrama, A. (1995) *De-hegemonizing Language Standards*, London: Macmillan.

Parasher S. (2001) 'Communication in multilingual India: a sociolinguistic perspective for the 21st century', *AILA Review*, 14, The English Company (UK) Ltd.

Peng, L. and Setter, J. (2000) 'The emergence of systematicity in the English pronunciations of two Cantonese-speaking adults in Hong Kong', *English World-Wide*, 21: 81–108.

Pennycook, A. (1994) *The Cultural Politics of English as an International Language*, London: Longman.

Pennycook, A. (1998) *English and the Discourses of Colonialism*, London: Routledge.

Pennycook, A. (2006) 'The myth of English as an international language' in S. Makoni and A. Pennycook (eds) *Disinventing and Reconstituting Languages*, Clevedon, UK: Multilingual Matters.

Pennycook, A. (2007) *Global Englishes and Transcultural Flows*, London: Routledge.

Phillipson, R. (1992) *Linguistic Imperialism*, Oxford: Oxford University Press.

Phillipson, R. (1996) 'Linguistic imperialism: African perspectives', *ELT Journal*, 50/2: 160–7.

Phillipson, R. (2003a) *English-only Europe? Challenging Language Policy*, London: Routledge.

Phillipson, R. (2003b) '"World English" or "World Englishes"?: on negating polyphony and multicanonicity of Englishes: two perspectives. Perspective 2: Robert Phillipson', *World Englishes*, 22/3: 324–6.

Phillipson, R. (2007) 'Reviewing a book and how it relates to "global" English: Ngũgĩ wa Thiong'o, *Wizard of the Crow*', *The European English Messenger*, 16/1: 50–4.

Pinker, S. (1994) *The Language Instinct*, London: Penguin.

Platt, J., Weber, H. and Ho, M. (1984) *The New Englishes*, London: Routledge and Kegan Paul.

Pölzl, U. (2005) 'Exploring the third space: negotiating culture in English as a lingua franca', doctoral thesis submitted at the University of Vienna.

Prodromou, L. (1997) 'From corpus to octopus', *IATEFL Newsletter*, no. 137: 18–21.

Przedlacka, J. (2001) 'Estuary English and RP: some recent findings, *Studia Anglica Posnaniensia*, 36: 35–50.

Przedlacka, J. (2002) *Estuary English?* Frankfurt am Main: Peter Lang.

Quirk, R. (1990) 'Language varieties and standard language', *English Today*, 21: 3–10.

Rampton, B. (1990) 'Displacing the "native speaker": expertise, affiliation and inheritance', *ELT Journal*, 44/2: 97–101.

Rampton, B. (1995) *Crossing: Language and Ethnicity among Adolescents*, London: Longman (republished 2005 by St Jerome Publishing).

Rolleston, C. (1911) *The Age of Folly: A Study of Imperial Needs, Duties, and Warning*, London: John Milne.

Romaine, S. (1988) *Pidgin and Creole Languages*, London: Longman.

Rosewarne, D. (1996) 'Changes in English pronunciation and some implications for teachers and non-native learners', *Speak Out!*, newsletter of the IATEFL Pronunciation Special Interest Group, no. 18: 15–21.

Rubagumya, C. (2004) 'English in Africa and the emergence of Afro-Saxons: globali-
    zation or marginalization?' in M. Baynham, A. Deignan and G. White (eds)
    (2004) *Applied Linguistics at the Interface*, London: Equinox.
Rubdy, R. (2001) 'Creative destruction: Singapore's Speak Good English movement',
    World Englishes, 20/3: 341–55.
Rubdy, R. and Saraceni, M. (eds) (2006) *English in the World: Global Rules, Global
    Roles*, London: Continuum.
Rudzka, B. (1985) 'Vocabulary teaching: a cognitive approach' in A.-M. Cornu and
    T. Scovel (1994) *Genes and Teens – Sociobiological Explanations for the Presence of
    Accents after Puberty*.
Sampson, G. (1924) 'The problem of grammar', *English Association Pamphlet*, 56,
    London: English Association.
Saxena, M. (2008) 'Ideology, policy and practice in bilingual classrooms: Brunei
    Darussalam' in A. Creese and P. Martin (eds) (2008), *Encyclopedia of Language
    and Education*, vol. 9 *Ecology of Language*, New York: Springer.
Schneider, E. (2003) 'The dynamics of New Englishes: from identity construction to
    dialect birth', *Language*, 79/2: 233–81.
Schneider, E. (2007) *Postcolonial Englishes: Varieties around the World*, Cambridge:
    Cambridge University Press.
Sebba, M. (1993) *London Jamaican*, London: Longman.
Sebba, M. (1997) *Contact Languages: Pidgins and Creoles*, London: Macmillan.
Sebba, M. (2007) 'Caribbean creoles and black English' in D. Britain (ed.) (2007).
Seidlhofer, B. (1999) 'Double standards: teacher education in the Expanding Circle',
    World Englishes, 18/2: 233–45.
Seidlhofer B. (2001) 'Closing a conceptual gap: the case for a description of English as
    a lingua franca', *International Journal of Applied Linguistics*, 11/2: 133–58.
Seidlhofer, B. (2002) '*Habeas corpus* and *divide et impera*: "Global English" and applied
    linguistics' in K. Spelman Miller and P. Thompson (eds) (2002) *Unity and Diver-
    sity in Language Use*, London: Continuum.
Seidlhofer, B. (2004) 'Research perspectives on teaching English as a lingua franca',
    Annual Review of Applied Linguistics, vol. 24: 209–39.
Seidlhofer, B. (2005) 'Standard future or half-baked quackery?: descriptive and peda-
    gogic bearings on the globalisation of English' in C. Gnutzmann and F. Intemann
    (eds) (2005).
Seidlhofer, B. (2006) 'English as a lingua franca and communities of practice' in
    S. Volk-Birke and J. Lippert (eds) (2007) *Anglistentag 2006 Halle Proceedings*,
    Trier: Wissenschaftlicher Verlag: 307–18.
Seidlhofer, B. (forthcoming) *Understanding English as a Lingua Franca*, Oxford:
    Oxford University Press.
Seidlhofer, B., Breiteneder, A. and Pitzl, M.-L. (2006) 'English as a lingua franca in
    Europe: challenges for applied linguistics', *Annual Review of Applied Linguistics*,
    vol. 26: 3–34.
Selinker, L. (1972) 'Interlanguage', *International Review of Applied Linguistics*, 10: 209–31.
Shim, R. (1999) 'Codified Korean English: process, characteristics and consequence',
    World Englishes, 18/2: 247–58.
Siegel, J. (1991) 'Variation in Fiji English' in J. Cheshire (ed.) (1991).
Siegel, M. (1996) 'The role of learner subjectivity in second language sociolinguistic

competency: Western women learning Japanese', *Applied Linguistics*, 17/3: 356–82.

Singh, I. (2001) *Pidgins and Creoles*, London: Arnold.

Skuttnab-Kangas, T. (1999) 'What fate awaits the world's languages?', *Media Development Journal of the World Association for Christian Communication*, XLVI 4/1999: 3–7.

Skuttnab-Kangas, T. and Phillipson, R. (1994) 'Linguistic human rights, past and present' in T. Skuttnab-Kangas and R. Phillipson (eds) (1994) *Linguistic Human Rights: Overcoming Linguistic Discrimination*, Berlin and New York: Mouton de Gruyter.

Skuttnab-Kangas, T. and R. Phillipson (1996) 'Linguicide and linguicism' in G. Hans et al. (eds) *Kontaktlinguistic/Contact Linguistics/Linguistique de contact*, vol. 1, Berlin and New York: de Gruyter.

Smith, L. and Forman, M. (eds) (1997) *World Englishes 2000*, Honolulu, Hawai'i: University of Hawai'i Press.

Sobkowiak, W. (2005) 'Why not LFC?' in K. Dziubalska-Kołaczyk and J. Przedlacka (eds) (2005).

Sridhar, S. (1994) 'A reality check for SLA theories', *TESOL Quarterly*, 28/4: 800–5.

Sridhar, K. and Sridhar, S. (1986) 'Bridging the paradigm gap: second language acquisition theory and indigenized varieties of English', *World Englishes*, 5/1: 3–14.

Sridhar, K. and Sridhar, S. (1992) 'Bridging the paradigm gap: second-language acquisition theory and indigenized varieties of English' in B. B. Kachru (ed.) (1992).

Strevens, P. (1985) 'Standards and the standard language', *English Today*, no. 1/2: 5–8.

Strevens, P. (1992) 'English as an international language: directions in the 1990s' in B. B. Kachru (ed.) (1992).

Stubbs, M. (1986) *Educational Linguistics*, Oxford: Blackwell.

Sutcliffe, D. (1982) *British Black English*, Oxford: Blackwell.

Talib, I. (2002) *The Language of Postcolonial Literatures*, London: Routledge.

Tay, M. (1991) 'Southeast Asia and Hongkong' in J. Cheshire (ed.) (1991).

Taylor, L. (2006) 'The changing landscape of English: implications for language assessment', *ELT Journal*, 60/1: 51–60.

Thumboo, E. (1992) 'The literary dimension of the spread of English' in B. B. Kachru (ed.) (1992).

Titlestad, P. (1998) 'South Africa's language ghosts', *English Today*, 14/2: 33–9.

Todd, L. (1990) *Pidgins and Creoles*, 2nd edition, London: Routledge.

Todd, L. (1997) 'Ebonics: an evaluation', *English Today*, 13/3: 13–17.

Toolan, M. (1997) 'Recentring English: new English and global', *English Today*, 13/4: 3–10.

Tripathi, P. (1998) 'Redefining Kachru's "Outer Circle" of English', *English Today*, 14/4: 55–8.

Trudgill, P. (1984) *Language in the British Isles*, Cambridge: Cambridge University Press.

Trudgill, P. (1998) 'World Englishes: convergence or divergence?' in H. Lindquist et al. (eds) (1998).

Trudgill, P. (1999) 'Standard English: what it isn't' in T. Bex and R. Watts (eds) (1999).

Trudgill, P. (2002) *Sociolinguistic Variation and Change*, Edinburgh: Edinburgh University Press.

Trudgill, P. (2005) 'Native-speaker segmental phonological models and the English lingua franca core' in K. Dziubalska-Kołaczyk and J. Przedlacka (eds) (2005).

Trudgill, P. and Chambers J. K. (1991) 'Introduction: English dialect grammar' in J. K. Chambers and P. Trudgill (eds) *Dialects of English*, London: Longman.

Trudgill, P. and Hannah, J. (1982) *International English*, London: Arnold.

Trudgill, P. and Hannah, J. (2002) *International English*, 4th edition, London: Arnold.

Trudgill, P. and Hannah, J. (2008) *International English*, 5th edition, London: Arnold.

Tsui, A. and Bunton, D. (2000) 'The discourse and attitudes of English language teachers in Hong Kong', *World Englishes* 19/3: 287–303.

Vandenbroucke, J. P. (1989) 'On not being born a native speaker of English', *British Medical Journal*, 298: 1461–2.

Wang, R. (1991) 'China English does exist', *Journal of Luoyang Military Foreign Language Institute*, vol. 4.

Wardhaugh, R. (2006) *An Introduction to Sociolinguistics*, 5th edition, Oxford: Blackwell.

Waters, A. (2007) 'ELT and the "spirit of the times"', *ELT Journal*, 61/4: 353–9.

Watts, R. and Trudgill, P. (eds) (2002) *Alternative Histories of English*, London: Routledge.

Wee, L. (2002) 'When English is not a mother tongue: linguistic ownership and the Eurasian community in Singapore', *Journal of Multilingual and Multicultural Development*, 23/4: 282–95.

Wee, L. (2005) 'Intra-language discrimination and linguistic human rights', *Applied Linguistics*, 26/1: 48–69.

Weinberger, S. (1987) 'The influence of linguistic context on syllable simplification', in G. Ioup and S. H. Weinberger (eds) *Interlanguage Phonology*, Cambridge, MA: Newbury House.

Wells, J. (1998) 'Estuary English', lecture handout UCL, available at http://www.phon.ucl.ac.uk/home/estuary/wells.htm

Wenger, E. (1998) *Communities of Practice*, Cambridge: Cambridge University Press.

Wesley-Smith, P. (1994) 'Anti-Chinese legislation in Hong Kong' in M. K. Chan (ed.) *Precarious Balance: Hong Kong between China and Britain, 1842–1992*, Hong Kong: Hong Kong University Press.

Widdowson, H. G. (1993) 'The ownership of English', *IATEFL Annual Conference Report: Plenaries 1993*.

Widdowson, H. G. (1994a) 'Pragmatics and the pedagogic competence of language teachers' in Sebbage T. and S. Sebbage (eds) *Proceedings of the 4th International NELLE Conference*, Hamburg: NELLE.

Widdowson, H. G. (1994b) 'The ownership of English', *TESOL Quarterly*, 28/2: 377–89.

Widdowson, H. G. (1997) 'EIL, ESL, EFL: global issues and local interests', *World Englishes*, 16/1: 135–46.

Williams, A. (2007) 'Non-standard English and education' in D. Britain (ed.) (2007).

Winitz, H. (1977) 'Nonauditory auditory disorders', *Otorhinolaryngologic Clinics of N. America*, 10.

Wolfram, W. (2006) 'African American English' in B. B. Kachru, Y. Kachru and C. Nelson (eds) (2006).

Wolfram, W. and Schilling-Estes, N. (2006) *American English*, 2nd edition, Oxford: Blackwell.

Yano Y. (2001) 'World Englishes in 2000 and beyond', *World Englishes*, 20/2: 119–31.

GLOSSARIAL INDEX

The glossarial index is based on significant terms used in the text. The page numbers in bold refer to explanations or significant information.